浙江省“十四五”研究生教学改革项目资助
本书获杭州电子科技大学教材立项出版资助

Elementary Statistics

主编　薛　洁　付　荣　徐　姗　牛阿丹

西安电子科技大学出版社

Brief Introduction

This book mainly introduces the basic theories, methods and applications of statistics. The book has 8 chapters, including introduction to statistics, data collection, data grouping and data graphing, characteristics of data distribution, probability basis, parameter estimation, hypothesis testing, correlation analysis and regression analysis. On the basis of introducing the concepts and methods of statistics, this book introduces the practical applications of statistical methods.

This book can be used as a textbook for international students in colleges or universities to offer statistics courses in various majors, as a reference textbook for students to study statistics bilingual courses and professional English courses, or as a reference book for practitioners to understand statistics terminology.

图书在版编目（CIP）数据

基础统计学 = Elementary Statistics ：英文 / 薛洁等主编. -- 西安 ：西安电子科技大学出版社，2024.6. -- ISBN 978-7-5606-7321-9

Ⅰ. C8

中国国家版本馆 CIP 数据核字第 2024U5M794 号

策　　划　陈　婷
责任编辑　郭　静
出版发行　西安电子科技大学出版社（西安市太白南路 2 号）
电　　话　(029) 88202421　88201467　　邮　　编　710071
网　　址　www.xduph.com　　电子邮箱　xdupfxb001@163.com
经　　销　新华书店
印刷单位　广东虎彩云印刷有限公司
版　　次　2024 年 6 月第 1 版　　2024 年 6 月第 1 次印刷
开　　本　787 毫米×1092 毫米　1/16　　印张　12
字　　数　280 千字
定　　价　34.00 元

ISBN 978-7-5606-7321-9

XDUP 7622001-1

Preface

With the rapid development of the Internet of Things(IOT), Cloud Computing, Big Data, Artificial Intelligence(AI), Digital Economy and other new information technologies and the times, dozens of ZB data need to use statistical theory and methods to explore their inherent laws. LinkedIn, a famous professional social network, once analyzed the work skills of more than 330 million users worldwide, and published 25 skills that are most popular and popular with employers, of which statistical analysis skills ranked first. From this point of view, the professional skills of statistics have become a necessary ability for every high-quality compound talent.

Statistics is a science that collects, processes, analyzes and interprets data and draws conclusions from data. It provides a set of data analysis methods that are common to all disciplines. As an introductory textbook for statistics, the book consists of 8 chapters, including descriptive statistics and inferential statistics, as well as statistical methods commonly used in economic management. The first part is descriptive statistics, including introduction to statistics, data collection, data grouping and data graphing, characteristics of data distribution; The second part is inferential statistics, including probability basis, parameter estimation, hypothesis testing, correlation analysis and regression analysis.

The completion of this book has condensed the efforts of many teachers. Chapters 1, 2 and 3 are prepared by Xue Jie, Chapters 5 and 8 are prepared by Fu Rong, Chapters 4, 6 and 7 are prepared by Niu Adan, and the whole book is integrated by Xue Jie and Xu Shan. We would also like to thank some postgraduate students for their work in the process of writing this book. The compilation of this book has been funded by the school level textbook construction project of Hangzhou Dianzi University, and some excellent statistics textbooks at home and abroad have been referred to. We would like to express our sincere gratitude.

Due to the limited level of the editors, it is inevitable that there are some mistakes in the book. We sincerely hope that the colleagues and readers can give us some advice.

Editors

March, 2024

Contents

Chapter 1

Introduction to Statistics

In our daily life, we are being submerged by data and exposed to all kinds of data. Such as the GDP (Gross Domestic Products) of one country, the technology statistics in each basketball match, the PMI (Purchasing Managers' Index), E-commerce business data, the ratio of unemployment, etc. There are also some conclusions obtained from statistical studies, such as taller fathers have children who are also taller, taking 500 ml of vitamin C every day can extend life by 6 years, etc. Are these conclusions correct? Do you believe them? Whatever your focus and your future career plans are, in order to understand these data correctly, it is likely that you will need statistical knowledge to make smart decisions in your field and in everyday life. In this chapter, we will introduce the development of statistics and basic concepts, and lays the foundation for learning the subsequent chapters.

1.1 An Overview of Statistics

With the advent of the era of the Internet of Things(IOT), Cloud Computing, Big Data and Digital Economy, government departments, large and medium-sized enterprises, financial institutions and consulting organizations are faced with a large amount of data processing work, including the collection, storage, analysis, presentation, inference, prediction and interpretation of massive and diverse types of data. What is the definition of statistics? What is the object of statistical research? How does statistics conduct research? These will be the main contents of this section.

1.1.1 A Definition of Statistics

Every day, we are exposed to statistics. For example, consider the following statements.

(1) "People who eat three daily servings of whole grains have been shown to reduce their risk of … stroke by 37%." (*Source: Whole Grains Council*)

(2) "70% of the 1500 U. S. spinal cord injuries to minors result from vehicle accidents, and 68% were not wearing a seatbelt." (*Source*: *UPI*)

(3) "Data from Iceland was used to determine that 90% of Icelanders have access to the Internet, the highest rate of any country." (*Source*: *The World Bank's All Countries dataset*)

The information among these statements is based on the collection of data. Data consist of information coming from observations, counts, measurements, or responses. For example, we can obtain the daily behavior data by observing animals, obtain the attendance of employees by counting, obtain the height and weight data of students by measuring tools, and obtain their views on problems by interviewing respondents. We will introduce the specific sources of data and how to obtain data in detail in Chapter 2.

The use of statistics dates back to census taking in ancient Babylonia, Egypt, and later in the Roman Empire, when data were collected about matters concerning the state, such as births and deaths. In fact, the word statistics is derived from the Latin word *status*, meaning "state". As can be seen in the definition, the modern practice of statistics is far beyond the calculation of birth and death and covers a wide range. ***Statistics science*** is a methodology science, which is the science of collecting, organizing, analyzing, and interpreting data in order to make decision, and it is the investigation and study of a large number of various social phenomena.

In addition to the above, statistics also has another two different meanings in different occasions: one is statistical practice activities, the other is statistical data.

Statistical practice activities, also known as statistical works, is the process of collecting, organizing and analyzing the objective quantity of social phenomena. For example, statistical competition points, statistical output and statistical deposit amount mentioned above are all engaged in a statistical practice activity.

Statistical data refers to the general term for various data and other related information obtained in the process of statistical practice activities. For example, the game points, output, deposit amount, number of confirmed coronavirus cases, consumer price index, real estate price index, economic growth rate, etc. mentioned above are all statistical data.

It is clear from the discussion above that there is a close connection between the three meanings of "statistics" in our daily life. As shown in Figure 1. 1, the relationship between statistical practice activities and statistical data are activity processes and results, while the relationship between practice and theory are statistical practice activities and statistics science.

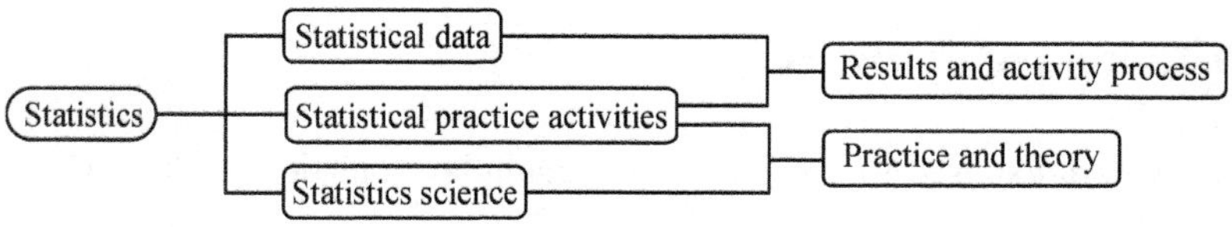

Figure 1. 1 Three meanings of statistics and their relationship

1.1.2 Research Objects and Properties of Statistics

In nature and production management practice, the phenomena observed by people can be summarized into two types, one is deterministic phenomena, the other is uncertain phenomena, namely random phenomena. Random phenomenon refers to repeated experiments under the same conditions, and the results may not be the same each time; or it is a phenomenon that we know its past performance, but cannot be completely sure of its future development in advance. For example, the waiting time for customers to receive a service, and the profits after the product advertisement is launched are all random phenomena.

In fact, the so-called uncertainty only refers to one or a few observations or practices. When a large number of observations are made under the same conditions, random phenomena show regularity, which is called statistical regularity of random phenomena. For example, the service time of a service to customers follows the law of exponential distribution, the height of people follows the law of normal distribution, and the test scores follow the law of normal distribution. Therefore, people can make scientific decisions on problems studied according to the discovered laws. Statistics is to study the statistical regularity of random phenomena, which is of great significance to scientific decision-making.

Generally speaking, the research objects of statistics have the following properties.

1. Randomness

There are two explanations for randomness. One is the uncertainty of the results of events. As mentioned above, the uncertainty of random phenomena; Second, different individuals have differences, these differences are not given in advance by some fixed reasons, but caused by random factors. For example, the population is large or small in an area, the income is high or low, and there are differences in consumption levels. So, it is necessary to study statistical indicators such as the total population of the region, the average income, and the level of average consumption. After all, if there are no differences between the units like twins, then there is no need for statistics.

2. Totality

The research object of statistics should include more than one individual, it means that a single individual does not need statistical analysis. Although statistical research starts from the investigation of individuals and observes the specific facts of individuals, the ultimate purpose is to understand the quantitative characteristics of the population. For example, to analyze the employees' wages, we do not want to analyze and study the wages of the individual but the overall wages situation and regularity of a region, a department and an institution. Of course, this does not mean that statistics ignore the in-depth study of the individual thing. On the contrary, it makes a specific analysis of representative typical units and an understanding of the internal relationship of phenomena, so as to understand the overall regularity better.

3. Quantitative

Quantitative are the basic feature of statistical research objects. Data is the language and core of statistics, and it is also the raw material of statistics. The occurrence of the event shall be expressed in quantity for statistical analysis. This can be done in most cases. If the occurrence of a matter is expressed qualitatively, it can be expressed in terms of quantity. For example, there may be three cases of sales of a product: high, medium and low, the distribution of these three cases can be recorded as 1, 2, 3; the occurrence of an event is recorded as 1, and the non-occurrence is recorded as 0; male is recorded as 1 and female as 0.

1.1.3 The Basic Process of Statistical Study

Generally speaking, the basic process of using statistics to study the statistical regularity of random phenomena includes statistical design, statistical survey, statistical organizing, statistical analysis, and information accumulation and applications of statistical data, which is shown in Figure 1.2.

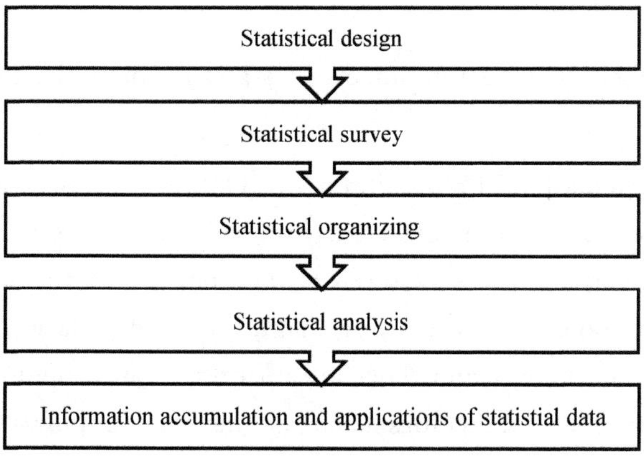

Figure 1.2 The basic process of statistical study

1. Statistical Design

Statistical design is the beginning of statistical research work, and it is a key link in the comprehensive arrangement of statistical activities. Generally speaking, after receiving a statistical research topic, the research topic should be considered as a whole. All aspects and links of statistical activities should be reasonably arranged, and a complete set of statistical design schemes should be formed. It is similar to the project plan and its content includes the objectives of statistical work, research objects, research content, data survey plan, organize plan, data analysis, provision and storage, work deadlines and schedules, etc. The final statistical research work will be carried out on the above basis. For example, in order to understand people's views on regional COVID-19 epidemic prevention and control, it is necessary to clarify the background and purpose of the investigation, the object, and the scope of the survey. Then we can design a questionnaire according to the content of the study, formulate a sampling plan, point out the data collection method, collation plan, data analysis method, and have a unified arrangement for personnel and time. Of course, when carrying out statistical design, it is not enough to have only general knowledge of statistical methods, but also to have theoretical knowledge of relevant research field.

2. Statistical Survey

The statistical survey is the collection of statistical data. According to the requirements of the statistical design scheme, the statistical survey is the process of collecting accurate and sufficient statistical data from the objective and actual information in a planned and organized way. And it also needs to use various forms of statistical survey organization and survey methods. The statistical survey is the stage of statistical cognitive activities from qualitative to quantitative cognition. All kinds of data in the process of statistical research are obtained from above process. Whether the information collected at this stage is objective, comprehensive, systematic, accurate and timely, will directly affect the quality of statistical organizing, and the correctness of statistical analysis conclusions. Therefore, the above process is the basis of statistical research work and determines the quality of statistical research work.

3. Statistical Organizing

Statistical organizing is the process of grouping and summarizing the data obtained from statistical surveys. Through the organizing of data to make the data systematized and organized, the data reflecting the individual characteristics of each unit is transformed into the data reflecting the population characteristics, which facilitates subsequent statistical analysis of data. Statistical organizing belongs to the third stage of statistical research work, which not only is the continuation of the statistical survey stage, but also is the basis and premise of statistical analysis. The steps of statistical organizing mainly include: ① formulating a statistical organizing plan; ② reviewing the statistical survey data; ③ selecting grouping signs according to the purpose of the study, and establishing frequency distribution; ④ summarizing and calculating the data after grouping to reflect the population quantitative characteristics; ⑤ visualizing the results with various statistical tables and figures.

4. Statistical Analysis

Statistical analysis is the process of analysis and research of grouping data. The data are mainly analyzed from both static and dynamic aspects through various statistical analysis methods, including hypothesis testing, regression models and variance analysis, etc. Its goal is to reveal the regularity and trend of phenomenon development. This is the most important process in statistical work and the main content of statistical research.

In the process of statistical organizing and statistical analysis, the methods used include two major categories: descriptive statistics and inferential statistics. And they are often referred to as the two branches of statistics.

(1) Descriptive statistics. Descriptive statistics is a branch of statistics, it involves the work of organization, summarization, display of data, using numerical formulas to describe the nature of data. Based on the data obtained from surveys or experiments, use charts to summarize and display the data, and calculate some data characteristic values, such as proportion, mean, standard deviation, etc. People can have a general understanding of the laws of the research object intuitively according to the statistical figures, and can analyze the central tendency, dispersion tendency, distribution characteristics and other aspects of the data through the data characteristic values, so as to enclose the trends and laws of the research object. Descriptive statistics is the basis of the statistical research process, providing a factual basis for statistical inference, statistical prediction and decision-making.

(2) Inferential statistics. Inferential statistics is the branch of statistics, it involves using a sample to draw conclusions about a population. A basic tool in the study of inferential statistics is probability. (You will learn more about probability in Chapter 5.). It mainly includes parameter estimation and hypothesis testing. Parameter estimation is to use sample information to infer the characteristics of the population concerned, hypothesis testing is to use sample information to determine whether a certain hypothesis of the population is true. For example, randomly select a few women from the female group aged 20 - 40 as samples, measure their mean weight, and then estimate the population mean weight using the sample mean weight; or use sample evidence to test a claim. For example, the population mean weight is 55 kilogram.

5. Information Accumulation and Applications of Statistical Data

After statistical analysis, organized statistics can be obtained, but the statistical process is not over. The purpose of statistics is to study the statistical regularity of random phenomena. With only one statistical data, it is far from being able to find the statistical regularity of objective phenomena. Therefore, it is necessary to accumulate the data collected, collated and analyzed, establish various statistical databases, and provide data to departments and society in various flexible ways through statistical information networks, so as to realize statistical informatization and data sharing. How to better apply statistical data and methods to various research fields is one of the important aspects of applied statistics research.

1.2 Statistical Origin and Development

1.2.1 Development History of Statistics

Statistics has a long history. In China, the knotted rope chronicle developed in primitive society is the germ of statistics. There is a record of population and land figures in slave society Xia Dynasty, which is the earliest statistical data in China. The earliest statistical reporting system was established in the Western Zhou Dynasty.

In Western countries, as you can see in the former contents, the use of statistics dates back to the survey of population and property in ancient Egypt and Roman Empire. From the word "statistics", it comes from Latin word "status", which means that with the state power, there is statistical practice activities. However, statistics came into being in the mid-17th century when governments established statistical departments. Since statistics became a professional work, population, social, and economic statistics have experienced rapid development. In short, statistics as a discipline has a history of more than 300 years. According to the evolution order of statistical methods and history, the development of statistics has roughly experienced three stages, namely, classical statistics period (from the mid-17th century to the mid-18th century), modern statistics period (from the end of the 18th century to the end of the 19th century) and modern statistics period (Since the 20th century).

1. Classical Statistics Period

The sprout of classical statistics can be traced back to the mid-17th century, when Europe was in the stage of the disintegration of feudal society and the rise of capitalism. Industry and handicraft industry developed rapidly, the level of social-economic development is improving. Political reformers support the data evidence of national operation and management to meet the needs of economic development. During this period, represented by William Petty (1623—1687), John Grant (1620—1674) and Hermann Corning (1606—1681).

Among them, William Petty's masterpiece *Political Arithmetic* (1676) is regarded as an important work in the history of economics and statistics, in which "political" means political economy and "arithmetic" means statistical methods. Karl Marx considers William Petty, the father of political economy, as the founder of statistics.

Another representative character, John Grant, regard the weekly *Death Bulletin* published by the Church of London in 1604 as his research material, and he published his book *Natural and Political Observations on the Death Bulletin* in 1662. The book discovered many quantitative patterns related to the population through many observations, such as the mortality rate of each age group, the sex ratio. He also compiled the *life table* firstly and analyzed the mortality rate and the life expectancy of the population in a more detailed way. Thus, he is considered to be the founder of demography.

Hermann Corning from Germany is the representative of the school of "State Power" (in German is "Staatskunde"), also known as the school of narrative. In 1660, Corning separated the science of state power from the disciplines of law, history, and geography. Since the word "state" and "statistics" have the same meaning in foreign languages, it was later officially named "statistics". And because the school of state power is only a written description of the national conditions, it emphasizes the qualitative analysis of the nature of things, and not pays attention to quantitative analysis. Therefore, people also call it the narrative school (the old school or the German school), and believe that the school of "State Power" has the name of statistics, not the reality of statistics.

2. Modern Statistics Period

Modern Statistics is roughly from the end of the 18th century to the end of the 19th century. In the past 100 years, European countries have successively completed the industrial revolution, and data in the fields of astronomy and meteorology, social population have accumulated to a certain extent. The demand for statistics has also expanded from the national level to various fields of social science. The famous laws of large numbers, the least squares method, the normal distribution curve and other theoretical methods were put forward during this period. The representative figure is the Belgian scholar Adolphe Jacques Quetelet (1796—1874), who founded the school of mathematical statistics; as well as the German scholar Knies (1821—1898), Engel (1841—1896) and Mayr (1841—1925), who founded the school of social statistics.

In the 18th century, the probability theory became increasingly mature. While in the mid-19th century, probability theory was introduced into statistics. The founder of mathematical statistics, Belgian scholar Quetelet, whose contribution to statistics is to introduce the research methods of natural science into the study of social phenomena. He believes that statistics is mathematical statistics. He founded the Law of Large Numbers, developed a large number of observation methods and laid the foundation for the development of mathematical statistics.

The school of social statistics arose in the end of the 19th century, the founder of which is Karl Gustav Addt Knies, a German economist and statistician. The main representatives are Ernst Engel, Georg von Mayr (1841—1925), and others. They believe that the research object of statistics is social phenomenon, the research method is a large number of observation methods, and statistics is a social science. During this period, people use social surveys to collect and analyze data to reveal social phenomena and problems. For example, Engel carried out a continuous survey of Belgian workers' families and put forward the famous "Engel's Law", that is, the more the family income, the less the percentage of food consumption expenditure in the family income, thus extending the "Engel coefficient" as a standard to measure the standard of living, which has been used until now.

3. Modern Statistics Period

The development speed of science and technology in the 20th century is faster than that in previous era. Descriptive methods can no longer meet the needs. The focus of statistics has shifted to inferential statistics. In 1900, the British statistician Karl Pearson (1857—1936) proposed the chi-square test method. In 1908, the William Seely Gossett (1876—1937) proposed a small sample theory, also known as the "student-*t* test", which enriched the theory of sampling distribution and laid the foundation for statistical inference. The famous British statistician R. A. Fisher (1890—1962) proposed the concept of maximum likelihood estimation, which became an important method for parameter estimation, and he also proposed the distribution of sample correlation coefficients, experimental design, and variance analysis. In 1930, the Polish scholar J. Neyman (1894—1981) created the theory of interval estimation and developed hypothesis theory with E. Pearson. The American statistician Wald proposed decision theory and sequential sampling methods; the American chemist Frank Wilcoxon developed a series of nonparametric statistical methods, which opened up a new field of statistics.

1.2.2 Development Direction and Trend of Statistics

In recent decades, the development of modern science and technology such as computer technology, Internet and Internet of Things has brought a huge impact on statistics, and new fields emerge in endlessly.

Mathematical statistics is an important branch of statistics, and has developed rapidly since the 20th century. At present, researches on mathematical statistics mainly focus on Bayesian research, survival analysis and high-dimensional statistics.

(1) Almost every issue has papers on "Bayesian statistics", such as Journal of the American Statistical Association (JASA), Journal of the Royal Statistical Society (JRSS). Bayesian statistics is a theorical method that uses prior information and posterior information to determine probability, and then makes statistical inference on this basis.

(2) Survival analysis is a statistical analysis method that combines the result of an event with the time it takes to produce the result. As an important subject of statistics, survival analysis has a wide range of applications, such as survival time and efficacy in biomedicine, engineering failure time, existence time of financial insurance companies, life span, and so on.

(3) High-dimensional statistics is widely used in financial, genetic and spectroscopy analysis, especially for the collection, storage and processing of large-scale data sets. The

accuracy of model prediction, the improvement of model estimation methods, and the testing of special types of high-dimensional data are hot issues in current research.

Meantime, with the development of the times, human society is surrounded by explosive growth of information. In 2011, McKinsey Global Research Institute put forward the concept of "Age of Big Data" for the first time, "Big data" arises spontaneously and affects the theories and methods of traditional statistics. Victor Mayer Schoenberg, a professor at Oxford University, is known as the "prophet of big data era". He and Kenneth Cook jointly wrote the book *The Age of Big Data*, which clearly points out that in the age of big data, three major changes should be made in the traditional data analysis idea.

(1) The first is to change the sampling idea. In the era of big data, the sample is the population, so we should analyze all relevant data instead of relying on a small number of data samples.

(2) The second is to change the idea of data measurement, be willing to accept the complexity of data, and no longer pursue accurate data.

(3) The third is to stop searching for elusive causality and focus instead on correlation. The terms of sampling, sample, population, causality and correlation mentioned here are the basic concepts and core contents of statistics.

In the context of rapid development of modern statistical theory and method research, we have to mention the statistical conference which is most related to the frontier of statistics. In 1853, the first World Statistics Congress (WSC) was successfully held in Brussels, Belgium, and has since been held every two years. The 50th WSC was held in Beijing in 1995. The 60th WSC was held in Rio de Janeiro, Brazil, in 2015. The theme of the conference was "sustainable development in data transformation". From July 11 to 16, 2021, the 63rd WSC was held online, with the theme of "Statistics and Data Science for a Better World". The 64th WSC was held July 16 – 20, 2023 in the magnificent Shaw Centre in Ottawa, Canada.

As a learner of a basic statistics course, it is necessary to know the authority level awards related to statistics. As is known to all, the Nobel Prize has set up awards in many fields, such as literature award, economics award, peace award and so on. However, there is no Nobel Prize for statistics. Because statistics and econometrics are relatively relevant, more than 2/3 of the research achievements of the Nobel Economics prize are related to statistical and econometric analysis. So, is there a similar prize in statistics? The answer is yes. It has its own Nobel prize, the COPSS (Committee of Presidents of Statistical Societies) Presidents' Award, which was established in 1976 and sponsored by the following five statistical societies: The American Statistical Association(ASA), Statistical Society of Canada (SSC), Institute of Mathematical Statistics (IMS), Econometric Association of North America (EANA) and Econometric Association of South America (EASA). Only one outstanding scholar of statistics under the age of 40 will be awarded each year. As of 2023, there are 43 scholars who have won the COPSS Presidents' Award worldwide, among which 9 are Chinese scholars. As shown in Table 1.1, most of them majored in statistics, mathematics or computer science during their undergraduate studies, which fully demonstrates the close connection between statistics, mathematics and computer science.

Table 1.1 List of COPSS Presidents' Award winners①

Time	Winners	Work unit when winning	Time	Winners	Work unit when winning
1979	Peter J. Bickel	University of California, Berkeley	2003	Andrew Gelman	Columbia University
1982	Stephen Fienberg	Carnegie Mellon University	2004	Michael A. Newton	University of Wisconsin
1983	Li Ziliang	Stanford University	2005	Mark J. van der Laan	University of California, Berkeley
1984	David V. Hinkley	University of California, Santa Barbara	2006	Lin Xihong	Harvard University
1985	James O. Berger	Duke University	2007	Jeffrey S. Rosenthal	University of Toronto
1986	Ross L. Prentice	Fred Hutchinson Cancer Research Center	2008	Cai Tianwen	University of Pennsylvania
1987	Wu Jianfu	University of Wisconsin	2009	Rafael Irizarry	Johns Hopkins University
1988	Raymond J. Carroll	Texas A&M University	2010	David Dunson	Duke University
1989	Peter Hall	Australian National University	2011	Nilanjan Chatterjee	National Cancer Institute
1990	Peter McCullagh	University of Chicago	2012	Kou Xingchang	Harvard University
1991	Bernard Silverman	University of Bristol	2013	Marc A. Suchard	University of California, Los Angeles
1992	Nancy Reid	University of Toronto	2014	Martin J. Wainwright	University of California, Los Angeles
1993	Wang Yongxiong	Harvard University	2015	John D. Storey	Princeton University
1994	David L. Donoho	Stanford University	2016	Nicolai Meinshausen	Zurich Federal Institute of Technology
1995	Iain M. Johnstone	University of California, Berkeley	2017	Tyler J. Vander Weele	Harvard University
1996	Robert J. Tibshirani	University of Toronto	2018	Richard Samworth	Cambridge University

① Data source: http://baike.baidu.com/item/COPSS Presidents' Award/53282396? fr=aladdin.

Continued Table

Time	Winners	Work unit when winning	Time	Winners	Work unit when winning
1997	Kathryn Roeder	Carnegie Mellon University	2019	Hadley Wickham	RStudio, Inc.
1998	Pascal Massart	Paris University Xi	2020	Rina Foygel Barber	Chicago University
1999	Larry A. Wasserman	Carnegie Mellon University	2021	Jeffrey T. Leek	Johns Hopkins University
2000	Fan Jianqing	University of North Carolina at Chapel Hill	2022	Daniela Witten	Washington University
2001	Meng Xiaoli	University of Chicago	2023	Ryan Tibshirani	University of California, Berkeley
2002	Liu Jun	Harvard University	Total		43

1.2.3 Applications of Statistics in Various Fields

C. R. Rao, an internationally renowned statistician, once mentioned that "statistics is essentially parasitic and survives by studying work in other fields". As shown in Figure 1.3, statistics is widely used in almost all fields. Only when statistics is closely combined with other disciplines, it can exert its powerful vitality, produce a series of professional fields of statistics and form a discipline system of statistics.

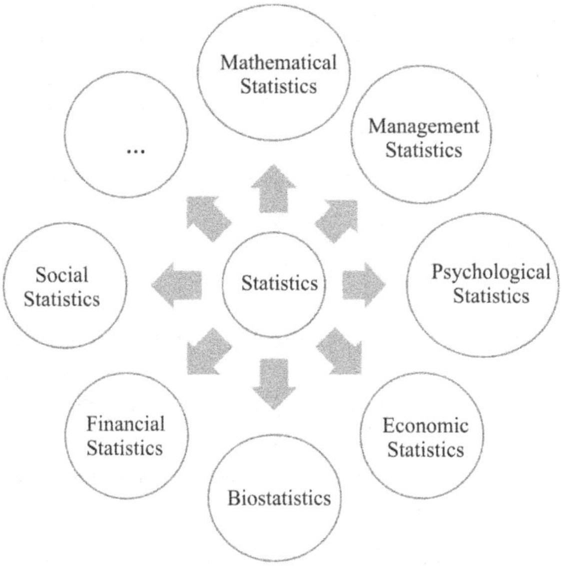

Figure 1.3 Discipline system of statistics

This section will mainly introduce the applications of statistics in the fields of economy, international trade, management, finance and computer science.

1. Applications in Economy

Statistics is a powerful tool for understanding the quantitative laws of the objective world. It is necessary to accurately grasp all kinds of quantitative information related to economic operation when conduct macro national economic management decision or micro enterprise management decision.

Cases, such as study the structure of the service industry and its impact on the national economy, study the relationship between unemployment rate and economic growth based on correlation and regression analysis, analyze the impact of technology, labor force and capital on a country's economic production based on Cobb-Douglas production function theory model, build regression models to analyze the relationship between household consumption and income, are the specific applications of statistical methods in the economic field.

2. Applications in International Trade

In the analysis and research of international trade, traditional trade theory, modern trade theory, as well as tariff, non-tariff and other trade policies, all rely on a large amount of statistical knowledge. For example, when calculate the degree of trade dependence, it is also necessary to collect and sort out a large number of relevant data by combining various statistical methods, including both import and export trade volume data and Gross Domestic Product(GDP) data. When compare China with other countries, it is also necessary to collect some country data on the United Nations Data Network, and sort out and analyze it in combination with statistical charts.

The theoretical analysis of international trade combines a large number of statistical data and analysis indicators, and the theory of comparative advantage makes data demonstration through the indicator of opportunity cost. The measurement of the global value chain position of a product or industry needs to make use of the input-output model in statistics. In the analysis of international trade policy, the import and export volume and tariff rate are usually combined, and the weighted arithmetic mean method is used to calculate and analyze the tariff level of each country. When analyze the effectiveness of foreign exchange dumping, the elasticity of supply and demand is calculated with the help of statistical data. It can be seen that statistical knowledge is widely used in both theoretical analysis and policy analysis of international trade.

3. Applications in Management

In order to survive and develop, enterprises must not only understand their own advantages and disadvantages, but also grasp the market, competitors, suppliers and consumers at all times, collect relevant data that can reflect the current situation of enterprises, and transform them into useful information for enterprises to provide reference for enterprises to make scientific decisions. The role of statistics in enterprise management is the process of transforming data into valuable information.

Statistics is applied in many aspects in management, such as inventory determination (analyze the demand and inventory of raw materials to determine the purchase quantity), production control (quality inspection of sample products), market analysis (forecast sales volume based on the trial sales of new products), customer management (segmentation of customer categories, precision marketing), risk investment (analyze the return on investment and its risks), etc.

4. Applications in Finance

As a research direction of statistics, financial statistics is one of the most popular directions at present and in the future. Statistics and finance penetrate each other.

On the one hand, with the prosperity and development of the financial industry, the emerging field of digital finance, the continuous innovation and development of financial instruments, and the increasing complexity of the financial market, more and more statistical methods are used for financial data analysis and financial market research. For example, the application of normal distribution curve in quantitative trading strategy, and the applications of quantile regression in risk measurement of stocks and futures, IPO pricing behavior, and analysis of determinants of fund flow.

On the other hand, financial data has high-dimensional and high-frequency data characteristics, and it needs to find its potentially useful information with the help of statistical methods. In recent years, data mining algorithms such as neural network, ensemble learning and text analysis have been applied more and more widely in financial market. For example, research on price-volume relationship of high-frequency financial data, research on stock price prediction based on ensemble learning algorithm, research on investor sentiment based on text analysis, etc.

5. Applications in Computer Science

Computer science is an important means of the development of statistics. At present, in the background of the Big Data and digital economy era, statistics is more inseparable from computer technology. It is necessary to use various computer software to simplify the complicated and difficult calculation process in statistical methods, and use various algorithms of software to data mining on Big Data. Therefore, we should also develop from the past statistics to the 21st century computer statistics and strengthen the applications of statistical software in statistics. At present, the main statistical softwares used include SAS, SPSS, Stata, MS Excel, etc. In addition, there are data mining software and programming languages such as IBM SPSS Modeler, R, Python, Markway, etc. In the process of learning statistical methods, if you can skillfully use statistical software to solve practical problems, you will get twice the result with half the effort.

1.3 Data Classification

1.3.1 Types of Data

Statistical data is the result of statistical practice activities, when doing a study, it is important to know the type of data involved. The type of data you use determines which statistical methods should be used for analysis. In this section, you will learn how to classify data by types and by levels of measurement. Data sets consists of two types of data: qualitative data and quantitative data.

1. Qualitative Data

Qualitative data, also known as categorical data or attribute data, it consists of attributes, labels, or nonnumerical entries. Qualitative data have labels (i.e., words). For example, gender; eye color; socioeconomic level; nationality; level of education; major; a list of the goods bought by different families at a grocery store expressed by {milk, eggs, toilet paper, …}; etc.

2. Quantitative Data

Quantitative data consist of numerical measurements or counts, for example, the weights of supermodels; the average speed on a busy expressway; the scores on a final exam; the daily temperatures in Beijing of China. Quantitative data can furtherly be described as discrete type and continuous type.

Discrete data are whole numbers. It makes sense when the number of possible values is a finite number or a "countable" number. For instance, one study might count how many pets' different families own or how many eggs that a hen lays; it wouldn't make sense to have half a goldfish or half an egg.

Continuous data, also known as measured data, in contrast to discrete data, are continuous, and thus may take on any real value. It results from infinitely many possible values that correspond to some continuous scale that covers a range of values without gaps, interruptions, or jumps. For example, the amount of milk that a cow produces per day is 18.34 kg, 20.48 kg, 23.05 kg ...

[**Example 1.1**] Classifying Data by Type

The suggested retail prices of several Tesla vehicles are shown in Table 1.2. Which data are qualitative data and which are quantitative data? Explain your reasoning.

Table 1.2 Suggested retail prices of several Tesla vehicles

Model	Suggested retail price
Model 3	￥229, 900
Model Y	￥259, 900
Model S	￥789, 900
Model X	￥879, 900

[**Solution**] The information shown in Table 1.2 can be separated into two data sets. One data set contains the names of vehicle models, and the other contains the suggested retail prices. The names of vehicle models are nonnumerical entries, so they are qualitative data. The suggested retail prices are numerical entries, so they are quantitative data. And because the suggested retail prices may take on any real value, so they are continuous data.

[**Example 1.2**] Determine whether the data are qualitative or quantitative.

(1) The career of some people.

(2) The daily high temperatures for month of August.

(3) The percentage scores of a class in an exam.

(4) The telephone numbers in a telephone directory.

[**Solution**] (1) The career is nonnumerical entries, we use words as the values(key words), so it's qualitative data;

(2) The daily high temperatures and the percentage scores can use the number to represent, so they are quantitative data;

(3) The telephone numbers are numerical entries, but each of them is just one label, the number has no quantitative meaning, so it is qualitative data, not quantitative data.

From the previous example, we can see that some qualitative data can be coded with numbers in reality, but this does not mean that they are quantitative data, unless the number itself has quantitative meaning. For example, we usually mark male as 1 and female as 2. Whereas, "gender" is still a qualitative variable, because we are more interested in the number of people in each category than the average value. In other cases, we can choose to convert quantitative data into qualitative data. For example, if we record specific income values, then "family income" is a quantitative data, but if we only record the income categories of each family ("low""medium""high"), then "family income" is a qualitative data.

1.3.2 Levels of Measurement

Statistical data is the measurement result of objective phenomena in statistical research. To measure objective phenomena, the first task is to clarify the levels of measurement of data. According to the levels of measurement, we can determine which statistical calculations are meaningful. The levels of measurement can be divided into four levels, arrange the order from the lowest to the highest and from rough to accurate, there are nominal level of measurement, ordinal level of measurement, interval level of measurement, and ratio level of measurement.

1. Nominal Level of Measurement

Nominal level of measurement is the coarsest and the lowest level of measurement. It is generally used to classify or group objects in parallel, and it is characterized by data that consist of names, labels, or categories only, and the data cannot be arranged in an ordering scheme. Such as gender, occupation, area code, place of birth and nationality, etc. Data at this level are qualitative only, and no mathematical computations can be made. If it is expressed in numbers, the numbers simply represent a label. For example, numbers on sport jerseys, student ID or telephone numbers. The main mathematical feature of nominal level is "$=$" or "$\neq$".

Classification using nominal level must conform to the principles of "exhaustion" and "mutual exclusion", that is, each individual or unit must belong to a certain category and can only belong to one category in all categories. Nominal level of measurement is the most basic measure of things, and it is the basis of other levels of measurement.

2. Ordinal Level of Measurement

Ordinal level of measurement is the difference measurement in a rank or an order between things. It is a level of measurement higher than nominal level of measurement. This level of measurement not only classifies things into different categories, but also reflects their strengths, weaknesses, or order, but differences between data entries are not meaningful. For example, (1) First-class, second-class, third-class and waste products of product quality grade; (2) First-class scholarship, second-class scholarship and third-class scholarship; (3) birth order of a person (first-born, second-born, etc.) (4) top five players; (5) size of clothes: S, M, L, XL, XXL; (6) Grade assessment of course examination: A, B, C, D, E.

Data at this level are qualitative or quantitative. Obviously, ordinal level of measurement is more accurately than nominal level of measurement, but it just measures the order between categories without measuring the exact difference between them. Like nominal level of measurement, ordinal level of measurement has no mathematical computations. The main mathematical feature of ordinal level is "$<$" or "$>$". The position of median or quantile can be determined in data analysis.

[**Example 1.3**] Try to judge which data set at the nominal level or which data set at the ordinal level?

(1) Movie genres: comedy, adventure, action or drama; (2) Top five grossing movies of 2022 in China.

[**Solution**] (1) Movie genres. No mathematical computations can be made with the names and the names cannot be ranked, so these data are at the nominal level.

(2) Top five grossing movies can be listed in order, and these data are at the ordinal

level. Note that the difference between a rank of 1 and 5 has no mathematical meaning.

3. Interval Level of Measurement

Interval level of measurement is a level of measurement higher than ordinal level of measurement. This level of measurement can not only represent the difference of various categories and order of phenomena with numbers, but also represent the meaningful differences between data entries to be calculated. Data at this level are quantitative only. It is worth noting that a zero entry simply represents a position on a scale at this level; the entry is not an inherent zero. For example, there is no absolute zero point for the values of Celsius temperature, test scores, IQ, etc. The 0℃ temperature is simply a position on the Celsius scale, not mean no temperature; a score of 0 does not mean that you have not learned anything; an IQ of 0 does not mean there is no IQ. Because of the existence of non-absolute zero value, so the main mathematical feature of interval level is "+" or "−". For example, a temperature of 30℃ is 15 different from 15℃, but it does not mean that 30℃ is twice as hot as 15℃.

4. Ratio Level of Measurement

Ratio level of measurement is the highest of the four level of measurement. In addition to all the characteristics of the above three levels of measurement, ratio level of measurement has a feature that it cannot only add and subtract, but also multiply and divide. That is, the main mathematical feature of ratio level is " * " or "/". This means a zero entry is an inherent zero for ratio level of measurement, which is also an important difference compared with the interval level of measurement. For example, people's age, height, weight, length, area, volume of objects, savings account, etc., all have absolute zero points, that is, "0" means "none". We can compare two related numbers to get relative number or average number, which reflects the quantitative relationship such as structure, speed, density or mean of a phenomenon. Therefore, ratio level of measurement has the widest application range.

Table 1.3 summarizes the mathematical characteristics at each of the four levels of measurement. High-level measurement can have the features of low-level measurement. For example, ratio level of measurement includes the features of interval level of measurement, interval level of measurement includes the features of ordinal level of

Table 1.3 Summary of the mathematical characteristics of four levels of measurement

Mathematical features	Levels of measurement			
	Nominal level	Ordinal level	Interval level	Ratio level
Classify(=, ≠)	√	√	√	√
Sort(<, >)	×	√	√	√
Space(+, −)	×	×	√	√
Ratio(* , /)	×	×	×	√

measurement, and so on. However, low-level measurement cannot have the features of high-level measurement.

1.3.3 Other Data Types

According to above four levels of measurement, statistical data can also be divided into nominal data, ordinal data, interval data and ratio data. Among them, nominal data is also called classified data, displayed in several categories, without inherent size and high or low order; ordinal data is also called sequential data, displayed in several categories, and listed in a sequence; interval data and ratio data are numerical values, which can do mathematical calculation of add, subtract or multiply, divide.

According to the data collection method, the statistical data can be divided into observation data and experimental data. Observation data is generally collected through investigation or observation. Types of statistical data related to social and economic phenomena are almost observation data. Experimental data is the data collected by controlling experimental objects through experiments. Types of most data in the field of natural science are experimental data.

According to the described phenomenon and time period relationship, the statistical data can be divided into cross-sectional data, time series data and panel data.

(1) Cross-sectional data refers to data collected at a certain point in time or at approximately the same time, this kind of data is usually obtained from different spaces, such as the number of international students in Chinese universities in 2022.

(2) Time series data refers to the data collected from an object at some time points, reflecting the change of phenomenon with time. For example, from January, 2018 to March, 2022, measure the height of the children once a month.

(3) Panel data refers to the data collected for the same batch of objects at multiple points in time. For example, from January, 2018 to March, 2022, the height and weight of fathers, mothers and children were collected every month.

1.4 Basic Concepts of Statistics

1.4.1 Population and Sample

1. Population and Population Unit

Population is the collection of all outcomes, responses, measurements, or counts in which people are interested. For example, all likely voters in the next election, all parts produced today, all sales receipts of November. It is a whole composed of many individual units that exist objectively and have some common properties. Population unit, can also be called as unit, is the individual that makes up the population. We can think of the population as a set, and the unit as the elements of the set.

For example, to study the working conditions of equipment in industrial enterprises, all equipment constitutes a population, and each equipment is a unit. If we study the consumption level of urban residents in China, then all urban residents in China constitute the population, and each urban resident is a unit.

Population and unit are two concepts at different levels, and the relationship between them will change timely with different research purposes, so their relationship is relative. For example, to study the canteen environment of a university, all the canteens of the university constitute the population, and each canteen of the university is a unit. If we study the teaching environment of universities in a region, all the universities in the region constitute the population, and each university in the region is a unit.

Population can be divided into finite population and infinite population. Finite population is the population composed of finite units, that is, the scope of the population can be clearly determined. For example, to investigate students' satisfaction with the course, all students who take the course belong to a finite population. Infinite population is the population made up of an infinite number of units, such as fishes in the sea or stars in the sky. The significance of distinguishing between finite population and infinite population is the different survey methods adopted. For a finite population, a census or sampling method can be used; for an infinite population, only sampling methods can be used.

2. Sample

The set of units drawn from one population is called a sample, which is a subset or part of the population. Sample can be used to represent population, so the sample data can be used to draw conclusions about population data. In the actual survey process, we can observe all units by census, but unless the population is small, it is usually impractical to obtain all units. In most studies, information are obtained from random sample, we use samples to infer the characteristics of population. Note, Sample must be collected through appropriate method, such as random sampling, we will introduce these contents in Chapter 2. When sample are collected through an inappropriate method, data cannot be used to draw conclusions about population.

Samples are drawn from population, the number of units contained in sample is called sample size, and the number of samples that be drawn from the same population is called sample number. How many samples may be drawn from a population depends on both the sample size and the sampling method.

In inferential statistics, sample size is very important. The larger the sample size, the higher the cost of sampling survey, but the smaller the error of sampling survey. Conversely, the smaller the sample size, the greater the error of the sampling survey, and even the act of sampling inference is meaningless. In many reference books, a sample with a sample size of no less than 30 is generally called large sample, and a sample with less than 30 is called a small sample. The sample size is different, so the sampling inference method is also different.

1.4.2 Population Parameters and Sample Statistic

1. Population Parameters

Population parameters, as known as parameters, are numerical measurements describing some characteristics of population. The value of each of population parameters is unique and constant, but it is usually unknown. Various parameters can be used to describe the comprehensive quantitative characteristics of population from different aspects. Common population parameters include: population mean, population variance, population standard deviation, population proportion (also known as population ratio), etc. Among them, population mean is the centralized trend of describing the population distribution, and population variance and population standard deviation are the dispersion trend of describing the population distribution. We will study these contents in Chapter 4.

2. Sample Statistic

Sample statistic, as known as statistic, are numerical measurements describing some characteristics of a sample. The estimated population parameters are used to express the functions of sample statistic. The calculation method of statistic is constant, but the values of them differ from sample to sample, so sample statistic is a random variable. Corresponding to the population parameters, common sample statistic includes sample mean, sample variance, sample standard deviation, sample proportion (also known as sample ratio), etc. For example, if we draw a sample of 40 students from a university and compute their mean GPA (that is, the grade point average, usually on a 4.2-point scale, for each student), we have the sample statistic. If we could compute the mean GPA for all students in a university, we would have the population parameters.

In inferential statistics, we use statistic to estimate parameters. The relationship of population parameters and sample statistic is shown in Figure 1.4.

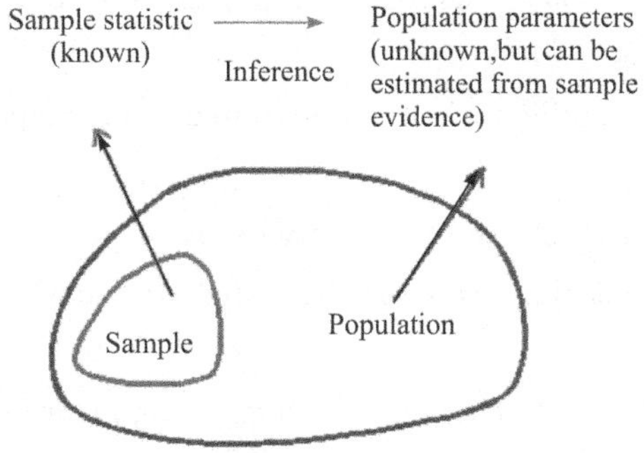

Figure 1.4 The relationship of population parameters and sample statistic

Chapter Review

In this chapter, we have presented the basic definition of statistics, the object of statistical research, the basic process of statistical study: statistical origin and development. Through the study of this chapter, on the basis of understanding the concepts of statistics, you should master the specific contents and relationships contained in two branches of statistics, namely descriptive statistics and inferential statistics. At the same time, understand the types of data: qualitative data and quantitative data, and the four levels of measurement; master the basic concepts of statistics, including population, unit, sample, population parameters and sample statistic, and can clearly identify the connections and differences between them. We hope students make a solid understanding of above concepts for future research. In a word, this chapter is the introduction of the book, and also provides readers with a general understanding of statistics, so as to facilitate the learning of the following chapters.

Exercise

1. What is the definition of statistics?

2. How to understand the relationship among statistical practice activities, statistical data and statistics?

3. How to understand the statistical research object?

4. What are the two main branches of statistics?

5. What are the main links in statistical research process?

6. What are the types of data?

7. True or false.

(1) Sample is a subset of population. (　　)

(2) Inferential statistics involves using a population to draw a conclusion about a corresponding sample. (　　)

(3) Population is the collection of some outcomes, responses, measurements, or counts that are of interest. (　　)

(4) Data at the ordinal level are quantitative only. (　　)

(5) More types of calculations can be performed with data at the ratio level than with data at the interval level. (　　)

8. Determine whether the data are qualitative or quantitative.

(1) Heights of hot air balloons.

(2) Carrying capacities of pickups.

(3) Eye colors of models.

(4) Student ID numbers.

(5) Weights of infants at a hospital.

(6) Species of trees in a forest.

(7) Responses on an opinion poll.

(8) Wait times at a grocery store.

9. Indicate which of the following variables are continuous and which are discrete.

(1) Product output value.

(2) Commodity sales volume.

(3) Number of staff and workers.

(4) Labor productivity.

(5) Unit product cost.

(6) Number of equipment.

(7) Monthly salaries.

(8) Number of product varieties.

10. Indicate the levels of measurement for the following variables:

(1) Gender; (2) Height; (3) Salary; (4) Weight; (5) Team ranking; (6) Nationality.

11. Identify the population and the sample.

(1) A survey of 202 pilots found that 20% admit that they have made a serious error due to sleepiness.

(2) To gather information about starting salaries at companies listed in the Standard & Poor's 500, a researcher contacts 65 of the 500 companies.

12. Determine whether the numerical value is a population parameter or a sample statistic.

(1) In a survey of a sample of China adults, 97% owned a mobile phone.

(2) Voter registration records show that 78% of all voters in a county are registered as Democrats.

(3) In a recent semester, the average score of statistics for all students was 85.6.

Chapter 2

Data Collection

Statistical data is the basis of statistical analysis, if there is no statistical data, there is no way to conduct any statistical analysis. Therefore, how to collect accurate and reliable statistical data is an important process of statistical research. For example, (1)If you want to know the situation of students' canteen, how to collect the related data? Which methods should you choose to collect data? (2) For the 2020 China's 7th Census, the Statistics Bureau sent short forms to every household. Short forms ask all members of every household such as their gender, age, race and so on. Then, a long form, which covered additional topics, was sent to about 10% of the population.

Statistical data can be divided into first-hand data and second-hand data according to different sources. The first-hand data is the statistical data collected directly from the respondents to reflect the situation of the survey unit through special statistical surveys, experiments or observations, generally known as the original data or primary data. The second-hand data, also known as secondary data, refers to data obtained from other people's surveys, observation or experiments, and had been organized and published. This chapter mainly introduces the theories and methods of collecting first-hand data.

2.1 Methods of Data Collection

The purpose of statistical research is to collect data, and then use these data for analysis and decision-making. So, there is one important question: How to collect data? Here we introduce three methods of data collection, including surveys, observations and experiments.

2.1.1 Surveys

Chairman Xi of the People's Republic of China stress repeatedly: "Investigation and research are the foundation of planning and the way to success. Without investigation, there is no voice, and without investigation, there is no decision-making power." Surveys are a method of obtaining data through direct or indirect contact between the investigator and the respondent. Most often, surveys are carried out by asking people questions. The most common types of surveys are done by interview, telephone, web, E-mail or focus group. Here we'll introduce some popular and commonly used methods.

1. Interview Survey

Interview is a method of collecting data through face-to-face conversation between the investigators and the respondents. The interview survey can be carried out in two forms: standard or non-standard. The standard interview is that the respondents answer according to the questionnaire designed by the investigators in advance; Non-standard interview means that there is no uniform questionnaire designed in advance, and the investigators talk freely with the interviewees(respondents) according to the topic or outline to obtain the required data. Interview surveys are often used in market surveys and social surveys.

2. Telephone Survey

Telephone survey is a method of communicating with interviewees to obtain data by telephone. Telephone survey has the characteristics of time-efficient and low cost. At present, telephone survey is a popular method. The telephone survey can be carried out according to a pre-designed questionnaire or a telephone interview on specific questions. The questionnaire used for telephone survey should be specific and not too many. Of course, because calls are often rejected, the visit rate of telephone survey is low.

3. Computer Assisted Telephone Interviewing (CATI)

The working form of CATI method is that the interviewer sits in front of the computer, faces the questionnaire on the screen, reads the question to the respondent at the other end of the call, and records the result of the respondent's answer into computer through mouse or keyboard; The supervisor shall monitor the whole interviewing on site in front of another computer with the help of LAN and telephone switch (Figure 2.1).

Figure 2.1 CATI work scenario

Another survey method similar to CATI is CAPI (Computer Assisted Personal Interviewing), which is also completed with the help of computers. The questionnaire is managed and presented by computers. The results of the respondents' answers are directly recorded into the computer by the respondents through mouse, keyboard, stylus or touch screen. At the end of the interview, the data is transmitted to the central server through the Internet, E-mail or wireless network. The summarized data can be directly used for statistical analysis without much sorting (Figure 2.2).

Figure 2.2 CAPI work scenario

With the wide applications of computers, we can use computers to complete the whole process of questionnaire design and display, sample selection, telephone dialing, survey records, data processing and analysis, etc.

4. Web Survey

Web survey, also known as internet-based survey or online survey, is investigators use Internet to distribute questionnaires to specific subjects, and also use the Internet to withdraw the questionnaires answered by respondents. In essence, the web survey is closer to the way of mailing the questionnaire, because none of the investigators participated in it, and all of it was completed by the respondents themselves, but it has changed the way of mailing the paper and pen questionnaire in the past into the way of sending the electronic questionnaire online. At present, there are some online survey platforms on the market, such as Questionstar (wjx.cn), Tencent Questionnaire, 51diaocha.cn, etc.

Compared with face-to-face and telephone interviews in the form of paper and pen, web survey saves the costs of recruitment, training, travel, labor and other costs of visitors (possibly supervisors and quality inspectors); Compared with CAPI and CATI, web survey also saves the cost of purchasing computers and internet equipment. In addition, web survey also has the advantages of fast access and timely information feedback; and it can reduce data entry errors and other advantages. Of course, this method also has shortcomings, such as the uncertainty of the population representativeness of the samples participating in the web survey. For example, the commonly used WeChat friend circle forwarding the questionnaire at present, the friend circle of each questionnaire issuer may be a group of people who are similar to themselves, so the final collected data may only represent the cognition, behavior and attitude of this group of people, and cannot be inferred to a broader group.

5. Focus Group

Focus group is a data collection method in which investigators (researchers) and respondents discuss some issues together to obtain necessary information. It is worth noting that this method is a one-to-many conversation, not a simple summary of one-to-one interviews. The interaction of respondents (participants) is also an important part of the interview. This method is often used in market research (See Figure 2.3).

Figure 2. 3 Focus group scenario

Before the group discussion, it is first necessary to draw up the discussion outline according to the research purpose and research conditions. The questions in the outline are usually open, and there must be a certain logical relationship. The number of people participating in the discussion should not be too large, usually 6 – 10, and investigators should be experts or experienced people in the subject under investigation. The way of discussion mainly depends on the habits and preferences of the host. Therefore, the moderators shall understand the background of the question, be familiar with the purpose of the survey, understand the basic situation of the group members, and be good at guiding the discussion, fully mobilize the enthusiasm of the group members to collect desired information.

The focus group has the advantages of high efficiency in collecting data, flexible structure, and more in-depth and extensive data. Of course, there are also some disadvantages, for example, scattered answers are not conducive to later collation and analysis, it is easy to cause judgment errors.

2. 1. 2 Observation and Experiment

1. Observational Study

In an observational study, the researcher observes and measures characteristics of interest of part of one population but does not change existing conditions. Generally speaking, during observation and research, observers or investigators go to important places (such as supermarkets, overpasses in busy areas, etc.) to observe and record people's behaviors and actions by themselves or by setting up instruments. Because the investigators are not forced to intervene, the respondents do not need to make any response, so they usually obtain data information without the respondents' awareness. For example, an observational study of traffic flow, or researchers observe the service and management level of a restaurant as a "mystery customer".

2. Experiment

An experiment is a special study, which conduct experiments on the survey objects to obtain the required data in a special test site and in a special state. In an experiment, the purpose was to determine the extent of the effect of treatment (explanatory variables) on the results (response variables). Usually, a treatment is applied to one part of population and whose responses are observed, which is called treatment group; another part of population is called the control group without any treatment (The subjects in the treatment group and the control group are often referred to as experimental units). In most cases, the same number of subjects are used in each group. For example, researchers may change the performance awards for employees in different departments, some departments change their employee awards, and others do not, so as to understand how this will affect the team's ability to perform specific tasks. Another example is there are two kinds of advertisement, A and B, are published in the same newspaper on the same day, the size and position of the two are basically the same, and then they are distributed to the readers in order to measure their response to the advertising.

2.2 Statistical Survey and Design

2.2.1 Statistical Survey Plan Design

Before the statistical survey, it is necessary to be familiar with how to design a statistical survey plan. Survey plan design is the overall planning of the survey. For large-scale surveys such as population census, perfect statistical survey plan design is particularly important. In general, a statistical survey plan should include the following items:

1. Determine the Purpose of the Survey

Whether it is a special topic survey, a large-scale comprehensive survey, a small symposium survey or even an individual in-depth interview survey, clarifying the purpose of the survey is the primary issue of the survey plan design. Only when the purpose of the survey is determined, can the content and main methods of the survey be determined.

The specific contents of a survey vary widely, it can be related to the views, attitudes, cognition and other issues of the people, for example, students' perceptions and attitudes towards cultural differences at home and abroad, people's views and attitudes towards love, and foreigners' views on Chinese tea culture. Besides this, the contents of a survey can also be specific habits or behaviors, such as people's shopping habits, preferences for goods, daily living habits, etc. In fact, the purpose of the survey is to solve the problem of "why do the survey?" "what is the type of problems to be solved?"

2. Determine the Object and the Scope of the Survey

After clarify the purpose of the survey, it is necessary to define the scope of the survey and the survey object. Different types or different subjects have different objects, the survey object of the "survey of citizens' shopping habits" is the citizens who have shopping activities; The survey object of "household daily consumption survey" is household; the object of the "college students' attitudes towards love" is college students. Therefore, it is necessary to determine the survey object according to the main purpose of the survey, and clarify that the survey object is to solve the question of "who should be the object of our survey?"

Clarifying the scope of the survey solves the problem of "where to do the survey?". For example, the scope of the "Hangzhou residents' energy consumption survey" is the households within 10 districts and counties in Hangzhou. The scope of the survey is of great significance for determining the workload of the survey and the arrangement of personnel and cost in the later stage. And the two factors (the object and the scope of survey) also have an important impact on the later sampling design, and the quality of the sampling design plays a vital role in the final data.

3. Determine the Survey Contents

After the purpose, the object and the scope of the survey are determined, specific survey contents must be determined. The question is "what is survey content?".

For example, in the 2020 China's 7th Population Census, the survey proposed contents such as name, gender, age, nationality, household registration status, education level, industry, occupation, migration and mobility, marriage, childbirth, death, housing, etc. Various survey contents are arranged in a certain order on a certain table, which constitutes the questionnaire. Questionnaire is the most commonly used way to express survey contents and an important tool to collect statistical survey data. Questionnaire design plays a significant role in the process of survey and statistical study, and it will be specially discussed in the Section 2.2.2 of this chapter.

4. Formulate the Survey Organization Plan

If you want to implement the survey design idea, you need to develop a detailed survey organization plan, such as how to train investigators, how to improve data quality through effective measures, how to input and delete data, and so on. For large-scale or inexperienced surveys, pilot survey should be carried out to gain experience and improve the survey scheme.

In the survey program, pilot survey (a thorough and detailed organization and implementation plan survey) can ensure a smooth progress of the whole statistical survey.

5. Selection of Data Processing and Analysis Methods

Most of the original data collected by the survey method are scattered and disordered, which can only reflect the appearance of things. It is required to make a large number of original data systematic and organized, by processing and summarizing and to design in advance what methods to be used for data collection and analysis. With the development of statistical theory and the wide applications of statistical software, there are more and more statistical methods available for statistical data analysis, such as visualization technology, descriptive analysis method, correlation analysis, regression analysis, etc. These methods will be introduced in the following chapters. Each analysis method has its own characteristics and applicabilities. In the survey design, appropriate analysis methods should be selected according to the needs of the survey.

2.2.2 Questionnaire Design

Questionnaire design is the process of quantifying survey purposes and survey needs into specific survey topics. Clarifying the purpose and content of the survey is one of the most important work in the questionnaire design. It is not only the premise of the questionnaire design, but also the basis. From the current statistical practice, in addition to the surveys conducted by professional statistical institutions of national statistical departments, a large number of small-scale and medium-scale social and market surveys are conducted by various specialized organizations, and most of these surveys are carried out by questionnaire. The questionnaire plays the role of "bridge" in the survey process, which is a key tool for communication between researchers and interviewees. A complete questionnaire usually includes the following structure.

1. Title

The title of the questionnaire is used to summarize the research topic of the survey, from which the respondents can clearly know the questions to be answered. Make sure the title is concise and likely to interest the respondents. For example, "automobile consumption survey" "Differences of eastern culture and western culture" "Internet and mobile usage of Chongqing city" "Relationships: differences between Chinese and foreigners" and so on. And do not simply use "questionnaire survey" as a title, it usually causes respondents to refuse to answer due to unnecessary doubts.

2. Preface

The preface of questionnaire is usually in the form of a paragraph, which aims to explain the purpose and significance of the survey to the respondents. The preface of the questionnaire is usually placed at the beginning of the questionnaire. Generally, it includes the following contents: the identity of the investigator, the description of the purpose of the investigation, the general content of the investigation, the selection method of the investigation object, the security measures for the investigation data and acknowledge, and sometimes it also includes the notes and specific instructions for filling in the questionnaire. By reading the preface of the questionnaire, the respondents can clearly understand the purpose of the survey, eliminate their concerns and complete the questionnaire as required.

3. Main Part

The main part should include the main contents of the survey and the explanation of some answers. Generally, the main body of the questionnaire is divided into two parts. The first part is the background information of the respondents, that is, questions about the individual's personal information. Such as in consumer survey, consumer's gender, nationality, marital status, education level, occupation, income, etc. Through these items, it is convenient for statistical grouping and analysis of the survey data. Some respondents will think that background information is personal privacy, unwilling to answer and expressing a contradiction or refusal, so it is suggested that background information should be placed at the end of the questionnaire. The second part is the basic question of the investigation that researchers need to understand, which is the most important part of the questionnaire. The design quality of this part directly affects the quality of the whole survey.

Both the background information and the basic questions of the investigation should be provided to the respondents in the form of questions. The types of questions are closed-end questions(select from a short list of defined choices, for example, your major is: Business, Management, International Trade, or Statistics); open-end questions (respondents are free to respond with any value, words, or statement, for example, what did you like best about this course?).

4. Coding

Coding is the working process of converting the survey items in the questionnaire into codes and numbers. Most questionnaires need to be coded, so that they can be sorted and easily processed by computer and statistical analysis. Therefore, in questionnaire design, the number of each survey item should be determined, and the corresponding coding should be prepared. At the same time, each questionnaire must be coded.

5. Other Materials and Concluding Remarks

Other materials refer to the records of some basic information of the investigation, such as the time and place of the investigation, the name of the investigator and the contact information of the respondent. Concluding remarks can be exampled as, "Finally, we would like to thank the respondents again for their cooperation." Take into account the connection with international standards, be aware that the above-mentioned records should be approved by the respondents before proceeding.

2.3 Sampling Techniques

A census is a count or a measurement of the entire population. A census can provide complete information about the population, but it usually takes a lot of time, energy and money. Especially when the population is very large, it is impractical to conduct a census. Interestingly, if the sample selection is appropriate, a relatively small sample will give a fairly good population value estimation. For example, about 1200 randomly selected students can provide reliable consume information about the population students in the university.

Sampling is to count or measure part of a population, which is more often used for statistical research than census. In order to collect unbiased data, we must ensure that the sample can represent the population, that is to say, the sample should have the basic characteristics of the population. As we all know, if a study uses the wrong data, then the results are meaningless. Therefore, appropriate sampling techniques must be adopted to ensure that the samples are representative and that the inference about the population is valid. Of course, even if the best sampling method is used, sampling errors may occur. Sampling error is the difference between the sample results and the population results. Next, we will learn common sampling methods, and sampling error will be introduced in Section 2.4.

According to whether each individual in the survey population has the same chance to be selected into the sample, the sampling can be divided into two categories: ① probability sampling; ② non-probability sampling. Probability sampling is sampling based on the principle of probability theory and the principle of equal probability, so it can avoid human error in the sampling process and ensure the representativeness of the sample. Non-probability sampling is mainly based on the subjective will, subjective judgment or convenience of the researcher to select the survey object, it does not consider whether the sampling is an equal probability or not, so it often produces large errors, and it is difficult to ensure the representativeness of the sample. Firstly, let's introduce some probability sampling methods.

2.3.1 Simple Random Sampling

A random sample is one in which every member of the population has an equal chance of being selected. Simple random sampling is the way to directly sampling n individuals from the population containing N individuals according to the principle of equal probability ($N>n$). That's means each individuals have equal chance to be selected. The resulting sample is called a simple random sample.

One way to collect a simple random sample is to assign a number different to each member of the population and then use a series of random numbers which can be generated by software such as MS Excel. Calculators and computer software programs are also used to generate random numbers. The specific steps are as follows: (1) Obtain a list of all members in the survey population (i.e., sampling frame). (2) Assign one number to each of the members in the population. (3) Use software such as MS Excel to generate a series of random numbers. (4) Select enough random numbers according to the sample size n. (5) Select the members in the sampling frame according to the selected random numbers correspondingly.

When simple random sampling is adopted, first sample and record a member, and then put it back into the original population to participate in the next sampling, this method is called sampling with replacement; If the selected member is no longer put back, the second element is extracted from the remaining members until n members are selected, this method is called sampling without replacement. When the population is large, sampling without replacement can be regarded as sampling with replacement.

Consider a study of the number of people who live in Qiantang New District in Hangzhou city. To use a simple random sample to count the number of households in Qiantang New District, we could assign a different number to each household, use a software or random numbers table to generate a sample of numbers, then count the number of people living in each selected household.

[**Example 2.1**] Use the Simple Random Sampling.

There are 520 students currently enrolled in a "microeconomy" course at your school. You wish to form a sample of 8 students to answer some survey questions. Select the students who will belong to the simple random sample.

[**Solution**] Firstly, assign numbers 1 to 520 to the students in the course. Second, we use function "randbetween (A,B)" in MS Excel to generate 8 random numbers from 1 to 520 like 494, 484, 326, 104, 180, 70, 134 and 51. Then, the students assigned these numbers will make up the sample.

2.3.2 Stratified Sampling

When it is required to have members from each part of the population, a stratified sampling should be used. Stratified sampling is to divide the population elements into several subgroups (also called strata) before sampling, and then randomly select a certain number of elements from each subgroup to form a sample. Stratified sampling requires small differences within stratum and large differences between stratum, it aims to ensure that the sample can represent the population.

For example, in order to collect a stratified sample of the number of people living in the West Lake District households, households could be divided into three levels as low income, middle income and high income, and then randomly select households from each level, as shown in Figure 2.4.

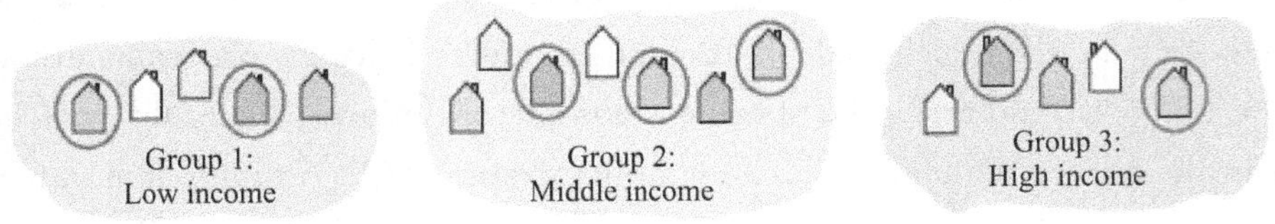

Figure 2.4 Stratified sampling method example

When a population with several strata is sampled, we often require that the number of items collected from each stratum be proportional to the strata, here we need to use the method of proportional stratified sampling. After stratifying the population or sampling frame, the researcher should select a number of items in proportion to the size of the strata from each stratum by means of a simple random sampling. For instance, if 30% of the people in West Lake District belong to the high-income group, then the sample should have 30% proportion from this group.

2.3.3 Cluster Sampling

When the population need to be divided into naturally occurring subgroups (groups), and each subgroup has similar characteristics, the cluster sampling may be the most appropriate method. Cluster sampling is to divide the population into several subgroups (called clusters), and then take the clusters as the sampling unit (to select one or more but not all of the clusters) to form a sample, and then investigate all the elements contained in each cluster in the sample. For instance, to collect a cluster sample of the voters who live in East County of United States, divide the voters into groups according to precincts, as in Figure 2.5, then select all voters (members) in one or more, but not all groups, interview all voters in shaded precincts.

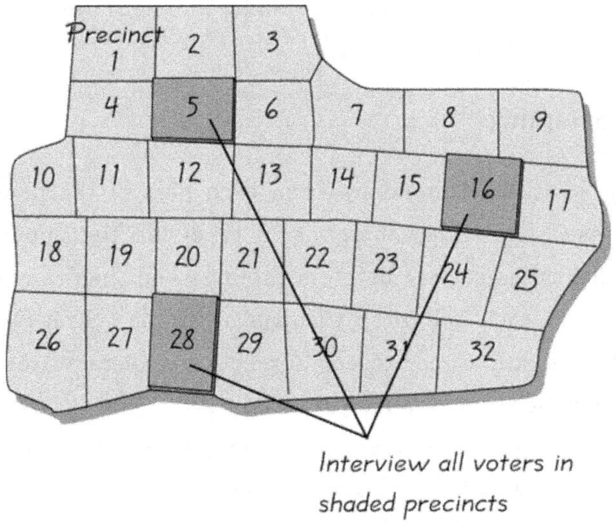

Figure 2.5 Cluster sampling method example

For another example, students' dormitories can be regarded as a cluster. A certain number of dormitories are selected from the dormitories of the whole university, and then each student in the selected dormitories is investigated. When using the cluster sampling, it is necessary to ensure that all clusters have similar characteristics, that is, small differences between clusters and large differences within clusters. For example, if the proportion of high-income people in one cluster is high, the sample may not be used to represent the population.

2.3.4 Systematic Sampling

Systematic sampling, also known as interval sampling, is to assign a number to each member of the population and sort the members in some way, a starting number is randomly selected, then calculate a certain interval, and extract members at this fixed interval until n elements are extracted to form a sample, like the Figure 2.6. (For instance, every 3rd, 6th, or 100th member is selected.)

Figure 2.6 Systematic sampling method example

Generally speaking, for the sampling interval $k=N/n$, N is the population size, n is the sample size. If we choose one start point A randomly, then the numbers in which each element counts up the selected members are A, $A+k$, $A+2k$, $\cdots$, $A+(n-1)k$. For instance, to collect a systematic sample in which each element counts up the number of households who live in West Lake District, you could assign different number to each household, randomly choose a starting number, select every 100th household, and count the number of people living in each. One advantage of systematic sampling is that it is easy to use. However, if there are any regular patterns in the data, this method should be avoided.

2.3.5 Non-probability Sampling

The above sampling methods are probability sampling methods, in addition to these, at times, people try to obtain samples by processes that are non-random but still hope, through design or faith, that the resulting sample is representative, that is non-probability sampling. The non-probability sampling methods includes convenience sampling, quota sampling, judgmental sampling, and snowball sampling.

1. Convenience Sampling

Convenience sampling, also called accidental sampling, it means that the researcher selects the people meet by chance (in a convenient way according to the actual situation) as the survey object, or only chooses the closest and easiest way to find people as the survey object. For example, handing out questionnaires to every member of a given class at school would be convenience sampling. The key issue here is that the surveyor makes the decision that whom to be included in the sample.

2. Quota Sampling

Quota sampling refers to dividing all members in the population into several categories or subgroups according to certain attributes or characteristics of the respondents, and then sampling in proportion in each subgroup. Random sampling is not required here. For instance, there are 2000 students in a university, of which 60% are boys, 40% are girls, and students in grades 1, 2, 3 and 4, respectively, accounting for 40%, 30%, 20% and 10%. A sample of 100 can be selected by quota sampling method according to the above proportion, the result of sampling is list in Table 2. 1.

Table 2. 1 Quota sampling result

	Boys (60)				Girls (40)			
Grade	1	2	3	4	1	2	3	4
Sample numbers	24	18	12	6	16	12	8	4

3. Judgmental Sampling

Judgmental sampling, also be called as purposive sampling, it is the method by which the investigators select and determine the respondents according to the research objectives and their own subjective analysis (the requirements for the investigators are relatively high).

4. Snowball Sampling

Snowball sampling(as in Figure 2. 7) is a sampling method that starts with a few suitable individuals, and then obtains more members through their interpersonal relationship network, so as to expand the sample size step by step. This method is often used to find members with the same nature, just like snowball. For example, if you want to study the life of retired elderly people, you can go to the park in the morning to meet a few walking elderly people, and then make friends with their friends. You can make a large number of elderly friends in a short time.

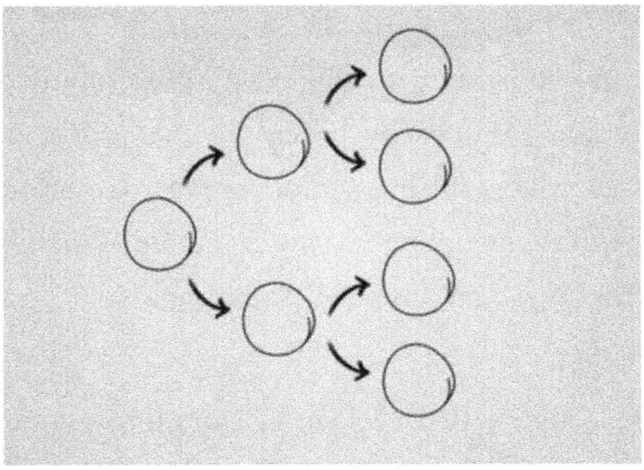

Figure 2. 7 Snowball sampling

[**Example 2.2**] Identify Sampling Techniques.

Choose a sampling technique to select the samples listed as below. Explain your reasons.

(1) Twenty-five students are randomly selected from each grade level at a high school to survey about their study habits.

(2) You assign each student a number and generate random numbers. You then question each student whose number is randomly selected.

(3) Select a class at random and question each student in the class.

(4) Law enforcement officials use a radar gun to measure the speed of every tenth vehicle on an interstate.

(5) You select students who are in your biology class.

[**Solution**] (1) Because students are divided into strata (grade level) and a sample is selected from each level, so this is stratified sampling.

(2) Each sample of the same size has an equal chance of being selected and each student has an equal chance of being selected, so this is simple random sampling.

(3) Because students are divided into cluster (classes) and choose one class at random, ask everyone in the class, this is cluster sampling.

(4) Because the radar gun measures the speed of every tenth vehicle, that's mean a certain interval, so this is systematic sampling.

(5) Because the sample is taken from students that are readily available, this is a convenience sampling. The sample may be biased because biology students may be more familiar with stem cell research than other students and may have stronger opinions.

2.4 Sampling Error and Non-Sampling Error

2.4.1 Sampling Error

Sampling error is the difference between a sample result and the true population result, such an error results from chance sample fluctuations. When using sample data to infer the population, there will inevitably be statistical inference errors, but the size of this error can be calculated and controlled in advance to ensure that the sampling inference results achieve the expected reliability. In other words, the sampling survey is carried out according to the error allowable range determined in advance, so the population inferred from part has a certain probability guarantee.

2.4.2 Non-sampling Error

Non-sampling error is also called "working error". It can be divided into three categories. The first is the sampling frame error, that is, the sampling frame error caused by the possible inclusion of heterogeneous units, by the acts of missing target units at the stage of defining the survey population or establishing the sampling frame based on the research population. The second is the answer error, that is, the answer error caused by the subjective and objective reasons of the respondents or of the investigators themselves. The third is the measurement error, which may be caused by the unscientific design of the statistical survey plan, improper coding in data processing, or improper measurement tools and methods. In short, it is very difficult to control the non-sampling error because of various causes. From the perspective of statistical study, the proportion of non-sampling error in statistical error has exceeded the sampling error, and has become the main factor restricting the accuracy of statistical data.

Extended reading

Why did the prediction of "Literary Digest" fail? ①

The American *Literary Digest* is a popular news magazine published in the United States from 1890 to 1938. Accurate predictions were made by it before the US presidential elections in 1920, 1924, 1928 and 1932.

In 1936, Franklin Delano Roosevelt and Alfred Landon jointly ran for President of the United States. At this time, the number of unemployed people in the United States was as high as 9 million. During the period of 1929—1935, the real income fell by about 1/3, and the economy was gradually recovering from the Great Depression. Landon's campaign theme is "small government", and the slogan is "those who spend money and waste must leave office", "we should concentrate on our own affairs". Roosevelt's campaign theme is "expanding domestic demand", and the slogan is "before we can balance the budget of the federal government, we must balance the budget of the American people". Most observers believe that Roosevelt will win without difficulty.

In 1936, *Literary Digest* conducted the most ambitious public opinion poll: the votes were sent to 10 million people selected from the telephone book and the registration information of car owners. The poll received more than 2 million responses. The results showed that 57% of the people supported the Communist Party candidate Alfred Landon, while the incumbent US President Franklin Roosevelt's support rate was 43%.

Two weeks later, the results of the national election came out. Roosevelt won the second term of office with the largest advantage of 62% in history. The failure of the prediction of *Literary Digest*, it is the biggest error ever made by an important public opinion poll.

---

① https://baike.baidu.com/item/%E6%8A%BD%E6%A0%B7%E5%81%8F%E5%B7%AE/10389453?fr=aladdin.

How did such a large prediction error of *Literary Digest* come about?

1. Sampling frame question: 10 million questionnaires were mailed and 2 million were recovered, but the respondents were selected from the phone book and the registration data of car owners. During the Great Depression, telephones and cars were not as common as they are now. At that time, only 11 million people owned residential telephones, but 9 million people were unemployed. It is not representative to investigate only a few people who owned automobiles and telephones, even though these lists are relatively easy to obtain.

2. Sampling bias: the sample contains too many rich people, and the election tendency between the rich and the poor is very different in the year. Those rich people supported the Republican candidate Landon, and those low-income people who failed to be surveyed supported the Democratic Roosevelt, which led to the distortion of the survey results. When there is sampling bias, more samples should be used.

3. Error caused by response or non-response, or low response rate. There are about 10 million questionnaires sent by mail, but only a few of them have been rolled back, and the effective response rate is only 23%. Landon was very popular in the questionnaire returned. So, the magazine predicted that Landon would win the election. Take Chicago as an example. The questionnaire was sent to 1/3 of the registered voters, and 20% of the questionnaires were collected. More than half of them said they would vote for Landon, but Roosevelt got 2/3 of the votes in final election results.

Chapter Review

This chapter first introduces two sources of raw data: first-hand data and second-hand data; then it introduces three main methods of data collection: surveys, observation and experiment. Next, it introduces the statistical survey plan design and questionnaire design. Finally, the probability sampling methods, non-probability sampling methods, the sampling error and non-sampling error are introduced.

Through the study of this chapter, we should first understand and master the different sources of data and the methods of data collection such as surveys, observation and experiment, understand the advantages and disadvantages of each method, and reasonably select and apply one in practice. Secondly, we should learn the statistical survey plan design and questionnaire design, which is the first work to collect raw data. Finally, we should understand several different sampling methods and clarify their application occasions and differences, so as to make these methods be flexibly used in daily investigation.

Exercise

1. What is the difference between an observational study and an experiment?

2. What is the difference between a census and a sampling?

3. What is the difference between stratified sampling and cluster sampling?

4. True or False.

(1) Use a systematic sample to guarantee that members of each group within a population be sampled. ( )

(2) A census is a count of part of a population. ( )

(3) To select a stratified sample, a population is ordered in some way and then members of the population are selected at regular intervals. ( )

(4) To select a cluster sample, a population is divided into groups and then select all of the members in at least one (but not all) of the groups. ( )

5. What is sampling error?

6. What is non-sampling error? Give some examples.

7. Determine whether you would take a census or use a sampling. If you would use a sampling, decide which sampling technique you would use. Explain your reasons.

(1) The average age of the 115 residents of a retirement community.

(2) The most popular type of movie among 100 000 online movie viewers.

8. Find an article that describes a statistical study under the following requirements.

(a) Identify the population and the sample.

(b) Classify the data as qualitative or quantitative. Determine the level of measurement.

(c) Is the study an observational one or an experimental one? If it is an experiment, identify the treatment.

(d) Identify the sampling technique used to collect the data.

Chapter 3

Data Grouping and Data Graphing

Based on the statistical survey, we can obtain the first-hand data, but these data were originally disorderly. If you want to find the characteristics and laws of the data, you need to organized the original data first, which is the basis of statistical analysis. There are many methods for data organization processing, such as arranging data in the form of tables and visualizing data in the form of graphs to observe the distribution of data. From Chapter 1, we have learnt that there are two types of data, qualitative data and quantitative data. In this chapter, you will learn how to organize data sets by grouping data to form frequency distribution, and how to use frequency distribution to create graphs, that is, statistical data visualization technology.

3.1 Frequency Distribution

3.1.1 Definition of Frequency Distribution

As an important form of statistical data organization, frequency distribution forms the distribution of each unit in each group in the whole through the orderly collection of scattered original data. The frequency distribution presented in a tabular form shows the categories or intervals of data items and the number of entries in each class. The frequency distribution includes two elements, one is the group divided by its variable value which called class, and the other is the number of data entries in the class, we call it frequency and which is expressed by f.

3.1.2 Construction of Frequency Distribution

1. Frequency Distribution of Qualitative Data

Qualitative data is mainly used to describe the classification of things. Therefore, when sorting out qualitative data collected through surveys, in addition to classifying these data and listing all categories, it is also necessary to calculate the frequency and relative frequency of each category, and present them in a tabular form, namely, the frequency distribution table of qualitative data. For example, a frequency distribution formed by grouping of gender, major, and occupation. Next, we will introduce examples to introduce the construction of such frequency distribution tables.

[**Example 3.1**] Construct a frequency distribution table.

In order to test consumers' acceptance for new perfume, a company designed five perfumes of A, B, C, D, E, randomly selected 150 consumers for the experiment, and asked them "Which of the five perfume do you like best?"

[**Solution**] The variable is perfume type which is qualitative data, and the variable value is A, B, C, D, E. After organizing the data set, we can construct a frequency distribution Table 3.1.

Table 3.1 Frequency distribution of consumers' preference for different types of perfume

Perfume Type	Frequency (f)	Relative frequency
A	65	0.43
B	30	0.20
C	22	0.15
D	15	0.10
E	18	0.12
Total	150	1.00

Obviously, after classification and organization, data can be greatly simplified. From Table 3.1, we can see that most people like type A of perfume. Then, what is the proportion of consumers like different types of perfume? Here we have,

$$\text{Relative frequency of people like type A} = \frac{\text{number of people like type A}}{\text{total number}} = \frac{65}{150} = 0.43$$

This relative frequency is a summary statistic that helps describe the qualitative variable, we see that proportion who like type A is 0.43 or 43%.

Definition 3.1 Relative frequency The relative frequency of a class is the portion, or percentage, the amount of data that falls in that class, also called proportion. To find the relative frequency of a class, divide the frequency f by the sample size n.

$$\text{Relative frequency in a class} = \frac{\text{number in that class}}{\text{total number}} = \frac{f}{n} \tag{3.1}$$

[**Example 3.2**] Construct a frequency distribution using the data set.

There is one web survey about "Some people say there is only one true love for each person. Do you agree or disagree?" Finally, received $n=2210$ people who responded to the survey, 520 people agree with the statement that there is only one true love for each person, while 1600 people disagree and 90 say they don't know. Please construct a frequency distribution table include relative frequency.

[**Solution**] The frequency distribution is as Table 3.2.

Table 3.2 Frequency distribution of response to the question

Response	Frequency (f)	Relative frequency
Agree	520	0.24
Disagree	1600	0.72
Don't know	90	0.04
Total	2210	1.00

From Table 3.2, we see the proportion of responders who agree is $520/2210=0.24$, the proportion of responders who disagree is $1600/2210=0.72$ and the proportion who responded that they don't know is $90/2210=0.04$. The proportions are added up to 1, as we expect.

2. Frequency Distribution of Quantitative Data

Constructing frequency distribution for quantitative data is an important aspect of data organization. From Chapter 1, it can be seen that quantitative data can be divided into discrete data and continuous data. If a variable is discrete with a small number of data, the value of this variable can be used as a group, which is called individually grouping. By organizing the corresponding frequency of each group, the corresponding frequency distribution table can be obtained. For example, if families (20 households) are grouped by the number of occupants, they can be divided into 5 groups: 1 person, 2 people, 3 people, 4 people, 5 people and above(see Table 3.3).

Table 3.3 Frequency distribution of the number of occupants in 20 households

Number of occupants	Number of households
1	3
2	5
3	6
4	4
5 and above	2
Total	20

In fact, many of the data we analyze are continuous data, and even discrete data may have many values. In this case, it is necessary to use the form of grouping by interval to obtain the frequency distribution table, that is to say, the variable values are divided into several intervals or classes, and that each variable value belongs to which class is determined by its size. The distance between the intervals is the class width, the boundary between adjacent classes is the class limit, and the corresponding frequency for each class is obtained.

For example, the frequency distribution ages of best actresses is shown in Table 3.4, there are six classes. The frequencies for each of the six classes are 30, 25, 10, 2, 2, and 1. Each class has a lower class limit, which is the smallest number that can actually belong to the class, and an upper class limit, which is the largest number that can actually belong to the class. Like the frequency distribution shown in Table 3.4, the lower class limits are 21, 31, 41, 51, 61, and 71, and the upper class limits are 30, 40, 50, 60, 70, and 80. The class width is the difference between two consecutive lower (or upper) class limits. For instance, the class width in the frequency distribution shown is 41−31=10 or 51−41 =10. Notice that the classes do not overlap. If the data is discrete, such as the number of workers, age (it is continuous data but take integer value), and the number of products, we usually use this form to construct a frequency distribution.

Table 3.4 Frequency distribution of ages of best actresses

Age of actress	Frequency
21 - 30	30
31 - 40	25
41 - 50	10
51 - 60	2
61 - 70	2
71 - 80	1
Total	70

Then, if the classes are overlap, as in Table 3.5, the lower class limits are 50, 60, 70, 80, and 90, and the upper class limits are 60, 70, 80, 90, and 100, it can be seen that the upper limits and the lower limits of two consecutive classes are the same value. The class width is the difference between the upper limits and the lower limits of the class, for example, the class width in the frequency distribution shown is 60−50=10 or 90−80= 10. Because of the values of continuous variables are uninterrupted, like salary, height, stock price and so on, so we should use this form to construct the frequency distribution. There is one thing to note, in the process of list corresponding frequency for each class, if there is one data valued 80, we need to follow the principle of "excluding this value from the upper limit value and include it in the class that serves as the lower limit value" in order to avoid duplicate counting.

Table 3.5 Frequency distribution of scores of "Statistics" course

Scores of "Statistics" course	Frequency
50 - 60	3
60 - 70	7
70 - 80	8
80 - 90	15
90 - 100	12
Total	45

Next, we will introduce the process of compiling such frequency distribution tables in detail.

3. Steps to Construct a Frequency Distribution from a Data Set

(1) Decide on the number of classes included in the frequency distribution. The number of classes should be between 5 and 20; otherwise, it may be difficult to detect any patterns. When in determining the number of classes in practice, we can refer to the empirical formula of American scholar H. A. Sturges:

$$n = 1 + 3.3\lg N \tag{3.2}$$

where n is the number of classes and N is the amount of data.

(2) Find the class width as follows. Determine the range of the data, divide the range by the number of classes, and round up to the next convenient number, for example, times of 5 or 10.

$$d = \frac{R}{n} = \frac{x_{max} - x_{min}}{1 + 3.3\lg N} \tag{3.3}$$

where d is the class width, R is the range of the data which is the difference between the maximum (x_{max}) data entry and minimum (x_{min}) data entry, n is the number of classes.

(3) Find the class limits. You can use the minimum data entry as the lower limit of the first class. Next to find the remaining lower limits and upper limits, we should divide the question into two situations:

① If the classes do not overlap, as in Table 3.4, you can add the class width to the lower limit of the preceding class. Then find the upper limit of the first class by the lower limit of the second class minus 1. Follow this approach, we can find the remaining upper class limits.

② If the classes are overlap, as in Table 3.5, because class width is the difference between the upper limit and lower limit of this class. So, you can find the upper class limit of the first class, then find the remaining lower class limit and upper class limit.

(4) Make a tally mark for each data entry in the row of the appropriate class.

(5) Count the tally marks to find the total frequency f for each class.

(6) Calculate the midpoint of each class by the Formula (3.4) if needed, it can be

found by adding the lower class limit and the upper class limit, and dividing the sum by two.

$$\text{Midpoint}=\frac{\text{Lower Limit}+\text{Upper Limit}}{2} \tag{3.4}$$

[**Example 3.3**] Construct a frequency distribution using the data set of the newspaper reading times (the classes do not overlap).

(1) The number of classes is five.

(2) Data set: time spent reading the newspaper in a day.

7	39	13	9	25	8	22	0	2	18	2	30	7
35	12	15	8	6	5	29	0	11	39	16	15	

[**Solution**] We have known the number of classes n is 5, the minimum number and maximum number of the data set are 0 and 39, so we can use formula (3.3) to calculate the class width

$$d=\frac{R}{n}=\frac{x_{\max}-x_{\min}}{n}=\frac{39-0}{5}=7.8\approx 8$$

Then, notice that the classes do not overlap, we find the lower limit (L_i) and upper limit (U_i) of each class, let $L_1=0$, $L_2=L_1+8=0+8=8$, like this, $L_3=16$, $L_4=24$, $L_5=32$; $U_1=L_2-1=8-1=7$, $U_2=15$, $U_3=23$, $U_4=31$, $U_5=39$. So, we can get each class list as Table 3.6. Next, count the tally marks to find the total frequency f for each class, and get the relative frequency by Formula (3.1). Finally, if needed, we use the Formula (3.4) to find the class midpoint, like $(0+7)/2=3.5$ is the first class midpoint.

Table 3.6 Frequency distribution of newspaper reading times

Class	Frequency	Relative frequency/%	Midpoint
0 - 7	8	32	3.5
8 - 15	8	32	11.5
16 - 23	3	12	19.5
24 - 31	3	12	27.5
32 - 39	3	12	35.5
Total	25	100	—

[**Example 3.4**] Construct a frequency distribution using the data set (the classes are overlap).

The scores of 40 students in the statistics exam are listed below:

66	89	88	84	86	87	75	73	72	68
75	82	97	58	81	54	79	76	95	76
71	60	90	65	76	72	76	85	89	92
64	57	83	81	78	77	72	61	70	81

[**Solution**] Due to the fact that student exam scores' are continuous variables, so we should use the overlap type of the classes. Firstly, sort the raw data in ascending sequence as follows.

54	57	58	60	61	64	65	66	68	70
71	72	72	72	73	75	75	76	76	76
76	77	78	79	81	81	81	82	83	84
85	86	87	88	89	89	90	92	95	97

According to Formula (3.2), the number of groups is calculated to be 6. However, due to the distribution characteristics of exam scores, it is generally accepted that a score of 60 is the passing line. A score below 60 is a failure, a score of 60 - 70 is a pass, a score of 70 - 80 is moderate, a score of 80 - 90 is good, and a score above 90 is excellent. So, the final number of classes was determined to be 5 and the class width to be 10. Then establish a variable sequence as shown in Table 3.7.

Table 3.7 Frequency distribution of 40 students' statistics scores

Scores	Number of students	Relative frequency/%
Below 60	3	7.5
60 - 70	6	15.0
70 - 80	15	37.5
80 - 90	12	30.0
Above 90	4	10.0
Total	40	100.0

3.1.3 Cumulative Frequency and Cumulative Relative Frequency

For the purpose of statistical analysis, it is sometimes necessary to observe how many observations lie above or below a given value. So, it is necessary to calculate the cumulative frequency or cumulative relative frequency of each class by adding each successive frequency (or relative frequency) figure to the previous cumulative figure.

The cumulative frequency distribution has two characteristics:

(1) The cumulative frequency of the first class is equal to the frequency of the first class itself;

(2) The cumulative relative frequency of the last class is equal to the total number of units (1 or 100%).

[**Example 3.5**] Given the Table 3.4, find the cumulative frequency and cumulative relative frequency.

[**Solution**] Make the cumulative frequency and cumulative relative frequency distribution as Table 3.8.

Table 3. 8 Cumulative frequency and cumulative relative frequency distribution of age of actress

Age of actress	Frequency	Cumulative frequency	Relative frequency/%	Cumulative relative frequency/%
Less than 31	30	30	42. 9	42. 9
Less than 41	25	55	35. 7	78. 6
Less than 51	10	65	14. 2	92. 8
Less than 61	2	67	2. 9	95. 8
Less than 71	2	69	2. 9	98. 7
Less than 81	1	70	1. 4	100
Total	70	—	100	—

From Table 3. 8, there are 55 actresses whose age is less than 41, there are 65 actresses whose age is less than 51, there are 69 actresses whose age is less than 71.

3. 2 Graphs of Frequency Distributions

Data visualization is a scientific and technological research of the visual representation of data, it can display the results of statistical survey data in a intuitive and effective way.

According to the above, we know that data can be divided into qualitative data and quantitative data, among which, qualitative data can be represented by bar chart, pie chart, ring chart and rose chart; For quantitative data, grouped data are usually represented by histogram, polygon, ogive, curve, etc., while ungrouped data can be represented by dot plot, stem-and-leaf plot, box plot and so on. In addition, pair data can be represented by scatter plot. Here we introduce the graphs for qualitative data and grouped quantitative data represention. The plots for ungrouped quantitative data will be introduced in Section 3. 3.

3. 2. 1 Qualitative Data Visualization

1. Bar Chart

A bar chart for qualitative data, with the bars arranged in order according to frequencies. When drawing a bar chart, each data can be placed on the x-axis (horizontal axis) or y-axis (vertical axis). A bar chart with data placed on the x-axis is called a vertical bar chart or a column chart, while a bar chart with data placed on the y-axis is called a horizontal bar chart. As in Figure 3. 1, it is a bar chart based on the data in Example 3. 2. Among them, (a) is a vertical bar chart, (b) is a horizontal bar chart.

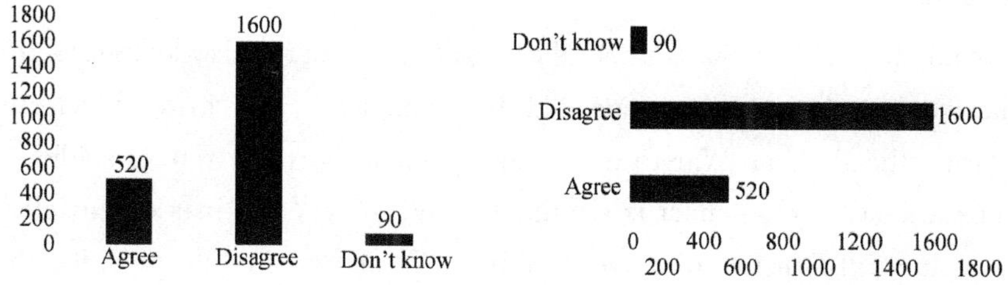

(a) Vertical bar chart (b) Horizontal bar chart

Figure 3. 1 Bar chart of response to one question

2. Pie Chart

A graph depicting qualitative data is as slices of a pie, used to represent the proportional relationship between various parts of the population. A pie chart based on the data in Example 3. 1 is shown in Figure 3. 2, which shows the proportion of consumers' preferences for different types of perfume.

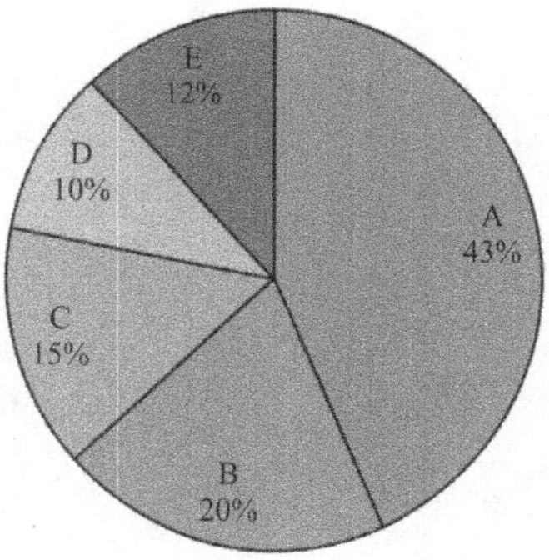

Figure 3. 2 Pie chart of consumers' preference for different types of perfume

3. Ring Chart

If multiple populations need to be compared, another form of pie chart can be used, which is ring chart. This graph hollows out the center of the circle and represents the structure of each population with a ring. A ring chart based on the final exam grades of Class A and Class B is shown as in Figure 3. 3.

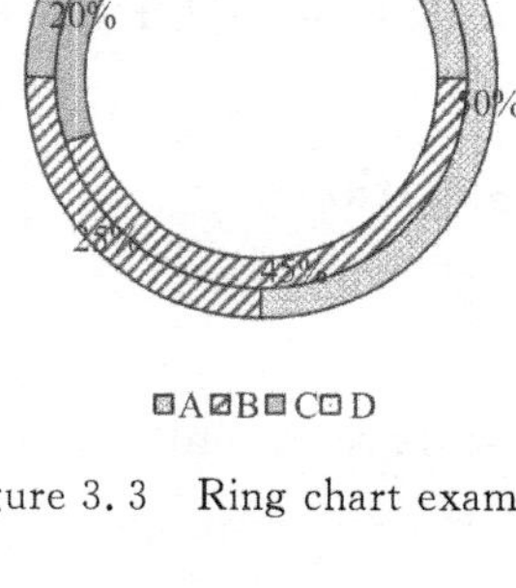

Figure 3. 3 Ring chart example

4. Rose Chart

The full name of the rose chart is the Nightingale rose chart, also known as the cockscomb chart or polar region chart. It was created by statistician and medical reformer Florence Nightingale during the Crimean War to reflect the seasonal mortality rate of soldiers.

The appearance of a rose chart is similar to a pie chart, but it is essentially a bar chart or stacked bar chart drawn in polar coordinates. As shown in Figure 3.4, this chart are based on the cumulative number of COVID-19 confirmed cases in some provinces of China (as of 12 o'clock on Nov 3, 2022). The ring chart represents the size of the data using the radius of the arc, while the pie chart represents the data using the radians of the sector. Due to the square relationship between radius and area, the rose chart visually exaggerates the size of the data. Therefore, this chart is commonly used to compare the sizes of different classifications, and the condition that differences in the values of each classification are not too significant.

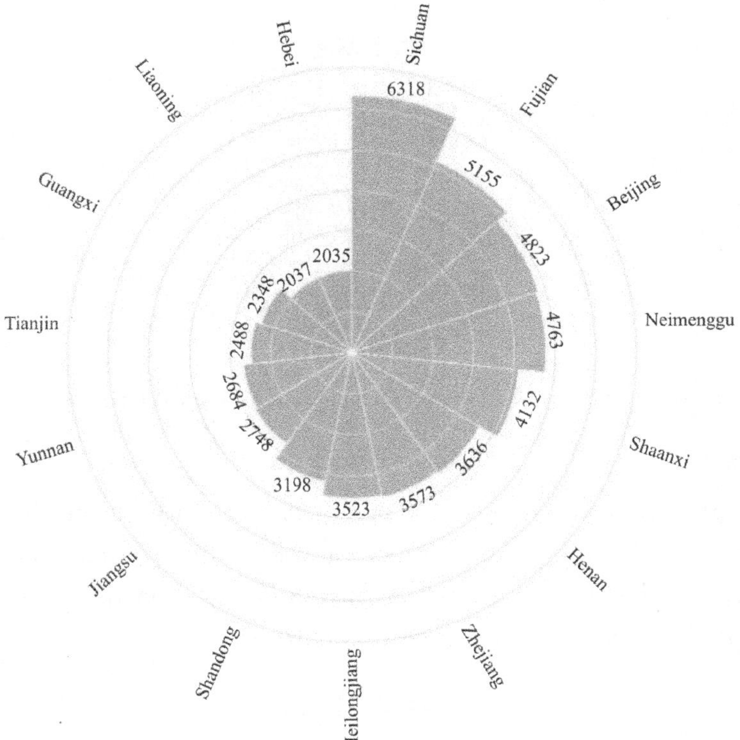

Figure 3.4 Rose chart example

3.2.2 Quantitative Data Visualization

1. Histogram

A bar chart has the horizontal scale representing the classes of data values, the vertical scale representing the frequencies (or relative frequency) of the classes, and additionally, when the bars are consecutive, we get histogram. A histogram based on the data set of Table 3.5 is shown as in Figure 3.5.

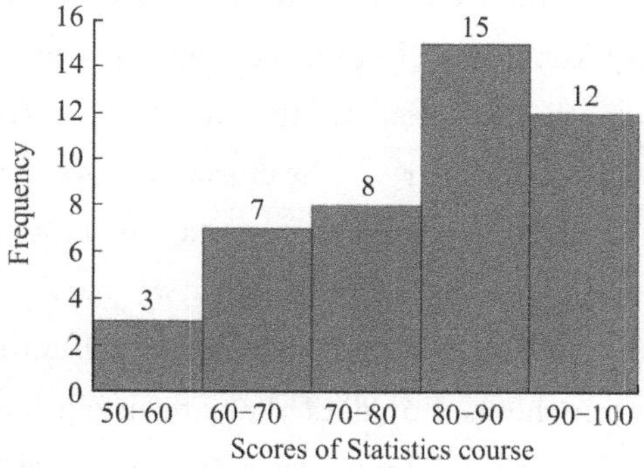

Figure 3.5 Histogram of frequency distribution of statistics scores

2. Polygon

Another way to plot a frequency distribution is to use polygon. Polygon is a line graph that emphasizes the continuous change in frequencies. This graph uses line segments connected to points directly above class midpoint values. Figure 3.6 is a polygon based on data of Figure 3.5.

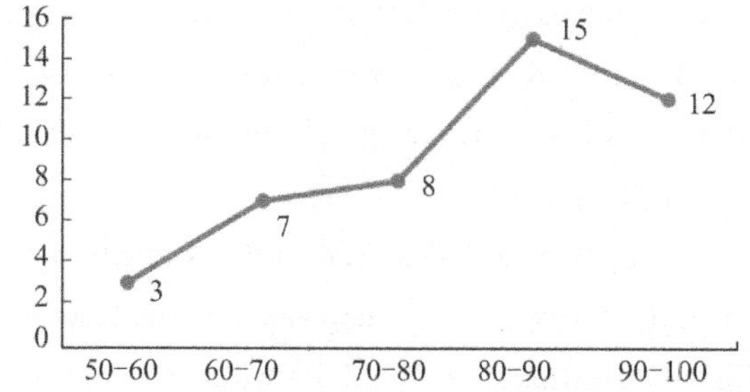

Figure 3.6 Polygon example

In addition, in practice, polygon is often used to represent the shape and trend of time series data over time. The horizontal scale represents time, and the vertical scale is the value of variable, as shown in Figure 3.7.

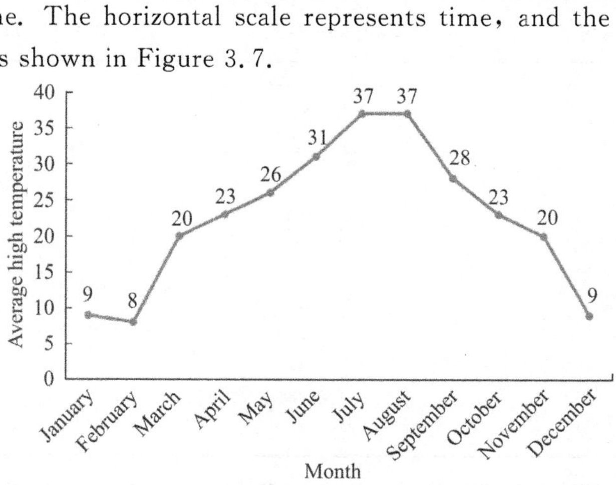

Figure 3.7 Polygon of average high temperature of each month

3. Ogive

To describe the number of data entries that are less than or equal to a certain value, we can construct ogive, also known as cumulative frequency graph.

An ogive, is a line graph that depicts the cumulative frequency of each class in corresponding to its upper class boundary. The horizontal axis represents the upper class boundaries and the vertical axis represents the cumulative frequencies.

When the limits of each class are not overlap, we need to construct the graph by means of the class boundary. Class boundaries are the numbers that separate classes without forming gaps between them. For data that are integers, you can minus 0.5 from each lower limit to find the lower class boundaries, you can add 0.5 to each upper limit to find the upper class boundaries.

How to construct an ogive, please see the next guidelines:

(1) Construct a frequency distribution that includes cumulative frequencies.

(2) Specify the horizontal and vertical scales. The horizontal consists of upper class boundaries, vertical scale measures cumulative frequencies.

(3) Plot points.

(4) Connect the points in order from left to right with line segments.

(5) The graph should start at the lower boundary of the first class (cumulative frequency is 0) and should end at the upper boundary of the last class (cumulative frequency is equal to the sample size).

[**Example 3.6**] According to the Table 3.4 and Example 3.5, draw an ogive.

[**Solution**] Given the cumulative frequencies, we can construct the ogive as in Figure 3.8. The upper class boundaries, frequencies, and cumulative frequencies are shown in the Table 3.9.

Table 3.9 Cumulative frequency of age of actress

Upper class boundary	Frequency	Cumulative frequency
30.5	30	30
40.5	25	55
50.5	10	65
60.5	2	67
70.5	2	69
80.5	1	70

Notice that the graph starts at 20.5, where the cumulative frequency is 0, and the graph ends at 80.5, where the cumulative frequency is 70, the sample size.

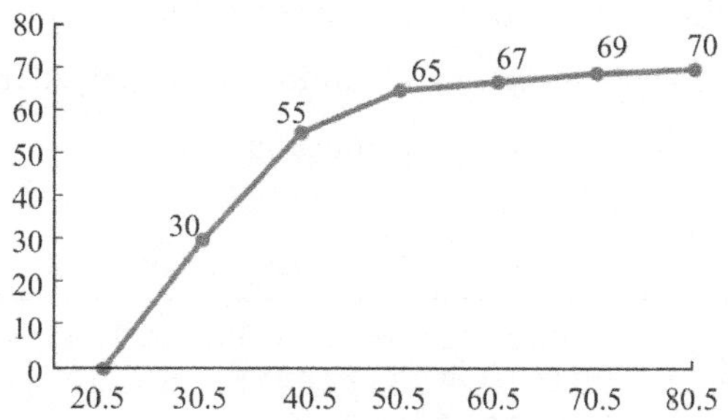

Figure 3. 8 Ogive example

4. Curve

As the number of classes in the frequency distribution increases, the polygon can approximately appear as a smooth curve. The curve is based on the polygon and replaces the line segment with a smooth curve representation, as shown in Figure 3. 9.

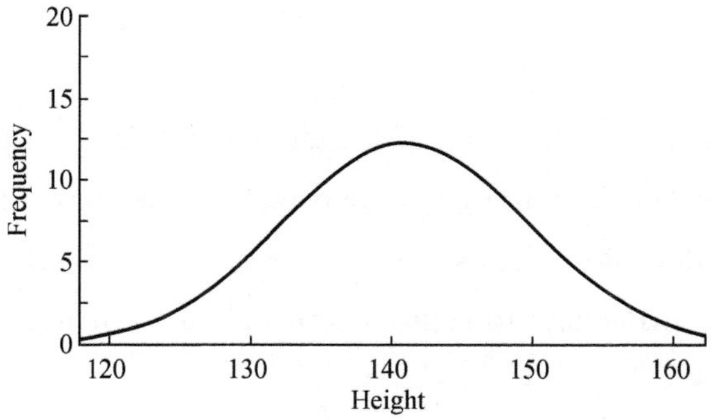

Figure 3. 9 Curve example

3. 3 More Graphs and Displays

In Section 3. 2, we introduce several ways to display qualitative or quantitative data graphically. In this section, other graphs commonly used in statistical analysis are introduced, the main objective is to understand a data set by using a suitable graph that is effective in revealing some important characteristic.

3. 3. 1 Stem-and-leaf Plot

Stem-and-leaf plots, or stemplot, are used to make examples of exploratory data analysis (EDA), which was developed by John Tukey in 1977. In a stem-and-leaf plot, represents data by separating each value into two parts: the stem (such as the leftmost digit) and the leaf (such as the rightmost digit), as shown in Figure 3. 10. The graph should have as many leaves as the number of original data, and the leaves should be single digits. A stem-and-leaf plot is similar to an inverted histogram, from which all the raw data can be seen, this is one advantage of stemplot. Another advantage of a stem-and-leaf plot is that it provides a simple data sorting method.

Stem (tens)	Leaves (units)
2	12445555666677778888999999
3	0011122333334445555555677888899
4	011111223569
5	04 ←Values are 50 and 54.
6	013
7	4
8	0 ←Value is 80.

Figure 3.10 Stem-and-leaf plot

3.3.2 Dot Plot

You can also use a dot plot to graph quantitative data. In a dot plot, each data entry is plotted by using a point (or dot) along a scale of values, as shown in Figure 3.11. Like a stem-and-leaf plot, a dot plot allows you to see how data are distributed, so as to determine specific data entries and to identify unusual data entries.

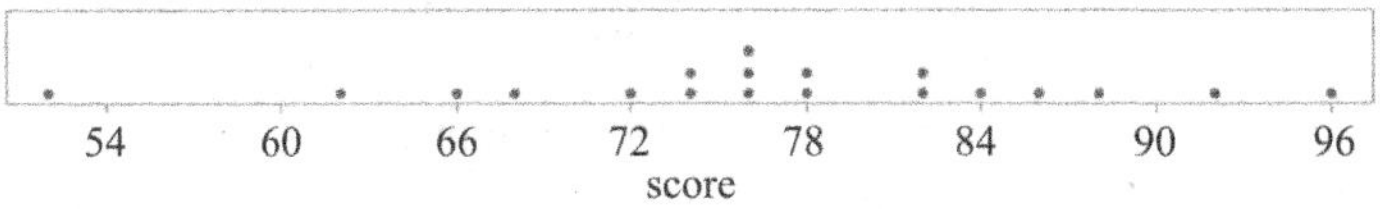

Figure 3.11 Dot plot example

3.3.3 Box Plot

A box plot, also known as a box and whisker plot, can not only display the characteristics of a set of data distribution, such as whether the distribution is symmetrical and whether there are outliers, but also compare the distribution characteristics of multiple sets of data.

The box plot consists of 5 numbers, they are Q_2, the median of entire set; Q_1, the median of bottom half of the set; Q_3, the median of top half of the set, and the maximum non-outlier number of the set and the minimum non-outlier number of the set.

The box and whisker display is a graphical representation of the five-number summary. Horizontal lines are drawn at Q_1, Q_2, and Q_3; a box is then drawn around these lines, forming a double box with a shared side. Two perpendicular lines (whiskers) are drawn from the top and bottom of the box to the maximum non-outlier number and minimum non-outlier number. Any outliers are then plotted as individual points. Figure 3.12 shows the basic box plot format.

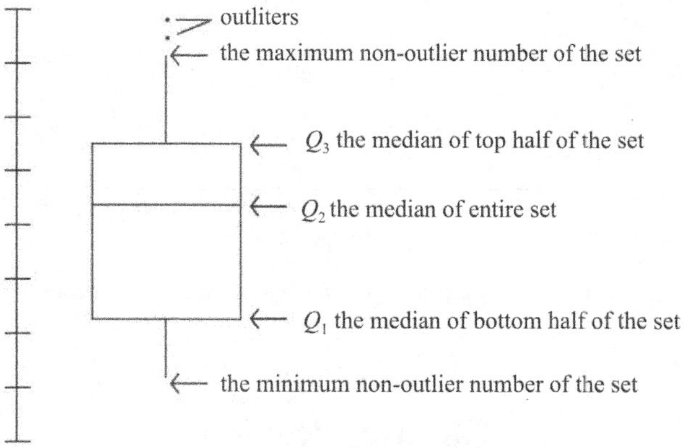

Figure 3.12 The basic box plot format

For example, randomly select ten students in the field of economic management, and conduct a survey on their exam scores in five major courses. According to the data set, the box plot is shown as in Figure 3.13. From this graph, the scores of English and Economics are better than other courses, the distribution of Mathematics score is relatively scattered.

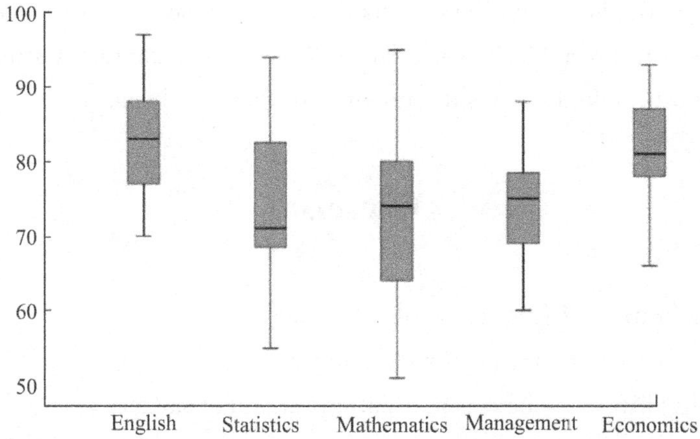

Figure 3.13 The box plot of exam scores in five major courses

3.3.4 Scatter Plot

When each entry in one data set corresponds to one entry in a second data set, the sets are called paired data sets. When two variables are analyzed, a scatter plot can be drawn, a plot of paired (x, y) data with a horizontal x-axis and a vertical y-axis, like Figure 3.14, it shows the relationship between temperature and production. You will learn these contents in detail in Chapter 8.

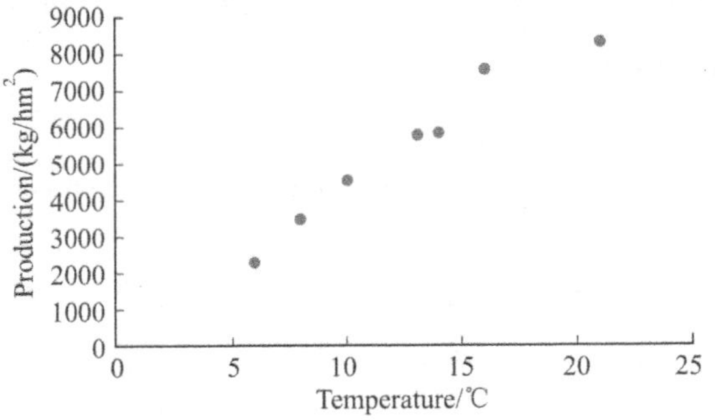

Figure 3.14 Scatter plot between temperature and production

Chapter Review

This chapter mainly introduces the principles, steps and methods of frequency distribution and data visualization. First, it introduces the specific concepts and methods of constructing frequency distribution based on qualitative data and quantitative data. Then it introduces common data visualization types for different types of data.

Through the learning of this chapter, it is necessary to understand the basic concepts and compilation methods of frequency distribution. Based on the needs of analysis, corresponding statistical graphs are selected to illustrate the characteristics and patterns of data, laying a solid foundation for subsequent statistical analysis.

Exercise

1. What is definition of frequency distribution?

2. How to construct the frequency distribution?

3. What is the difference between a histogram and a bar chart?

4. What are the advantages of using a stem-and-leaf plot compared to a histogram? What is the disadvantage?

5. Use a bar chart to display the data. The data represent the 2001 NASA space shuttle operations expenditures (in millions of dollars).

Orbiter and integration: 720.6, Reusable solid rocket motor: 425.3

External tank: 346.5, Solid rocket booster: 143.7

Main engine: 265.1, Mission/launch operations: 783.2

6. Thirty people were randomly selected, count up the number of trips to supermarket in past week as Figure 3.13. The responses are given in the bar graph. Make a frequency distribution for the data.

7. A survey of 100 resort club managers on their annual salaries is listed in the following frequency distribution as Table 3.10:

Table 3. 10

Annual Salary ($ 1000s)	15 - 25	25 - 35	35 - 45	45 - 55	55 - 65
No. of Managers	12	35	27	20	6

(1) Find the lower/upper limits, class width, midpoint, relative frequency of each class.

(2) Prepare a cumulative relative frequency distribution for the annual salaries.

8. The following Table 3. 11 shows the sales volume of a department store for 40 consecutive days (million dollars):

Table 3. 11

41	25	29	47	38	34	30	38	43	40
36	37	34	37	30	45	36	26	38	44
28	37	42	45	37	44	39	43	36	44
36	46	35	46	49	37	42	32	33	35

(1) Group the above data.

(2) Plot the histogram.

9. Use the following data set representing the actual liquid volume (in ounces) in 24 twelve-ounce cans.

11.95	11.91	11.86	11.94	12.00	11.93	12.00	11.94
12.10	11.95	11.99	11.94	11.89	12.01	11.99	11.94
11.92	11.98	11.88	11.94	11.98	11.92	11.95	11.93

(1) Make a frequency distribution of the data set with seven classes.

(2) Make a relative frequency distribution of the data set with seven classes.

10. Use the following data set. The data represent the number of meals purchased during one night's business at a sample of represent.

153	104	118	166	89	104	100	79	93	96	116
94	140	84	81	96	108	111	87	126	101	111
122	108	126	93	108	87	103	95	129	93	

(1) Make a frequency distribution of the data set with six classes and draw a frequency polygon.

(2) Make an ogive of the data set using six classes.

11. Use the following data set as Table 3.12 representing the top seven American Kennel Club registrations (in thousands) in 2000. (Source American Kennel Club, New York, NY)

Table 3.12

Breed	Labrador Retriever	Golden Retriever	German Shepherd	Dachshund	Beagle	Poodle	Yorkshire Terrier
Number registered (in thousands)	173	66	58	55	52	46	44

(1) Make a bar chart of the data set.

(2) Make a pie chart of the data set.

12. Use the following data set representing the average daily high temperature (in degrees Fahrenheit) during the month of January for Chicago, Illinois. (Source: American Oceanic and Atmospheric Administration)

33 31 25 22 38 51 32 23 23 34 44 43 47 37 29 25

28 35 21 24 20 19 23 27 24 13 18 28 17 25 31

(1) Make a stem-and-leaf plot of the data set. Use one line per stem.

(2) Make a dot plot of the data set.

13. Students in an experimental psychology class did research on depression as a sign of stress. A test was administered to a sample of 30 students. The scores are given.

44 51 11 90 76 36 64 37 40 73 56 62 36 77 55

37 28 38 61 44 66 38 45 22 37 51 46 85 13 78

(1) Construct a frequency distribution of the data.

(2) Find the midpoint, relative frequency, cumulative frequency of each class.

Chapter 4

Characteristics of Data Distribution

With the statistical investigation, many effective data points can be obtained after statistical analysis of the original data, and the data can be displayed by graphs/charts, so that we can have a general understanding of the shape and characteristics of the data distribution, but more deeply and importantly, it is necessary to fully grasp the quantity of the data from the data regularity and distribution characteristics, specifically, the necessarity and core work of descriptive statistics is to find representative values reflecting the characteristics of the overall quantity. For example, if we want to describe the quantitative characteristics of the employees, we need to know the proportion of female employees to the total number of employees, the average salary of employees, the standard deviation of employee wages, etc. In this chapter, we will introduce measures of center and measures of variation, etc.

4.1 Measures of Center

4.1.1 Meaning of Measures of Center

The measures of center is an important part of descriptive analysis of data. To understand the degree of data concentration, representative level and other information, it is necessary to measure the central tendency. Generally speaking, there are two types of commonly used central tendency measurement indicators, one is the numerical mean, that is, the average index calculated based on all the marker values of each unit in the population, including the arithmetic mean, harmonic mean, geometric mean, etc.; The other type is the position average, which is to sort the variable values of each unit, and then take the representative value corresponding to a certain position that can reflect the general level, including mode and median.

Measuring central tendency has a wide range of functions, specifically introduced as follows:

(1) It reflects the central tendency and general level of the overall unit variable distribution. Usually, in objective phenomena, the number of units with very small or very large unit variable values in the population unit is relatively small, and the number of units with variable values closer to the average number gradually increases, that is, the number of units with variable values around the mean number in the population occupies the largest proportion, showing the tendency of the population units to concentrate on the average. Therefore, the average indices are indices to measure the central tendency of variables.

(2) Compare the development levels of similar phenomena in different units at the same time. If we want to compare the development level of similar phenomena in different units at the same time, it is recommended not to use aggregate indicators for direct comparison, because aggregate indicators will be affected by factors from different scales, so the comparability of aggregate indicators is poor. If the average index is used for comparison, the problem can be explained more objectively. Average index is widely used in many occasions such as explaining production levels, economic benefits, investment project evaluation, and product cost calculation.

(3) Compare the trends or rules of similar phenomena in different periods. The individual units or the total indicators of phenomena are easily affected by accidental factors from different scales. For the average index used for analysis, only when it eliminates the effect of random factors and avoids being affected by factors from different scale, can it more accurately reflect the basic trend of the overall phenomena. For example, the total salary of employees is easily affected by the number of employees. If the average salary of employees used for comparative analysis are data from over years, it can reflect the trend of salary changes.

4.1.2 Mean, Median and Mode

A measure of central tendency is a value that represents atypical, or central, entry of a data set. The most commonly used indicators to measure the central tendency are the mean, the median, and the mode. We will introduce the mean firstly.

1. Mean

The mean includes the arithmetic mean, the harmonic mean and the geometric mean. In this section, we will focus on the arithmetic mean. The basic formula for the arithmetic mean is:

$$\text{Arithmetic Mean} = \frac{\text{Sum of all values}}{\text{Number of values}} \tag{4.1}$$

One thing to emphasize here is that the numerator and denominator of the arithmetic mean are compatible. That is to say, the total amount of the population variable values must be the sum of the variable value of each unit in the population, and there is a one-to-one correspondence between the variable and the unit. For example, the national per capita wheat consumption indicator is the ratio of the national total wheat consumption to the national population. Because every citizen has a wheat consumption indicator, the per capita wheat consumption is an average indicator. However, the per capita wheat output index is not an average index, because the wheat output is not an indicator that every citizen has, so we call the per capita wheat output an intensity relative index.

The arithmetic mean has two forms: simple arithmetic mean and weighted arithmetic mean.

1) Simple arithmetic mean

If the ungrouped data is known, it can be obtained and calculated as the ratio of the simple sum of the values of the population unit to the number of the population unit, which we call the simple arithmetic mean. The formulas for the population and sample simple arithmetic mean are as follows:

$$\bar{X}=\frac{X_1+X_2+\cdots+X_N}{N}=\frac{\sum X}{N} \tag{4.2}$$

$$\bar{x}=\frac{x_1+x_2+\cdots+x_n}{n}=\frac{\sum x}{n} \tag{4.3}$$

In Formula (4. 2), $\bar{X}$ is the population mean, X_i is the value of each unit of the population, and $N$is the number of population units; In Formula (4. 3), x is the sample average, $\bar{x}$ is the sample mean, x_i is the value of each unit of the sample, n is the number of sample units.

[**Example 4. 1**] There are 5 people in a production group, and the daily output is 25, 28, 30, 40, 47 pieces, then the mean daily output of workers is:

$$\bar{X}=\frac{\sum X}{N}=\frac{25+28+30+40+47}{5}=\frac{170}{5}=34 \textit{ pieces}$$

2) Weighted arithmetic mean

The weighted arithmetic mean is mainly used for the grouped data of the frequency distribution. If the variable value X of each class is assigned a corresponding frequency, we also call it as positive weight f, the weighted arithmetic mean is defined as the sum of their products Xf divided by the sum of their frequencies or weights.

$$\bar{X}=\frac{X_1f_1+X_2f_2+\cdots+X_Nf_N}{f_1+f_2+\cdots+f_N}=\frac{\sum Xf}{\sum f} \tag{4.4}$$

$$\bar{x}=\frac{x_1f_1+x_2f_2+\cdots+x_nf_n}{f_1+f_2+\cdots+f_n}=\frac{\sum xf}{\sum f} \tag{4.5}$$

where f is the frequency of each class.

[**Example 4. 2**] The bonus of an enterprise in June is shown in Table 4. 1:

Table 4.1 Bonus for employees of an enterprise (frequency weighted) in June

Bonus/Yuan	Number of employees (person)(f)	group median(X)	Xf
100 - 150	6	125	750
150 - 200	10	175	1750
200 - 250	12	225	2700
250 - 300	35	275	9625
300 - 350	15	325	4875
350 - 400	8	375	3000
total	86	—	22700

Then the mean bonus of employees of this enterprise in June is:

$$\bar{X} = \frac{\sum Xf}{\sum f} = \frac{22700}{86} = 263.95 \text{ Yuan}$$

Since this example is known to be a series of group distance distributions, it is necessary to first obtain the group median value of each group as the representative of each group of data, and then multiply the group median value by the frequency of the corresponding group to obtain the total number of signs, then the average is calculated by Formula (4.4). At this time, in applying the median value of the group, it is assumed that the data of each group is evenly distributed within the group, and the results are approximate.

When is calculating the weighted arithmetic mean, one issue should be paid attention to: the significance and function of weights.

The reason we call the frequency of each class as the weight is that in addition to the variable value of each group, the frequency of each class also has a weighing effect on the average.

(1) The greater the number of times of each group, the greater the share of the mark value recorded in the average, and the greater the impact on the average.

(2) The smaller the number of times of each group, the smaller the share of the mark value recorded in the average, and the greater its impact on the average.

(3) If the number of times of each group is equal, the influence of the sign value corresponding to the number of times on the average does not exist, that is, the number of times does not have the so-called trade-off effect on the average. This form is a special case of the weighted arithmetic mean, where the weighted arithmetic mean is equal to the simple arithmetic mean. Instantly, $f_1 = f_2 = f_3 = \cdots = f_N$, then, the formula for the weighted arithmetic mean becomes:

$$\bar{X}=\frac{\sum_{i=1}^{N}X_i\cdot f_i}{\sum_{i=1}^{N}f_i}=\frac{f\sum_{i=1}^{N}X}{Nf}=\frac{\sum_{i=1}^{N}X}{N} \tag{4.6}$$

In addition to considering the frequency as the weight, we can also use the method of frequency weighted. The formula is as follows:

$$\bar{X}=\frac{\sum Xf}{\sum f}=\sum X\frac{f}{\sum f} \tag{4.7}$$

where $\frac{f}{\sum f}$ is the frequency of each group.

[**Example 4.3**] Based on the information in Table 4.1, we can calculate the result by using the method of frequency weighted, the calculation is specified as Table 4.2:

Table 4.2 Bonus for employees of an enterprise in June (frequency weighted)

Bonus/Yuan	Number of employees (person)(f)	group median(X)	proportion ($f/\sum f$)	$Xf/\sum f$
100 - 150	6	125	6.98	8.7250
150 - 200	10	175	11.63	20.3525
200 - 250	12	225	13.95	31.3875
250 - 300	35	275	40.70	111.9250
300 - 350	15	325	17.44	56.6800
350 - 400	8	375	9.30	34.8750
total	86	—	100	263.9450

$$\bar{X}=\frac{\sum Xf}{\sum f}=\sum X\frac{f}{\sum f}=263.945\approx 263.95\text{ Yuan}$$

The result of the calculation by Formula(4.7) is the same as that of Formula(4.4).

3) Mathematical properties of the arithmetic mean

Property 4.1 The sum of the deviations of each variable value minus the mean is equal to zero.

For simple arithmetic mean:

$$\sum(X-\bar{X})=0 \tag{4.8}$$

Proof: $\sum(X-\bar{X})=\sum X-n\bar{X}=\sum X-n\frac{\sum X}{n}=\sum X-\sum X=0$

For weighted arithmetic mean:

$$\sum(X-\bar{X})f=0 \tag{4.9}$$

Proof: $\sum (X-\bar{X}) f = \sum Xf - \sum \bar{X}f = \sum Xf - \bar{X}\sum f = \sum Xf - \frac{\sum Xf}{\sum f}\sum f = 0$

Property 4.2 The sum of the squared deviations of each variable value minus the mean is the minimum value.

For simple arithmetic mean:

$$\sum (X-\bar{X})^2 = X_{\min} \tag{4.10}$$

For weighted arithmetic mean:

$$\sum (X-\bar{X})^2 f = X_{\min} \tag{4.11}$$

Proof: X_0 is set to any value, $X_0 \neq \bar{X}$ when

$$\begin{aligned}\sum (X_i - X_0)^2 &= \sum (_i - \bar{X} + \bar{X} - X_0)^2 \\ &= \sum [(X_i - \bar{X}) + (\bar{X} - X_0)]^2 \\ &= \sum [(X_i - \bar{X})^2 + 2(X_i - \bar{X})(\bar{X} - X_0) + \\ &\quad (\bar{X} - X_0)^2] \\ &= \sum (X_i - \bar{X})^2 + \sum (\bar{X} - X_0)^2\end{aligned}$$

$\because \sum (X - X_0)^2 - \sum (X - \bar{X})^2 = \sum (\bar{X} - X_0)^2 > 0$

$\therefore \sum (X - \bar{X})^2 = X_{\min}$

This mathematical property of the arithmetic mean is the basis for measuring the degree of dispersion, error analysis, least squares estimation and other statistical methods.

4) Mean of binary variable

The so-called true sign and false sign means that some units in the population have a certain property on the sign, while another type of unit does not have this property. For example, product quality is divided into qualified products and unqualified products. In statistics, the difference in nature of these signs is often transferred to the variation in quantity, and then the mean is calculated. We usually use 1 to represent a variable value with a certain attribute, and 0 to represent a variable value without a certain attribute.

In a batch of products, the qualified products are considered to have the attribute of "yes", then the unqualified products have the attribute of "no". Let the qualified rate be P and the unqualified rate be Q, take 1 as the variable value of the unit of "yes"(qualified product), and take 0 as the variable value of the unit of "no" (unqualified product), so that the quality sign expressed is transformed into a quantity sign. Calculated according to the weighted arithmetic mean formula, there is:

$$\bar{X} = \frac{\sum Xf}{\sum f} = \frac{1 \times P + 0 \times Q}{P + Q} = P \tag{4.12}$$

P is also called the number of units with certain attributes in the population, or proportion. The number is a special average, which is the average of true sign and false sign.

2. Median

The median is the variable value in the middle of a set of sorted data. From the concept of the median, we can see that in the population, the units whose marker value is less than or greater than the median account for half. Since the median can avoid the influence of extreme values in the series, when there are extreme values in the data, it can be considered to use the median to represent the general level of the overall marker value.

(1) To determine the median for ungrouped data, first arrange the flag values of the overall unit in order of size, and then determine the position of the median. The flag value at the median position is the median.

If the number sequence is an odd number sequence and the median position is $(N+1)/2$, then the sign value in the middle position is the median.

If the number sequence is an even number sequence, the arithmetic mean of the two unit marker values in the middle is median.

(2) To determine the median of grouped data, it is necessary to distinguish between univariate distribution sequence and grouped distribution sequence. Then use the 50% principle of the median to find out the position of median at $\sum f/2$.

① Univariate Distribution Sequence, sort the marker values of the data, determine the position of the median, then use the upward cumulative frequency to find the group where the median is located, and finally determine the median.

[**Example 4.4**] The distribution data of workers processing products in an enterprise is shown in Table 4.3. Calculate the median based on the data.

[**Solution**] Since $\sum f/2=30$, it means that the median position is the 30th, then calculate its cumulative frequency, and get Table 4.3.

Table 4.3 The number of products processed by workers in an enterprise

Number of processed products X	10	11	12	13	14	15	16	total
number of workers f	5	7	10	15	13	6	4	60
Cumulative upward	5	12	22	37	50	56	60	—

From the upward cumulative frequency, the median is at the position of products as 13.

② For the group-distance distribution series, first find the position of the median, because of the group-distance series, the variable value corresponding to the median array is not uniquely determined, which needs to be calculated by using the lower limit or upper limit formula.

Lower bound formula:

$$M_e = L_{M_e} + \frac{\frac{\sum f}{2} - S_{M_e-1}}{f_{M_e}} \times d_{M_e} \tag{4.13}$$

Upper limit formula:

$$M_e = U_{M_e} - \frac{\frac{\sum f}{2} - S_{M_e+1}}{f_{M_e}} \times d_{M_e} \tag{4.14}$$

where, M_e is the median; L_{M_e} and U_{M_e} are the lower limit and upper limit of the median array respectively; d_{M_e} is the group distance of the median array; f_{M_e} is the number of occurrences of the median array; S_{M_e-1} and S_{M_e+1} are the number of cumulative frequencies upward (downward) until the group before (after) the group containing the median.

[**Example 4.5**] Calculate the median based on the data in Table 4.4, and the cumulative frequency is shown in Table 4.4.

Table 4.4 Cumulative frequency of employee wages in an enterprise

Salary level/ $	Number of employees person	Cumulative frequency upward	Cumulative frequency downward
5000 - 6000	10	10	255
6000 - 7000	20	30	245
7000 - 8000	120	150	225
8000 - 9000	80	230	105
9000 - 10000	25	255	25
total	255	—	—

[**Solution**] From the median position formula and cumulative frequency, the median array is the group of 7000 - 8000 $.

We have:

$$M_e = L_{M_e} + \frac{\frac{\sum f}{2} - S_{M_e-1}}{f_{M_e}} \times d_{M_e} = 7000 + \frac{\frac{255}{2} - 30}{120} \times 1000 = 7812.59 \ \$$$

and

$$M_e = U_{M_e} - \frac{\frac{\sum f}{2} - S_{M_e+1}}{f_{M_e}} \times d_{M_e} = 8000 - \frac{\frac{255}{2} - 105}{120} \times 1000 = 7812.59 \ \$$$

3. Mode

Mode was first proposed by British statistician Pearson. The so-called mode is the sign value that appears most frequently in the distribution sequence. From the perspective of distribution, mode is the value with obvious central tendency; from the perspective of distribution curve, mode is the sign value corresponding to the highest peak of the curve. Since the variable value appears most frequently, it occupies an important position in the population. Therefore, the mode can be used to represent a general level of the phenomenon. For example, in order to grasp the fashion trend of clothing styles in the market, it is not necessary to have a comprehensive understanding of the clothing styles, but to investigate what are the most sold clothing styles.

A set of data may have one mode only, multiple modes or no mode. In order to obtain mode accurately, we can resort to the preparation of distribution series as follows.

(1) For the sequence of Binomial distribution, it is only necessary to find out the indicator value with the highest frequency.

[Example 4.6] Please find the mode based on the data in Table 4.5.

Table 4.5 The number of products processed by workers in an enterprise

Number of processed products X	10	11	12	13	14	15	16	total
Number of workers f	5	7	10	15	13	6	4	60

[Solution] It can be seen from the question that there are 15 workers who process 13 pieces of products, the corresponding times(frequency) are the highest, that is, the mode for this set of data is 13 pieces.

(2) It is more complicated for grouped frequency distribution. First, determine the group in which the mode is located, and then calculate the mode value by the formulas. Because each group has a lower limit and an upper limit, it can be calculated separately by the lower limit formula and the upper limit formula, and the results of the two are equal.

Lower limit formula:

$$M_o = L_{M_o} + \frac{\Delta_1}{\Delta_1 + \Delta_2} \times d_{M_o} \tag{4.15}$$

Upper limit formula:

$$M_o = U_{M_o} - \frac{\Delta_2}{\Delta_1 + \Delta_2} \times d_{M_o} \tag{4.16}$$

where, M_o is the mode number; L_{M_o} and U_{M_o} are respectively the lower limit and the upper limit of the mode group; d_{M_o} is the group distance of the mode group; $\Delta_1 = f_{M_o} - f_{M_o-1}$ is the difference between the times of the majority group and its previous group; $\Delta_2 = f_{M_o} - f_{M_o+1}$ is the difference between the times of the majority group and latter group.

[Example 4.7] Grouped data on an enterprise's employee salaries are shown in Table 4.6, find the mode of the grouped data.

Table 4.6 Employee salary

Salary level/ $	Number of employees/person
5000 - 6000	10
6000 - 7000	20
7000 - 8000	120
8000 - 9000	80
9000 - 10000	25
total	255

【**Solution**】 Obviously, the mode of the grouped data is 7000 - 8000 $.

Calculate according to the lower limit Formula(4.15):

$$M_o = L_{M_o} + \frac{\Delta_1}{\Delta_1 + \Delta_2} \times d_{M_o} = 7000 + \frac{120-20}{(120-20)+(120-80)} \times 1000 = 7714.29 \$$$

Calculated according to the upper limit Formula(4.16):

$$M_o = U_{M_o} - \frac{\Delta_2}{\Delta_1 + \Delta_2} \times d_{M_o} = 8000 - \frac{120-80}{(120-20)+(120-80)} \times 1000 = 7714.29 \$$$

4. The Relationship of Arithmetic Mean, Median and mode

The mean, median, and mode are calculated in different ways, and their applicable occasions are also different. The median and mode are not affected by extreme values, while the arithmetic mean considers all data and is easily affected by extreme values. But all three are average indicators that reflect the overall general level, and there is a certain quantitative relationship among them.

Under the condition of symmetrical normal distribution, the arithmetic mean, median and mode are equal as shown $\bar{X} = M_e = M_o$ in Figure 4.1; In the case of an asymmetric normal distribution, the difference of the three of mode, median and arithmetic mean depends on the degree of skewness, the greater the degree of skewness, the greater the difference of the three; the smaller the degree of skewness, the smaller the difference of the three.

When the distribution sequence is left-skewed (or negatively skewed), the arithmetic mean is affected by the minimum value, as shown $\bar{X} < M_e < M_o$ in Figure 4.2. When the distribution sequence is right-skewed (or positively skewed), the arithmetic mean is affected by the maximum value, as shown $M_o < M_e < \bar{X}$ in Figure 4.3.

From the relationship of the three, we find that no matter how skewed, the median is always between the mode and the mean. Experience tells that, in the case of moderate skewness, the distance between the arithmetic mean and the mode is about three times the distance between the arithmetic mean and the median, namely:

$$\bar{X} - M_o \approx 3(\bar{X} - M_e) \tag{4.17}$$

According to this relationship, knowing two of the values, the third value can be approximated to determine the direction of skewness.

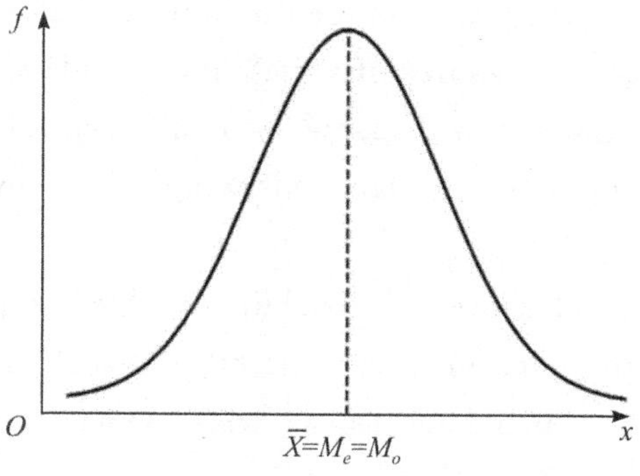

Figure 4.1 Symmetrical distribution

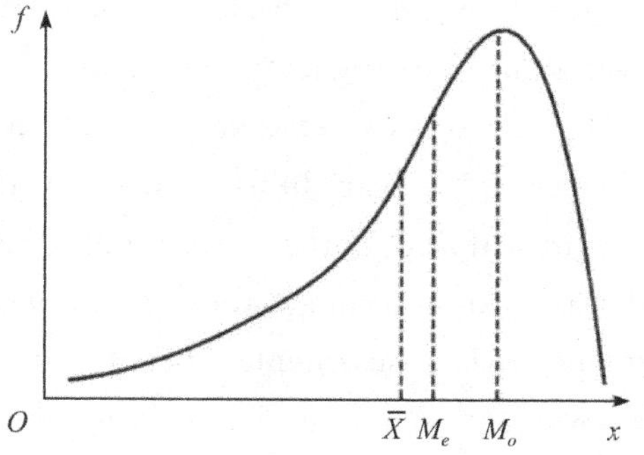

Figure 4.2 Left-skewed distribution

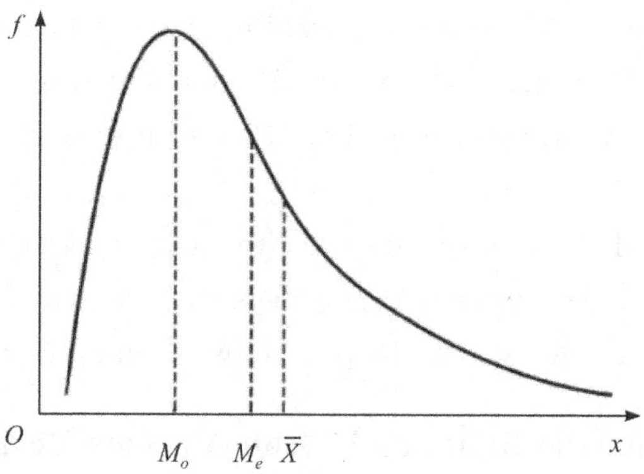

Figure 4.3 Right-skewed distribution

4.2 Measures of Variability

4.2.1 Significance of Measures of Variability

Measures of variability play a significant role in statistical analysis and data interpretation. Here are some key reasons for the importance of measures of variability:

(1) Describe data spread. Measures of variability provide a quantitative description of how the data points are spread out or dispersed around a central value. They give insights into the range and distribution of the data, allowing us to understand the diversity or uniformity of the values.

(2) Compare data sets. Measures of variability enable comparisons between different datasets. By comparing the measures of variability, such as the range or standard deviation, we can determine which dataset has a wider or narrower spread, or whether two datasets have similar or different levels of dispersion.

(3) Assess data quality. Measures of variability can indicate the quality or reliability of data. High variability may suggest a lack of consistency or precision in the measurements, while low variability may indicate more consistent or precise data.

(4) Identify outliers. Outliers are extreme values that significantly differ from the majority of the values. Measures of variability, such as the standard deviation or interquartile range, help in identifying outliers that fall outside the expected range. Outliers can provide valuable insights into unusual or exceptional observations about data.

(5) Decision making and risk assessment. Variability measures are essential in decision making and risk assessment. They provide information about the spread of data, which is crucial for understanding the potential risks and uncertainties associated with certain outcomes or variables.

(6) Statistical inference. Measures of variability play a vital role in statistical inference and hypothesis testing. They help in assessing the likelihood of observing certain sample statistics under different hypotheses, providing a basis for drawing conclusions and making statistical inferences.

Overall, measures of variability allow us to quantify and understand the spread, diversity, and potential uncertainties within a dataset. They provide valuable information for data analysis, decision making, and help to draw meaningful conclusions from data.

4.2.2 Range, Interquartile Range and Mean Absolute Deviation

1. Range

Range is the difference between the maximum and minimum values in a dataset. It provides a simple measure of the overall variability, indicating the spread between the highest value and lowest value. However, range only considers the extreme values and does not provide information about the distribution of the data, usually represented by R.

$$R=\max(X_i)-\min(X_i) \tag{4.18}$$

or

$$R=\max(x_i)-\min(x_i) \tag{4.19}$$

[**Example 4.8**] English test scores of students in Group A and Group B are as follows:

Group A: 80, 83, 85, 88, 90

Group B: 75, 81, 85, 90, 95

The average scores of both groups A and B are 85.2, but the ranges of the two groups are different.

The range of Group A: $R=90-80=10$ points

The range of Group B: $R=95-75=20$ points

It shows that the test scores of group B vary greatly, and the average score of group A is highly representative.

Range is the simplest method to measure the dispersion trend of data, but because it does not make full use of all the information of the data and is easily affected by extreme values, it often cannot fully and accurately reflect the degree of dispersion of the data.

2. Interquartile Range (IQR)

The interquartile range is the difference between the third quartile (75th percentile value) and the first quartile (25th percentile value) of a dataset. It measures the spread of the middle 50% of the data and is less affected by outliers compared to the range. The IQR provides a robust measure of variability, the calculation formula is:

$$Q_d=Q_3-Q_1 \tag{4.20}$$

In Formula(4.20), Q_3 denotes the third quartile; Q_1 denotes the first quartile.

[**Example 4.9**] Assume that there are 7 people in a tourist group whose ages are respectively: 17, 19, 22, 24, 25, 28, 34, and the interquartile range of age can be calculated as:

The positioning value of Q_1 is $\frac{n+1}{4}=\frac{7+1}{4}=2$;

The positioning value of Q_3 is $\frac{3(n+1)}{4}=\frac{3(7+1)}{4}=6$

So the first quartile corresponds to the second sign value, which is 19 years old, and the third quartile corresponds to the sixth sign value, which is 28 years old. Then the interquartile range is $Q_d=Q_3-Q_1=28-19=9$.

50% of the people in this small tourist group are between the ages of 19 and 28, and the maximum difference is 9 years.

3. Mean Absolute Deviation (MAD)

The mean absolute deviation is the average of the absolute differences between each data point and the mean of the dataset. It measures the average degree of deviation of each data point from the mean, providing a measure of dispersion that is less influenced by outliers compared to variance. MAD provides a robust and interpretable measure of variability. Here introduce the calculation methods of MAD.

(1) For ungrouped data:

$$A \cdot D = \frac{\sum |X - \bar{X}|}{N} \tag{4.21}$$

or

$$A \cdot D = \frac{\sum |x - \bar{x}|}{n} \tag{4.22}$$

[Example 4.10] Calculate the average difference from the data in Example 4.8 and Table 4.7.

Table 4.7 Calculation of the average difference of test scores in each group

Group A ($\bar{x}$=85.2)			Group B ($\bar{x}$=85.2)		
Score x	Dispersion ($x-\bar{x}$)	Absolute Deviation ($\|x-\bar{x}\|$)	Score x	Dispersion ($x-\bar{x}$)	Absolute Deviation ($\|x-\bar{x}\|$)
80	−5.2	5.2	75	−10.2	10.2
83	−2.2	2.2	81	−4.2	4.2
85	−0.2	0.2	85	−0.2	0.2
88	2.8	2.8	90	4.8	4.8
90	4.8	4.8	95	9.8	9.8
total	0	15.2	total	0	29.2

[Solution] Since the data are sample data, we can calculate the MAD as:

The average difference of scores in group A is

$$A \cdot D = \frac{\sum |x - \bar{x}|}{n} = \frac{15.2}{5} = 3.04$$

The average difference of scores in group B is

$$A \cdot D = \frac{\sum |x - \bar{x}|}{n} = \frac{29.2}{5} = 5.84$$

Therefore, the average degree of deviation of scores of group B is larger than that of group A.

(2) For grouped data:

$$A \cdot D = \frac{\sum |X - \bar{X}| f}{\sum f} \tag{4.23}$$

or

$$A \cdot D = \frac{\sum |x - \bar{x}| f}{\sum f} \tag{4.24}$$

[Example 4.11] It is known that the monthly wages of employees in a company are grouped as shown in Table 4.8. Please calculate the average monthly wage difference of the employees. (The average monthly wage is known to be 2500 $)

Table 4.8 Calculation of the average monthly wage difference of employees

Monthly salary/ $	Number of employees f	Group median x	$x-\bar{x}$	$\|x-\bar{x}\|$	$\|x-\bar{x}\|f$
1000 - 1500	4	1250	−1250	1250	5000
1500 - 2000	8	1750	−750	750	6000
2000 - 2500	12	2250	−250	250	3000
2500 - 3000	15	2750	250	250	3750
3000 - 3500	7	3250	750	750	5250
3500 - 4000	4	3750	1250	1250	5000
total	50	—	—	—	28000

According to Formula (4.24), there is

$$A \cdot D = \frac{\sum |x-\bar{x}| f}{\sum f} = \frac{28000}{50} = 560$$

MAD measures variability by averaging the absolute differences between each data point and the mean. MAD is less sensitive to outliers compared to variance and standard deviation, providing a robust measure of variability.

4.2.3 Variance and Standard Deviation

In order to overcome the defect of the MAD, consider replacing the absolute value of the deviation with the square of the deviation, and then calculate the mean value of the deviation, which is the variance or standard deviation. Variance and standard deviation utilize the $\sum (X-\bar{X})^2 = \min$ mathematical properties of the arithmetic mean, so they are the most sensitive indicators for determining the degree of marker variability.

1. Variance and Standard Deviation

Variance and standard deviation are two commonly used measures of dispersion or variability in a dataset. They provide insights into how data points are spread out or deviate from the mean.

The variance is the average of the squared deviations between the values of each variable and the mean, and the standard deviation is the result of the square root of the variance, also known as the mean square error. According on the data type, the calculation methods for variance and standard deviation are different.

1) Formulas to calculate the variance and standard deviation for ungrouped data

Population variance:

$$\sigma^2 = \frac{\sum (X-\bar{X})^2}{N} \tag{4.25}$$

Population standard deviation:

$$\sigma = \sqrt{\frac{\sum (X - \bar{X})^2}{N}} \tag{4.26}$$

where, σ^2 and σ represent the population overall variance and standard deviation, respectively, $\bar{X}$ is the population mean.

Sample variance:

$$S^2 = \frac{\sum (x - \bar{x})^2}{n - 1} \tag{4.27}$$

Sample standard deviation:

$$S = \sqrt{\frac{\sum (x - \bar{x})^2}{n - 1}} \tag{4.28}$$

where S^2 and S are the sample variance and sample standard deviation, respectively, $\bar{x}$ is the sample mean.

When calculating the population variance, or population standard deviation and sample sample variance and standard deviation, there are differences in the denominators of the two. The denominator of the population variance is the number of population units, and the denominator of the sample variance is the number of sample units minus 1, which is called one less degree of freedom in statistics. From a practical point of view, the sample variance is used to estimate the population variance, and the denominator of S^2 minus 1 can ensure σ^2 an unbiased estimator.

[**Example 4. 12**] Still use the data in Example 4. 8 to calculate the sample variance and standard deviation.

[**Solution**] Calculate the variance based on the data in Table 4. 9.

Table 4. 9 Calculation of the variance of scores for each group

Group A ($\bar{x}$=85. 2)			Group B ($\bar{x}$=85. 2)		
Score x	$(x-\bar{x})$	$(x-\bar{x})^2$	Score x	$(x-\bar{x})$	$(x-\bar{x})^2$
80	−5. 2	27. 04	75	−10. 2	104. 04
83	−2. 2	4. 84	81	−4. 2	17. 64
85	−0. 2	0. 04	85	−0. 2	0. 04
88	2. 8	7. 84	90	4. 8	23. 04
90	4. 8	23. 04	95	9. 8	96. 04
total	0	62. 8	total	0	240. 8

The variance of test scores of group A: $S^2 = \frac{\sum (x - \bar{x})^2}{n - 1} = \frac{62.8}{4} = 15.7$

Standard deviation of scores of Group A:

$$S = \sqrt{\frac{\sum (x - \bar{x})^2}{n - 1}} = \sqrt{\frac{62.8}{4}} = 3.96$$

The variance of scores of Group B:

$$S^2=\frac{\sum(x-\bar{x})^2}{n-1}=\frac{240.8}{4}=60.2$$

Standard deviation of scores of Group B:

$$S=\sqrt{\frac{\sum(x-\bar{x})^2}{n-1}}=\sqrt{\frac{240.8}{4}}=7.76$$

The average test scores of the students in Group A and B are equal. By comparing the variance and standard deviation in Group A and Group B, a conclusion that the variance and standard deviation of the scores of the students in Group A are smaller than those in Group B, which indicates that the representativeness of the average test scores of the students in Group A is better.

2) Formulas to Calculate the variance and standard deviation of the group data

Overall variance:

$$\sigma^2=\frac{\sum(X-\bar{X})^2 f}{\sum f} \tag{4.29}$$

Population standard deviation:

$$\sigma=\sqrt{\frac{\sum(X-\bar{X})^2 f}{\sum f}} \tag{4.30}$$

Sample variance:

$$S^2=\frac{\sum(x-\bar{x})^2 f}{\sum f-1} \tag{4.31}$$

Sample standard deviation:

$$S=\sqrt{\frac{\sum(x-\bar{x})^2 f}{\sum f-1}} \tag{4.32}$$

[**Example 4.13**] Use the data in Example 4.11, calculate the sample variance and standard deviation.

[**Solution**] Calculate the variance based on the data in Table 4.10.

Table 4.10 Monthly salary variance calculation table for employees

Monthly salary/ $	Number of employees f	Group median X	$x-\bar{x}$	$(x-\bar{x})^2$	$(x-\bar{x})^2 f$
1000 - 1500	4	1250	−1250	1 562 500	6 250 000
1500 - 2000	8	1750	−750	562 500	4 500 000
2000 - 2500	12	2250	−250	62 500	750 000
2500 - 3000	15	2750	250	62 500	937 500
3000 - 3500	7	3250	750	562 500	3 937 500
3500 - 4000	4	3750	1250	1 562 500	6 250 000
total	50	—	—	—	22 625 000

The variance of the monthly salaries:

$$S^2 = \frac{\sum (x-\bar{x})^2 f}{\sum f - 1} = \frac{22625000}{50-1} = 461734.7$$

The standard deviation of the monthly wages:

$$S = \sqrt{\frac{\sum (x-\bar{x})^2 f}{\sum f - 1}} = \sqrt{\frac{22625000}{50-1}} = 679.51$$

2. Variance of A Binary Variable

The variance of a binary variable refers to the measure of dispersion or variability when the data consists of only two possible outcomes or categories. In the case of a binary variable, the variance can be calculated as the product of the probability of success (e.g., "yes" or "true") and the probability of failure (e.g., "no" or "false"). It represents the spread or variability of the binary data points around the mean. The variance of a binary variable can be calculated as follows:

The mean of X is known as $\bar{X}=P$, and if it is substituted into the Formula (4.29), the variance of a binary variable is:

$$\sigma^2 = \frac{\sum (X-\bar{X})^2 f}{\sum f} = (1-P)^2 \times P + (0-P)^2 \times (1-P) = P \times (1-P) \quad (4.33)$$

The standard deviation of a binary variable is:

$$\sigma = \sqrt{P \times (1-P)} \quad (4.34)$$

This formula assumes that the binary variable follows a Bernoulli distribution, where there are only two possible outcomes, typically labeled as success (1) and failure (0). The variance quantifies the spread or variability of these outcomes around the mean probability of success.

3. Classic Application of Standard Deviation

1) Empirical Rule

The "empirical rule" is also known as the "68-95-99.7 rule". It is a statistical rule that provides a rough estimate of the spread of data in a normal distribution.

According to the empirical rule: Approximately 68% of the data falls within one standard deviation of the mean in a normal distribution. Approximately 95% of the data falls within two standard deviations of the mean in a normal distribution. Approximately 99.7% of the data falls within three standard deviations of the mean in a normal distribution.

The empirical rule is based on the properties of a normal distribution, also known as a bell curve or Gaussian distribution. It implies that the majority of the data points in a normal distribution are clustered around the mean, with fewer data points further away from the mean, as shown in Figure 4.4. This rule applies to both population and sample data.

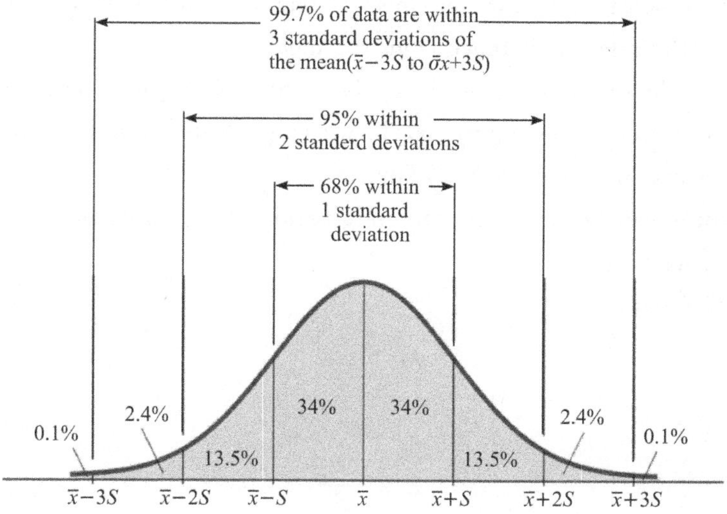

Figure 4. 4 Empirical rule

[**Example 4. 14**] Assume that the overall body weight of males aged 18 - 25 follows a normal distribution, with a mean of 60 kg and a standard deviation of 5 kg, what conclusions can be drawn by empirical rule?

[**Solution**] According to the Empirical Rule, conclusions can be made as follows:

① 68% of males aged 18 - 25 weighed 55 - 65 kg (60±5). It can be seen from the symmetrical distribution that 16% of young men aged 18 - 25 weighed less than 55 kg (50%- 34%).

② 95% of young men aged 18 - 25 weighed 50 - 70 kg (60±10), and a total of 5% of young men aged 18 - 25 weighed less than 50 - 70 kg. The thinnest 2. 5% of young men aged 18 - 25 weighed is less than 50 kg.

③ 99. 7% of them are almost all males aged 18 - 25, and their body weight ranges from 45 - 75 kg (60±15).

There are very few data points in a set of data that are lower or higher than 3 times the standard deviation of the mean, that is to say, almost all the data are included within the range of the mean, whose value is 3 times the standard deviation. For data other than, we call them outliers. For example, in the above example, if an 18-year-old male weighs 40 kg, then the weight is outside the range of 3 times the standard deviation, which is an outlier.

2) Z-Score

The standard score is also known as the Z-score, and is a statistical measure that quantifies the distance of a data point from the mean in terms of standard deviations. It indicates how many standard deviations a particular data point is above or below the mean of a distribution.

The resulting Z-score indicates the number of standard deviations that the data point is away from the mean. If the Z-score is positive, the data point is above the mean; if it is negative, the data point is below the mean. The magnitude of the Z-score provides information about the relative distance from the mean.

Z-scores are widely used in statistical analysis for various purposes, such as comparing data points across different distributions, identifying outliers, and standardizing data to facilitate comparisons and hypothesis testing.

Standard scores can be used for both population and sample data. The formulas to calculate the Z-score are:

For population data

$$Z=\frac{X-\bar{X}}{\sigma} \tag{4.35}$$

For sample data

$$Z=\frac{x-\bar{x}}{S} \tag{4.36}$$

[**Example 4.15**] According to the test scores of the students in Group A in Example 4.8, calculate the standard score of each student in Group A.

[**Solution**] $\bar{x}=85.2$, $S=3.96$, use the Formula (4.36) to calculate the standard score of each student in Group A, as shown in Table 4.11:

Table 4.11 The standard scores of each student in group A

Student ID	Score/points	Standard deviation
1	80	−1.313
2	83	−0.556
3	85	−0.051
4	88	0.707
5	90	1.212

It can be seen from Table 4.11 that student with the lowest score is 1.313 standard deviation lower than the mean score; while the student with the highest score is 1.212 standard deviation higher than the mean score.

4.2.4 Coefficient of Variation

The coefficient of variation (CV) is a statistical measure used to assess the relative variability or dispersion of a dataset compared to its mean. It is a dimensionless quantity expressed as a percentage. The formula to calculate the coefficient of variation is:

$$V_{\sigma}=\frac{\sigma}{\bar{X}}\times 100\% \tag{4.37}$$

The coefficient of variation is particularly useful in comparing the variability of datasets with different scales or units. It allows for the comparison of datasets with different means and standard deviations. A higher coefficient of variation indicates greater relative variability, while a lower coefficient of variation suggests less relative variability.

The coefficient of variation is commonly used in fields such as finance, economics, and biology to compare the variability of variables or datasets and assess the relative risk or stability of different measurements. Similarly, Formula (4.37) can be used to compare the variability of standard deviation as $v_\sigma = \frac{\sigma}{\bar{X}}$.

[**Example 4.16**] The average annual income of employees of enterprises A and B is 20 000 \$ and 50 000 \$ respectively, and the standard deviation of income is 3000 \$ and 5000 \$ respectively. Which enterprise has the smaller income gap?

[**Solution**] The average annual income of different enterprises is different, the standard deviation cannot be directly compared, only the standard deviation coefficient can be compared.

The standard deviation coefficient of enterprise A:

$$v_{\sigma A} = \frac{\sigma_A}{\bar{X}_A} = \frac{3000}{20000} \times 100\% = 15\%$$

The standard deviation coefficient of enterprise B:

$$v_{\sigma B} = \frac{\sigma_B}{\bar{X}_B} = \frac{5000}{50000} \times 100\% = 10\%$$

If we simply look at the standard deviation of enterprises A and B, the standard deviation of enterprise B is greater than the standard deviation of enterprise A, but the average annual income of the two is different. At this time, we need to analyze the standard deviation coefficients of enterprises A and B, and the standard deviation coefficient of enterprise B is smaller than that of enterprise A. Therefore, the income gap between employees of enterprise B is smaller than that of enterprise A.

4.3 Skewness and Kurtosis

Central tendency and discrete tendency are two important features to describe the data distribution, but to fully understand the characteristics of the data distribution, you also need to know whether the shape of the distribution is symmetrical, the degree of skewness, and the degree of flatness, so it is necessary to understand the two indicators: skewness and kurtosis, which take the normal distribution as the comparison standard, are important indicators to describe the distribution variation.

4.3.1 Moment

A moment is a mathematical concept used to describe the shape, characteristics, and properties of a probability distribution or a set of data points. Moments provide quantitative measures that capture various aspects of the distribution, such as its location, spread, and shape.

There are different orders of moments, including the first-order moment (mean), second-order moment (variance), third-order moment (skewness), and higher-order moments. Each moment provides unique insights into the distribution.

Given a central point $A \geqslant 0$, measure the deviation of each variable value from a central point A, the average of the k-th powers of deviations is called the order k moment of the variable about the point A, M_k expressed as:

$$M_k = \frac{\sum (X - A)^k}{N} \tag{4.38}$$

When $A=0$, it is the origin moment, which represents the deviation of each variable value in the population from the origin, and expressed as μ_k:

$$\mu_k = \frac{\sum (X - 0)^k}{N} = \frac{\sum X^k}{N} \tag{4.39}$$

Obviously, the zero-order origin moment is always equal to 1:

$$\mu_0 = \frac{\sum X^0}{N} = 1 \tag{4.40}$$

The first-order origin moment is the arithmetic mean:

$$\mu_1 = \frac{\sum X}{N} = \bar{X} \tag{4.41}$$

The second origin moment is simply the mean of the variable values:

$$\mu_2 = \frac{\sum X^2}{N} = \overline{X^2} \tag{4.42}$$

When $A = \bar{X}$, it was called the k-order central moment, which represents the deviation of each variable value from the arithmetic mean, and we used ν_k to denote:

$$\nu_k = \frac{\sum (X - \bar{X})^k}{N} \tag{4.43}$$

It can be seen that the zero-order central moment is equal to 1:

$$\nu_0 = \frac{\sum (X - \bar{X})^0}{N} = 1 \tag{4.44}$$

The first-order central moment is equal to 0:

$$\nu_1 = \frac{\sum (X - \bar{X})}{N} = 0 \tag{4.45}$$

The second-order central moment is the variance:

$$\nu_2 = \frac{\sum (X - \bar{X})^2}{N} = \sigma^2 \tag{4.46}$$

If we calculate $(X - \bar{X})^k$, the relationship between the central moment and the origin moment can be obtained, thus:

$$\nu_2 = \mu_2 - \mu_1^2 \tag{4.47}$$

$$\nu_3 = \mu_3 - 3\mu_2\mu_1 + 2\mu_1^3 \tag{4.48}$$

$$\nu_4 = \mu_4 - 4\mu_3\mu_1 + 6\mu_2\mu_1^2 - 3\mu_1^4 \tag{4.49}$$

According to these relations, the central moment can be deduced from the origin moment, which simplifies the calculation process.

4.3.2 Skewness Coefficient

Skewness coefficient, also known as skewness, is a statistical measure that quantifies the asymmetry or departure from symmetry in the distribution of a dataset.

Skewness is used to assess the shape of a distribution and determine whether it is skewed to the left (negative skewness) or skewed to the right (positive skewness). A symmetric distribution has a skewness of approximately zero.

The formula to calculate skewness coefficient depends on the specific method used, but one commonly used formula is based on the third-order central moment and the standard deviation:

$$\alpha = \frac{\nu_3}{\sigma^3} = \frac{\nu_3}{\nu_2^{3/2}} \tag{4.50}$$

The different values of α represent different degrees of skewness of the distribution.

When $\alpha = 0$, the frequency distribution is completely symmetrical around the left and right sides of the mean, which indicates that the frequency distribution is normal, as line A shown in Figure 4.5;

When $\alpha \neq 0$, the frequency distribution is asymmetrical, and the distribution is skewed. The larger the absolute value of α, the greater the skewness of the distribution;

When $\alpha > 0$, the distribution of flag values greater than the average is more dispersed, and the distribution curve drags its tail to the right, which is called right skew (or positive skew), as line B shown in Figure 4.5;

When $\alpha < 0$, the distribution of flag values smaller than the average is relatively scattered, and the distribution curve drags its tail to the left, which is called left skew (or negative skew), as line C shown in Figure 4.5.

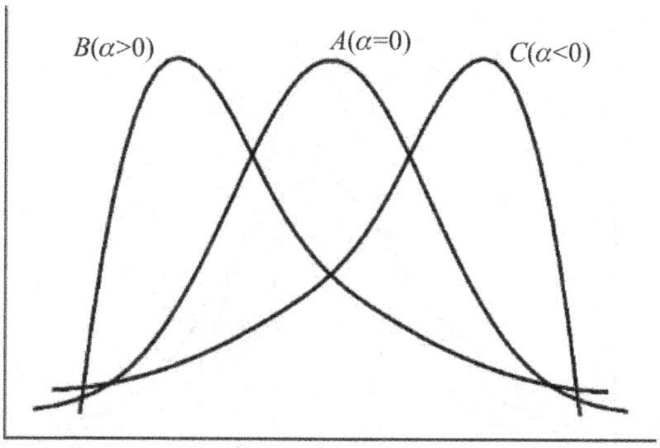

Figure 4.5 Distribution curves with different skewness

4.3.3 Kurtosis Coefficient

The kurtosis coefficient, also known as kurtosis, is a statistical measure that quantifies the degree of peakedness or flatness in the distribution of a dataset. It provides insights into the shape and characteristics of the tails of the distribution.

Kurtosis is used to assess the departure from the shape of a normal distribution. It compares the distribution's tail behavior with that of a normal distribution, which has a kurtosis of 3 (excess kurtosis of 0). Positive kurtosis indicates heavier tails or a more peaked distribution, while negative kurtosis indicates lighter tails or a flatter distribution.

There are many ways to calculate kurtosis, but one commonly used way based on the fourth central moment and the standard deviation is as follows:

$$\beta=\frac{\nu_4}{\sigma^4}-3=\frac{\nu_4}{\nu_2^2}-3 \tag{4.51}$$

A kurtosis coefficient greater than 3 indicates leptokurtic distribution, with heavier tails and a more peaked shape compared to a normality distribution. A kurtosis coefficient less than 3 indicates plat kurtic distribution, with lighter tails and a flatter shape compared to a normal distribution.

Kurtosis is used in various statistical analyses, including risk assessment, financial modeling, and outlier detection. It provides valuable information about the shape and behavior of data distributions, allowing for a deeper understanding of the data characteristics.

Also, different values of β have different kurtosis of the distribution.

When $\beta=0$, it indicates that the kurtosis of the distribution is the kurtosis of the normal distribution, as line A shown in Figure 4.6;

When $\beta>0$, it indicates that the marker values distributed near the average are more concentrated than the normal distribution, and the distribution curve is with a sharp peak, as the lines B shown in Figure 4.6;

When $\beta<0$, it indicates that the sign values distributed near the mean are more dispersed than the normal distribution, and the distribution curve is a flat peak, as line C shown in Figure 4.6;

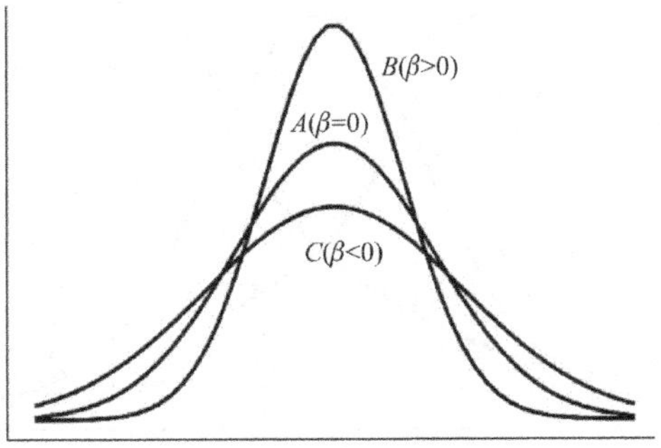

Figure 4.6 Distribution curves with different kurtosis

When β tends to -1.2, it indicates that the distribution curve tends to be horizontal and approximately evenly distributed;

When $\beta < -1.2$, it indicates that the distribution curve was U-shaped.

Chapter Review

On the basis of statistical data sorting, this chapter mainly describes the distribution characteristics of statistical data through simple index calculations. The content involves: use averages to describe the central tendency of data, including arithmetic mean, median and mode; use variation indicators to describe the discrete trend of data, such as range, variance and standard deviation, etc.; and use skewness coefficient and kurtosis coefficient to judge how skewed or steep the statistical data distribution compared to normal distribution.

Through the study of this chapter, students are required to master the calculation methods and applicable occasions of the central tendency measurement indicators of data, understand the relationship and difference between the mean, median and mode, and the relationship of the data in different data distributions; focus on understanding the calculation principles of variance, standard deviation and standard deviation coefficient; understand the skewness coefficient and kurtosis coefficient that reflect the variation of the shape of the overall distribution; at the same time, be able to use empirical rules and standard scores to analyze practical problems.

Exercise

1. What is the central tendency of a statistical distribution? What are the main indicators for determining the central tendency of a statistical distribution? What are their characteristics?

2. Where is the main performance of the determination of central tendency?

3. What is a weight? What is the essence of weight?

4. What is the median and mode? How are the median and mode related to and different from the arithmetic mean?

5. What is the coefficient of dispersion of a statistical distribution? What are the main variables for determining the discrete trend of a statistical distribution? What are their characteristics?

6. Why should we calculate the standard deviation coefficient?

7. What are the specific applications of standard deviation, the calculation and significance of Z-score.

8. What are the mean and standard deviation of a binary variable?

9. What are kurtosis and skewness? How to measure skewness and kurtosis?

10. The points per game scored by each NBA team during a recent season.

94.8	99.6	97.8	100.6	99.0	102.8	90.5	97.6
98.3	103.2	95.8	96.4	102.5	100.3	96.6	89.2
97.2	99.4	94.8	100.6	101.3	98.6	99.4	90.6

Please find and discuss the mean, median and mode.

11. The grouping information of annual net income of 300 rural households is as Table 4.13:

Table 4.13

Annual net income (100 \$)	Number of households
23 - 25	30
25 - 27	110
27 - 29	90
29 - 31	40
31 - 33	20
33 - 35	10

Find the arithmetic mean, median, mode and standard deviation of the annual net income of farmers.

12. The following data show the heights (in inches) and weights (in pounds) of the members of a basketball team. Find the coefficient of variation for each data set. What can you conclude?

Heights: 74 76 78 69 72 69 79 70 77 73 76 72

Weights: 180 168 224 200 188 195 197 160 176 172 184 210

13. An Internet site compares the strokes per round of two professional golfers. Which golfer is more consistent: Player A with $\mu=71.5$ strokes and $\sigma=2.3$ strokes, or Player B with $\mu=70.1$ strokes and $\sigma=1.2$ strokes?

14. The average daily output of a product line is 2600 pieces, with a standard deviation of 50 pieces. If the output of a day falls outside the range of ± 2 standard deviations of the average output, the production line is considered to be out of control. Answer the following questions:

(1) What range does the output fall in, and the production line is considered normal?

(2) What is the proportion of output falling within 2550 - 2700?

(3) What is the proportion of output higher than 2650 pieces? What is the proportion of output less than 2450 pieces?

(4) If the output of a certain day is 2750 pieces, try to judge whether the production line is out of control, why?

14. It is known that a company recruits employees to take an ability test, the average score is 130 points, and the standard deviation is 20 points. An interviewer's test score is

150 points, what is the standard score? What is the proportion for people with higher scores than the interviewer?

15. The Table 4.14 below shows the grouping data of 130 students in statistics:

Table 4.14

Test scores	Number of students
50 - 55	2
55 - 60	4
60 - 65	10
65 - 70	14
70 - 75	20
75 - 80	28
80 - 85	26
85 - 90	16
90 - 95	7
95 - 100	3

Find the skewness coefficient and kurtosis coefficient of the student achievement.

Chapter 5

Probability Basis

One of the fundamental tools of statistics is probability, which dates back as far as the 17th century and is discussed in Games of Chance. Games of Chance, as the name suggests, involve actions such as rolling dice and flipping a coin, in which the outcome of a trial is uncertain. Real life is full of similar uncertainties, such as the probability of rain falling in a particular city in the coming day, or the probability of winning a lottery ticket. Probability theory can provide a means for almost anything that could be considered as a random phenomenon. In this chapter, we will introduce some of the basic ideas of probability theory and provides a foundation for the subsequent study of statistical inference methods.

5.1 Basic Concepts of Probability

5.1.1 Random Experiments and Events

1. Random Experiments

Definition 5.1 A random experiment is an action, an observation, or a trial, which obtains specific results that cannot be predicted with certainty. A random experiment can be abbreviated as E.

As the following examples:

E_1: Toss a coin;

E_2: Roll a six-sided die;

E_3: Play a football game;

E_4: Observe the number of traffic accidents at an intersection in one month.

The set of all possible outcomes of a random experiment is called the sample space, which can be abbreviated as Ω. The sample space corresponding to the above four random experiments is:

$\Omega_1=\{\text{Head, Tail}\}$;

$\Omega_2=\{1, 2, 3, 4, 5, 6\}$;

$\Omega_3=\{\text{Win, Lose, Tie}\}$;

$\Omega_4=\{0, 1, 2, \cdots\}$.

2. Events

Definition 5.2 An event is a subset of the sample space. It may consist of one or more outcomes. Events are often represented by uppercase letters, such as A, B, C. Especially, if an event only consist of a single outcome, it can be called a simple event.

[**Example 5.1**] Roll a six-sided die. Event A is rolling an even number, event B is rolling a number no less than 3, event C is rolling one 6. Identify the sample space and determine the outcomes in each event. Then decide whether each event is simple or not.

[**Solution**] $\Omega=\{1, 2, 3, 4, 5, 6\}$, $A=\{2, 4, 6\}$, $B=\{3, 4, 5, 6\}$, $C=\{6\}$, event C is a simple event, event A and event B are not simple.

5.1.2 Set Theory

Each single result of a random experiment is called sample point or elements, which forms the sample space. If ω is a point belonging to the event A, we shall write $\omega \in A$; If ω is not a point of A, we shall write $\omega \notin A$. Then we define the following relationships between events.

(1) Containment: $A \subset B \Leftrightarrow x \in A \Rightarrow x \in B$.

(2) Equality: $A=B \Leftrightarrow A \subset B$ and $B \subset A$.

(3) Complement: The complement of A, written in $\bar{A}$, is the set of elements that are in Ω but not in A.

(4) Union: The union of A and B, written in $A \cup B$, is the set of elements that belong to either A or B or both.

$$A \cup B=\{x: x \in A \text{ or } x \in B\}$$

(5) Intersection: The intersection of A and B, written in $A \cap B$, is the set of elements that belong to both A and B.

$$A \cap B=\{x: x \in A \text{ and } x \in B\}$$

(6) Set difference: The set difference of A and B, written in $A-B$, is the set of elements that belong to A but not belong to B.

$$A-B=\{x: x \in A \text{ and } x \notin B\}$$

5.1.3 Types of Probability

How to calculate a probability depends on the type of probability. Since the 16th century, researchers have proposed three definitions of probability from different perspectives. They are classical probability, statistical probability and subjective probability.

Definition 5.3 Classical Probability If a random experiment can result in n equally likely outcomes and there are m outcomes in event A, then the classical probability of event A is given by

$$P(A)=\frac{\text{Number of outcomes in event } E}{\text{Total number of outcomes in sample space}}=\frac{m}{n} \tag{5.1}$$

[Example 5.2] You roll a six-sided die. Event A is rolling one 2, event B is rolling a number less than 4. Finding the probability of each event.

[Solution] The sample space consists of six outcomes: $\{1, 2, 3, 4, 5, 6\}$, and there is one outcome in event $A=\{2\}$, there are three outcomes in event $B=\{1, 2, 3\}$. So,

$$P(A)=\frac{1}{6},\ P(B)=\frac{3}{6}=\frac{1}{2}$$

However, not all probabilities of events are applicable to this method of calculation. When an experiment is repeated many times, regular patterns are formed. We can calculate statistical probability of each event and use it, even when each outcome of an event is not equally likely to occur based on these patterns.

Definition 5.4 Statistical Probability The statistical probability of an event E is the relative frequency of event E.

$$P(E)=\frac{\text{Frequency of event } E}{\text{Total frequency}}=\frac{f}{n} \tag{5.2}$$

For example, an insurance company determines that in every 1000 claims, 40 are fraudulent, then the statistical probability of the next claim that the company processes will be fraudulent is 4% approximately.

Definition 5.5 Subjective Probability Subjective probability is a type of probability derived from an individual's personal judgement or own experience about whether a specific outcome is likely to occur.

Classical probability and statistical probability calculations are based on objective facts or on the facts of a large number of repeated experiments. However, in real life, many events cannot be estimated by the frequency of a large number of repeated experiments. Thus, some scholars have proposed subjective probability which result from intuition, educated guesses, and estimates. For instance, a investment expert have empirically concluded that the probability of a certain company investing in a new project to be profitable is 0.7.

5.2 Addition Rule and Multiplication Rule

There are some basic properties about probability. Clearly for a certain inevitable event, the probability of it occurring is 1; the probability of an impossible event occurring is 0. Therefore, for any random event A, $0\leqslant P(A)\leqslant 1$.

5.2.1 Addition Rule

1. The Addition Rule of Mutually Exclusive Events

If A and B are two mutually exclusive events, then the probability of their union is

$$P(A \cup B)=P(A)+P(B) \tag{5.3}$$

[**Example 5.3**] In a survey of a sample of 100 workers in a company, 35 workers were found to be younger than 30 years old, 40 workers were between 30 and 40 years old, and 25 workers were older than 40 years old. Calculate the probability that a person is not older than 40.

[**Solution**] Assume event A is younger than 30, event B is between 30 and 40. Then $P(A)=\frac{35}{100}=\frac{7}{20}$, $P(B)=\frac{40}{100}=\frac{2}{5}$, $P(A \cup B)=P(A)+P(B)=\frac{7}{20}+\frac{2}{5}=\frac{3}{4}$.

So, the probability that a person is not older than 40 is $\frac{3}{4}$.

2. The Addition Rule of Any Two Events

If A and B are any two events, it typically implies that the events are not necessarily mutually exclusive. The events A and B can occur together, independently, or not at all, then the probability of their union is

$$P(A \cup B)=P(A)+P(B)-P(A \cap B) \tag{5.4}$$

[**Example 5.4**] A survey of special talents in a primary school found that 35% of the students could dance, 40% could sing and another 20% could both dance and sing. Calculate the probability of a student who can dance or sing.

[**Solution**] Assuming that being able to dance is event A and being able to sing is event B. It is obvious that $P(A)=35\%$, $P(B)=40\%$, $P(AB)=20\%$, So

$$P(A \cup B)=P(A)+P(B)-P(A \cap B)=35\%+40\%-20\%=55\%$$

5.2.2 Conditional Probability

In the application of probability theory to practical problems it is not infrequent that we are confronted with the following situation: Now what is the probability that something else will happen? Conditional probability is the probability of an event occurring, given that another event has already occurred. The conditional probability of event A given by event B, denoted by $P(A|B)$, is calculated by the following formula

$$P(A|B)=\frac{P(AB)}{P(B)} \text{ if } P(B)>0 \tag{5.5}$$

[**Example 5.5**] The two boxes contain a number of red balls and blue balls in quantities shown in the Table 5.1 below.

Table 5.1 Ball quantities in each box

Box	Red ball	Blue ball	Total
1	6	4	10
2	12	6	18
Total	18	10	28

Pick up any one ball from these 28 balls. Calculate:

(1) Probability of picking up a red ball;

(2) Probability of picking up a ball which is in Box 1;

(3) Probability of picking up a red ball which is in Box 1;

(4) Probability that a ball is red, given that this red ball is in Box 1.

[**Solution**] Assuming that event A is picking up a red ball, event B is picking up a ball which is in Box 1. So,

(1) $P(A)=\frac{18}{28}=0.6429$

(2) $P(B)=\frac{10}{28}=0.3571$

(3) $P(AB)=\frac{6}{28}=0.2143$

(4) $P(A|B)=\frac{P(AB)}{P(B)}=\frac{0.2143}{0.3571}=0.6001$

5.2.3 Multiplication Rule

According to the conditional probability, we can derive another formula called multiplication rule by deforming the equation. If $P(B)>0$,

$$P(AB)=P(B)P(A|B) \tag{5.6}$$

Similarly, if $P(A)>0$,

$$P(AB)=P(A)P(B|A) \tag{5.7}$$

where, $P(A)$ represents the probability of event A occurring, $P(B)$ represents the probability of event B occurring.

[**Example 5.6**] There are 18 girls and 22 boys in a class, from which 2 students are selected at random. Calculate the probability that the first student selected is a girl and the second student is also a girl.

[**Solution**] Assuming that event A is "the first is a girl", event B is "the second is also a girl". Clearly, $P(A)=\frac{18}{40}=\frac{9}{20}$, $P(B|A)=\frac{18-1}{40-1}=\frac{17}{39}$, according to the multiplication rule, the probability of the first student selected is a girl and the second student is also a girl is:

$$P(AB)=P(A)P(B|A)=\frac{9}{20}\times\frac{17}{39}=0.1962$$

5.2.4 Independent Events

$P(A|B)$ means the probability of A, given B. $P(A)$ means the probability of A whenever B occurs or not. If $P(A|B)=P(A)$, means event B does not affect the probability of A. In other words, the two events A and B are independent. Therefore,

$$P(AB)=P(A|B)P(B)=P(A)P(B)$$

Definition 5.6 Two events A and B are independent when

$$P(AB)=P(A)P(B) \tag{5.8}$$

[**Example 5.7**] A coin is tossed and a die is rolled once separately. Find the probability of tossing a head(A) and rolling one point 4(B).

[**Solution**] The events are independent. $P(A)=\frac{1}{2}$, $P(B)=\frac{1}{6}$, So

$$P(AB)=P(A)P(B)=\frac{1}{2}\times\frac{1}{6}=\frac{1}{12}=0.083$$

5.3 Discrete Probability Distributions

5.3.1 Probability Distribution

1. Random Variable

In random trials, many results are expressed by quantity identification. Due to the randomness of the results, the quantity is presented as a random variable. For example:

(1) Roll a dice and the number of points X is a random variable.

(2) The service life Y of air conditioner is a random variable.

(3) The flow of people entering a shopping mall Z is a random variable.

There are still many results in the random trials that are not expressed by quantitative identification. In order to facilitate the study of the results of random trials and the probability of their occurrence, we often associate the results of random trials with real numbers, that is, to quantify the results of random trials. For example:

(1) When checking whether a product is qualified, specify 0 as qualified and 1 as unqualified.

(2) When tossing a coin, specify 0 for the positive result and 1 for the negative result.

The definition of random variable is given below.

A random quantity is represented in the model by a *random variable*. Just as a random quantity attaches a value to each simple result of a random experiment, the corresponding random variable attaches a value to each simple event (By mathematics language, a random variable is thus a *function* of the simple event). We shall consistently use capital letters to denote random variables.

From the definition, we can see that a random variable is a function defined in the sample space, and its value is in the real number space. It is different from the normal function in that its independent variable is the result of a random trial.

According to the characteristics of random variables, random variables can generally be divided into two categories: discrete and continuous. If all values of random variable X

can be listed one by one, it is called a discrete random variable. For example, the number of defective products taken from a batch of products and the number of calls received by a certain exchange within a unit time are all discrete random variables. If all possible values of random variable X cannot be listed one by one, but take any point in an interval on the number axis, it is called a continuous random variable. For example, the life of a batch of electronic components and the measurement error of a batch of components are continuous random variables.

2. Discrete Probability Distributions

For discrete random variable, the distribution column is usually used to represent their distribution.

Assume that all possible values of discrete random variable X are x_1, x_2, ⋯, x_n, the corresponding probability is

$$p_i = p(x_i) = P(X = x_i),\ i = 1,\ 2,\ 3,\ \cdots \tag{5.9}$$

The above formula is called the probability distribution column or distribution column of discrete random variable X. Distribution columns can also be expressed in a list.

X	x_1	x_2	⋯	x_n	⋯
P	p_1	p_2	⋯	p_n	⋯

The probability of all possible values of discrete random variables is between 0 and 1, inclusive.

$$0 \leqslant p_i \leqslant 1,\ i = 1,\ 2,\ 3,\ \cdots$$

The sum of all the probabilities is 1.

$$\sum p_i = 1,\ i = 1,\ 2,\ 3,\ \cdots \tag{5.10}$$

3. Expected Value and Variance

In practical problems, it is difficult to determine the probability distribution of a random variable. And in many cases, we only need to know some numerical characteristics of random variable. Therefore, we need to calculate some common numerical characteristics, expected value and variance.

The sum of the products of all possible values of discrete random variables and their corresponding probabilities is called the expected value of random variable X, and is denoted as $E(X)$ or μ. Meanwhile, μ can also be expressed as the mean value of discrete random variable. The expected value represents the average level or concentration of the random variable, it is calculated as follows:

$$\mu = E(X) = \sum_{i=1}^{\infty} x_i p_i \tag{5.11}$$

The expected value of the square of the deviation between all possible values of the random variable and the expected value is called the variance of the random variable, and is denoted as $D(X)$ or σ^2. Variance represents the degree of dispersion of random variables. The variance of discrete random variables can be calculated as follows:

$$\sigma^2 = D(X) = E[X - E(X)]^2 = \sum_{i=1}^{\infty} [x_i - E(X)]^2 p_i \tag{5.12}$$

When calculating variance, the above formula can be simplified as

$$\sigma^2 = E(X^2) - [E(X)]^2 \tag{5.13}$$

The square root of the variance of a random variable is called the standard deviation.

$$\sigma = \sqrt{D(X)} \tag{5.14}$$

5.3.2 Binomial Distribution

1. Binomial Distribution

Bernoulli experiment is a kind of random trial that can be repeated and carried out independently in the same environment. There are only two possible outcomes of this random trial: success or failure. If this trial is repeated independently n times, then this series of repeated independent randomized trials is called n-fold Bernoulli trial.

If event A is recorded as "the result of n-fold Bernoulli test is success", and random variable X is the number of times event A occurs, then all possible values of X are 0, 1, …, n, and p is the probability of event A, that is, $P(A)=p$, $P(\bar{A})=1-p$.

Therefore, the probability function of X is given by the following formula:

$$P(X=k) = \binom{n}{k} p^k (1-p)^{n-k},\ k=0,\ 1,\ \cdots,\ n \tag{5.15}$$

The above formula can also be called binomial distribution and denoted as $X \sim b(n, p)$.

Binomial distribution is a common discrete distribution, such as

(1) Check 100 products, and the number X of defective products in 100 products follows binomial distribution $b(100, p)$.

(2) Shoot 10 times, and the number Y of shots in 10 times is subject to binomial distribution $b(10, p)$.

(3) After 6 traffic lights, the number Z of red lights in 6 times is subject to binomial distribution $b(6, p)$.

[**Example 5.8**] It is known that there are 10 defective products in 100 products. Now take any one of them and take it back five times. Find the probability of three defective products in the five products taken.

[**Solution**] "Take five times for those that have been put back" can ensure that the conditions of these five tests are consistent, so this test is Bernoulli test. Let X denote the number of defective products in the five products taken, then X follows a binomial distribution. The probability of getting defective products in each test is

$$p = \frac{10}{100} = 0.1$$

So $X \sim b(5, 0.1)$, the probability of three defective products in the five products taken is

$$P(X=3)=\binom{5}{3}(0.1)^3(0.9)^2=0.0081$$

[**Example 5.9**] Let random variables $X \sim b(3, p)$, $Y \sim b(4, p)$. If $P(X \geqslant 1)=\frac{7}{16}$, Try to find the value of $P(Y \geqslant 1)$.

[**Solution**] It can be seen from $P(X \geqslant 1)=\frac{7}{16}$ that$(X=0)=\frac{9}{16}$, that is, $(1-p)^2=\frac{9}{16}$, Thus, $p=\frac{1}{4}$ can be obtained. The value of $(Y \geqslant 1)$ is$(Y \geqslant 1)=1-(Y=0)=1-\left(1-\frac{1}{4}\right)^4=\frac{175}{256}$.

2. Two-point Distribution

When $n=1$, binomial distribution can also be called two-point distribution or 0—1 distribution. The random variable X of two-point distribution can only take two values: 0 or 1. Its distribution is calculated as follows:

$$(X=x)=p^x(1-p)^{1-x}, \quad x=0, 1 \tag{5.16}$$

It can also be expressed in tabular form.

X	0	1
P	$1-p$	p

The number of occurrences of event A in any Bernoulli test obeys the same two-point distribution $b(1, p)$, while the total number of occurrences of event A in the n-fold Bernoulli test obeys the binomial distribution $b(n, p)$. The two-point distribution is mainly used to describe the number of occurrences of event A in a Bernoulli test.

3. Expected Value and Variance

It is assumed that the random variable X follows a binomial distribution, that is, $X \sim b(n, p)$, then the expected value and variance of the random variable X can be calculated as

$$\mu=np, \quad \sigma^2=n(1-p) \tag{5.17}$$

The expected value and variance of the two-point distribution are

$$\mu=p, \quad \sigma^2=(1-p) \tag{5.18}$$

[**Example 5.10**] About 25% of the days in a year in a certain area are rainstorms, find the mean, variance, and standard deviation for the number of rainstorms during the month of June. Interpret the results and determine any unusual values.

[**Solution**] There are 30 days in June. Using $n=30$, $p=0.25$, you can find the expected value, variance, and standard deviation as shown below.

$$\mu=np=30\times 0.25=7.5$$

$$\sigma^2=n(1-p)=30\times 0.25\times 0.75=5.625$$

$$\sigma=\sqrt{n(1-p)}=\sqrt{5.625}\approx 2.37$$

Interpretation: On average, there are 3 rainstorms days during the month of June. The standard deviation is about 1.64 days. Values that are more than two standard deviations from the mean are considered unusual. Because $7.5-2\times 2.37=2.76$, a June with 2 rainstorms days or less would be unusual. Similarly, because $7.5+2\times 2.37=12.24$, a June with 13 rainstorms days or more would also be unusual.

5.3.3 Geometric Distribution

1. Geometric Distribution

In the n-fold Bernoulli test, if X is the number of tests in which event A occurs for the first time, then all possible values of X are 1, 2, 3, …. If the probability of event A in each test is p, then it is said that the random variable X follows the geometric distribution, and the probability distribution is given by the formula:

$$(X=k)=(1-p)^{k-1}p,\ k=1,\ 2,\ \cdots \tag{5.19}$$

The random variable X obeys the geometric distribution and can be abbreviated as $X\sim Ge(p)$.

There are many examples of geometric distribution in real life, such as

(1) If the non-conforming rate of a product is 0.01, the inspection times X of non-conforming products for the first time follow the geometric distribution Ge (0.01).

(2) If the shooting percentage of an athlete is 0.9, the number Y of shots in the first shot follows the geometric distribution Ge (0.9).

(3) After 6 traffic lights, the number Z of intersections with red light for the first time follows the geometric distribution Ge $\left(\frac{1}{3}\right)$.

[Example 5.11] Carry out the ball taking test in the box containing 3 black balls and 2 white balls. Take one ball each time when it is put back until the black ball is taken. Calculate the probability distribution of the number X of balls taken.

[Solution] If a white ball is taken, it needs to be put back. According to the definition of geometric distribution, the first $k-1$ times are all white balls, and the probability of the last time is black balls is

$$(X=k)=\left(\frac{3}{5}\right)\left(\frac{2}{5}\right)^{k-1}=0.6\times 0.4^{k-1},\ k=1,\ 2,\ 3$$

Similarly, the distribution column can also be expressed as

X	1	2	3
P	0.6	0.24	0.096

2. Expected Value and Variance

It is assumed that the random variable X follows geometric distribution, that is, $X\sim Ge(p)$, the expected value and variance of the random variable X can be calculated as

$$\mu=\frac{1}{p},\ \sigma^2=\frac{1-p}{p^2} \tag{5.20}$$

[Example 5.12] There are four intersections on a road, and each intersection has a traffic light. Find the expected value and variance of the number of intersections that a driver passes when he meets the traffic light for the first time.

[Solution] Each traffic light has three lights, namely, red light, green light and yellow light. Therefore, the probability of encountering a red light at an intersection is $p=1/3$. In addition, the number X of intersections that pass through when encountering a red light for the first time obeys the geometric distribution. According to the formula, the expected value and variance of the number X of intersections can be obtained.

$$\mu=\frac{1}{p}=3,\ \sigma^2=\frac{1-p}{p^2}=6$$

5.3.4 Poisson Distribution

1. Poisson Distribution

The probability distribution of Poisson distribution is listed as

$$(X=k)=\frac{\lambda^k}{k!}e^{-\lambda},\ k=0,\ 1,\ \cdots \tag{5.21}$$

where the parameter $\lambda>0$. We say the random variable X follows the Poisson distribution with parameter λ and is denoted as $X\sim(\lambda)$.

Poisson distribution is a commonly used discrete distribution, such as

(1) The number of people X passing through a station in a day follows Poisson distribution.

(2) The number of newborns Y in a certain area within a period of time follows Poisson distribution.

(3) In a certain time, the number Z of accidents at a traffic intersection obeys Poisson distribution.

[Example 5.13] The number of newborn babies X per day in a certain area follows the Poisson distribution of parameter $\lambda=0.5$. Try to find the probability that the number of newborns in a day in this area is 2 or more.

[Solution] Use the Poisson distribution formula to solve. The probability of 2 or more newborns per day in this area is

$$\begin{aligned}(X\geqslant 2)&=1-((X=0)+(X=1))\\&=1-e^{-0.5}\left(\frac{0.5^0}{0!}+\frac{0.5^1}{1!}\right)\\&\approx 0.0902\end{aligned}$$

2. Expected Value and Variance

Assuming that the random variable X follows a Poisson distribution, that is, $X\sim(\lambda)$, the expected value and variance of the random variable X can be expressed as

$$\mu=\sigma^2=\lambda \tag{5.22}$$

[**Example 5.14**] Suppose that the number X of employees of a state-owned enterprise who ask for leave in a week is approximately Poisson distribution, and if the average number of employees who ask for leave in a week is 3.5.

(1) The expected value and variance of the number X of people asking for leave.

(2) The number of people who ask for leave in a week is exactly 6.

[**Solution**] (1) Since the average is 3.5, we can know that the expected value and variance of X are both 3.5 according to the calculation formula of the expected value and variance of Poisson distribution, that is $\mu=\sigma^2=3.5$.

(2) The number X of people asking for leave follows the Poisson distribution with parameter $\lambda=3.5$. The probability that the number of people asking for leave in a week is exactly 6 is

$$(6)=\frac{(3.5)^6 e^{-3.5}}{6!}\approx 0.0771$$

5.4 Common Probability Distributions

As a very common continuous probability distribution, normal distribution was first obtained by Abraham De Moivre in the asymptotic formula of binomial distribution. Gauss first used normal distribution to describe the distribution of error when studying error theory, so normal distribution is also called Gaussian distribution. Normal distribution is very important in statistics and is widely used in natural and social sciences. Standard normal distribution is a special case of normal distribution, the expected value $\mu=0$, thus the symmetry axis of the function graph is y axis, the standard deviation $\sigma=1$, denoted as $N(0, 1)$.

5.4.1 Normal Distribution

1. Density Function of Normal Distribution

If the density function of random variable x is

$$f(x)=\frac{1}{\sqrt{2\pi}\sigma}e^{\frac{(x-\mu)^2}{2\sigma^2}}, \quad -\infty<x<\infty \tag{5.23}$$

Among Formula (5.23), μ, σ ($\sigma>0$) is a constant, then X follows the normal distribution or Gaussian distribution and is denoted as $X\sim N(\mu, \sigma^2)$. The graph of its density function is bell-shape shown in the Figure 5.1. It is a symmetric bell curve about, and takes the maximum value at $x=\mu$. And $f(\mu)=\frac{1}{\sqrt{2\pi}\sigma}$.

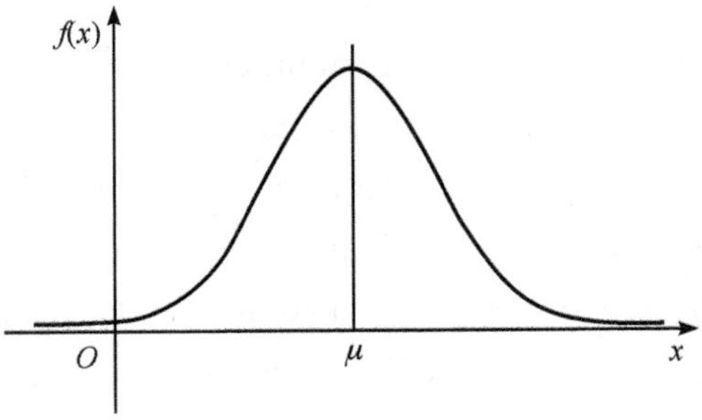

Figure 5.1 The density function diagram of normal distribution

2. Distribution Function of Normal Distribution

According to the density function, the distribution function of normal distribution $N(\mu, \sigma^2)$ is

$$F(x)=\frac{1}{\sqrt{2\pi}\sigma}\int_{-\infty}^{x} e^{\frac{(t-\mu)^2}{2\sigma^2}}dt \tag{5.24}$$

The image of the normal distribution function is a smooth rising S-shaped curve, as shown in the Figure 5.2.

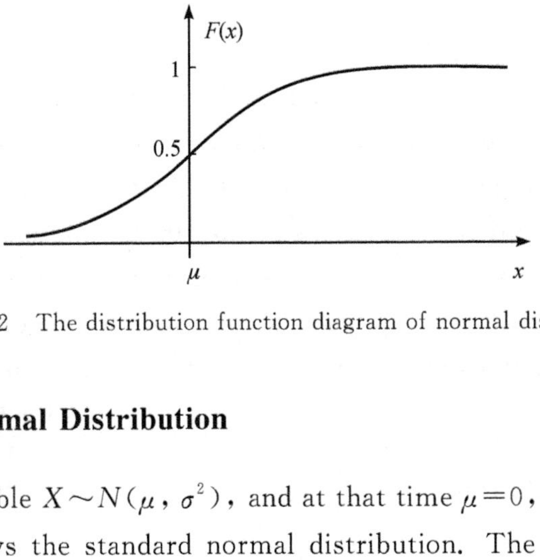

Figure 5.2 The distribution function diagram of normal distribution

5.4.2 Standard Normal Distribution

If the random variable $X \sim N(\mu, \sigma^2)$, and at that time $\mu=0$, $\sigma=1$, it is said that the random variable X obeys the standard normal distribution. The probability density and distribution function are expressed in terms of $\varphi(x)$, $\Phi(x)$.

$$\varphi(x)=\frac{1}{\sqrt{2\pi}}e^{-\frac{x^2}{2}}, \quad -\infty<x<\infty \tag{5.25}$$

$$\Phi(x)=\frac{1}{\sqrt{2\pi}}\int_{-\infty}^{x} e^{-\frac{t^2}{2}}dt, \quad -\infty<x<\infty \tag{5.26}$$

It is obviously that

$$\Phi(-x)=1-\Phi(x) \tag{5.27}$$

$$P(X>x)=1-\Phi(x) \tag{5.28}$$

$$P(a<X<b)=\Phi(b)-\Phi(a) \tag{5.29}$$

$$P(|X|<c)=2\Phi(c)-1,\ (c>0) \tag{5.30}$$

Theorem 5.1 If the random variable $X\sim N(\mu,\sigma^2)$, then $Z=\frac{(X-\mu)}{\sigma}\sim N(0,1)$.

Theorem 5.1 can transform any normal distribution into a standard normal distribution, and it is also known that if the random variable $X\sim N(\mu,\sigma^2)$, then we have:

$$P(X\leqslant c)=\Phi\left(\frac{c-\mu}{\sigma}\right) \tag{5.31}$$

$$P(a<X\leqslant b)=\Phi\left(\frac{b-\mu}{\sigma}\right)-\Phi\left(\frac{a-\mu}{\sigma}\right) \tag{5.32}$$

[**Example 5.15**] Given a random variable X that obeys a normal distribution $N(65,3^2)$, please find:

(1) $P(59<X<74)$;

(2) The constant α, such that $P(X<\alpha)=0.9505$.

[**Solution**]

(1) Using Equation (5.29) and checking the Appendix A: Standard normal distribution, we can see that

$$\begin{aligned}P(59<X<74)&=\Phi\left(\frac{74-65}{3}\right)-\Phi\left(\frac{59-65}{3}\right)\\&=\Phi(3)-\Phi(-2)\\&=\Phi(3)+\Phi(2)-1\\&=0.9987+0.9772-1\\&=0.9759\end{aligned}$$

(2) It is given by $P(X<\alpha)=\Phi\left(\frac{\alpha-65}{3}\right)=0.95$ or $\Phi^{-1}(0.95)=\frac{\alpha-65}{3}$

where Φ^{-1} is the inverse function of Φ. Check the Appendix A to know:

$$\Phi(1.65)=0.9505,$$

So

$$\frac{\alpha-65}{3}=1.65$$

Solve for

$$\alpha=69.95$$

[**Example 5.16**] A thermostat is placed in a container storing a certain liquid. The regulator is ordered at d℃, the temperature of the liquid X(in ℃) is a random variable, and $X\sim N(d,0.5^2)$.

(1) If $d=90$℃, find the probability of less than 89℃.

(2) If the probability of keeping the temperature of the liquid at least 80℃ is required to be not less than 0, please find the confidence interval of the temperature of the liquid.

[**Solution**] (1) The required probability is

$$P(X<89)=P\left(\frac{X-90}{0.5}<\frac{89-90}{0.5}\right)=\Phi\left(\frac{89-90}{0.5}\right)=\Phi(-2)$$
$$=1-\Phi(-2)=1-0.9772$$
$$=0.0228$$

(2) The demand d according to the question satisfies

$$0.99\leqslant P(X\geqslant 80)=P\left(\frac{X-d}{0.5}\geqslant\frac{80-d}{0.5}\right)$$
$$=1-P\left(\frac{X-d}{0.5}<\frac{80-d}{0.5}\right)$$
$$=1-\Phi\left(\frac{80-d}{0.5}\right)$$

Therefore,

$$\Phi\left(\frac{80-d}{0.5}\right)\geqslant 0.99=\Phi(2.327)$$

that is,

$$\frac{80-d}{0.5}\geqslant 2.327$$

So

$$d>81.1635$$

[**Example 5.17**] Let the height of an adult male follows $X\sim N(1.7,0.1^2)$.

(1) Observe a man at random and find the probability that his height exceeds 1.8.

(2) The height of the door of a city bus is designed so that it cannot be too high due to structural constraints. But in order to ensure that 95% of the men can board the bus smoothly, please find the most economic value for the height of the door.

[**Solution**]

(1) From Equation (5.28) and look up the Appendix A:

$$P(X>1.8)=P\left(\frac{X-1.7}{0.1}>\frac{1.8-1.7}{0.1}\right)$$
$$=1-\Phi\left(\frac{1.8-1.7}{0.1}\right)$$
$$=1-\Phi(1)=1-0.8413$$
$$=0.1587$$

(2) Since

$$P(X<x)=P\left(\frac{X-1.7}{0.1}<\frac{x-1.7}{0.1}\right)=\Phi\left(\frac{x-1.7}{0.1}\right)=0.95$$

Therefore

$$\frac{x-1.7}{0.1}=1.645$$

So

$$x=1.8645$$

5.4.3 Characteristics of Normal Distribution and Its Applications

1. Characteristics of Normal Distribution

Let the random variable follow $X \sim N(\mu, \sigma^2)$, because $Z=\frac{(X-\mu)}{\sigma} \sim N(0, 1)$, so the mathematical expectation of Z can be derived as

$$E(Z)=\frac{1}{\sqrt{2\pi}}\int_{-\infty}^{\infty} z\mathrm{e}^{-\frac{z^2}{2}}\mathrm{d}z=0 \tag{5.33}$$

Since $X=\mu+\sigma Z$, it follows that $E(X)=\mu+\sigma E(Z)=\mu$.

By the same token, we can see that

$$\begin{aligned}\operatorname{Var}(Z) &= E(Z^2)-[E(Z)]^2 \\ &= \frac{1}{\sqrt{2\pi}}\int_{-\infty}^{\infty} z^2\mathrm{e}^{-\frac{z^2}{2}}\mathrm{d}z \\ &= \frac{1}{\sqrt{2\pi}}\left(-z\mathrm{e}^{-\frac{z^2}{2}}\Big|_{-\infty}^{\infty}+\int_{-\infty}^{\infty}\mathrm{e}^{-\frac{z^2}{2}}\mathrm{d}z\right) \\ &= \frac{1}{\sqrt{2\pi}}\int_{-\infty}^{\infty}\mathrm{e}^{-\frac{z^2}{2}}\mathrm{d}z=1\end{aligned} \tag{5.34}$$

From the nature of the variance, it follows that $\operatorname{Var}(X)=\operatorname{Var}(\mu+\sigma Z)=\sigma^2$.

From above analysis, we know that

(1) if $X \sim N(\mu, \sigma^2)$, the mathematical expectation of X is μ, the variance is σ^2, i.e., $E(X)=\mu$, $\operatorname{Var}(X)=\sigma^2$.

(2) If X obeys the standard normal distribution, there is $E(X)=0$, $\operatorname{Var}(X)=\sigma^2$.

2. 3σ Guidelines

The "3σ guideline" is also known as"68—95—99.7 rule" or the "empirical rule".

Let the random variable $X \sim N(\mu, \sigma^2)$, then

$$\begin{aligned}P(\mu-k\sigma<X<\mu+k\sigma) &= P\left(\left|\frac{X-\mu}{\sigma}\right|<k\right) \\ &= \Phi(k)-\Phi(-k)=2\Phi(k)-1\end{aligned} \tag{5.35}$$

When $k=1, 2, 3$ there are

$$P(\mu-\sigma<X<\mu+\sigma)=0.6826$$
$$P(\mu-2\sigma<X<\mu+2\sigma)=0.9545$$
$$P(\mu-3\sigma<X<\mu+3\sigma)=0.9973$$

According to the 3σ guideline, approximately 99.7% of the observations falls within the interval $(\mu-3\sigma, \mu+3\sigma)$. These proportions are approximations and assume that the data follows a normal distribution. This is an important property of the normal distribution.

The 3σ guideline is often used in quality control, process improvement, and statistical analysis to assess the variability and identify potential issues. It helps in determining acceptable ranges or thresholds and in detecting observations that deviate significantly from the norm.

5.5 Other Sampling Distributions and Central Limit Theorem

From the Section 1. 4. 1, we have known the definition of population and sample. In practice, the distribution of the population is generally unknown, some individuals are often taken from the population. Based on the data obtained, the population distribution is inferred or analyzed, and the sampled individuals are called a sample of the population.

In order to understand the distribution of the population, n individuals are randomly selected from the population, and the value of the variable is X_1, X_2, …, X_n, which is called a sample of the population, n is called the sample size. The observed value x_1, x_2, …, x_n of a sample X_1, X_2, …, X_n is called the sample value.

There are different ways to draw a sample from the population. In order to make the sample more representative of the population, it is desirable that the sample be drawn in a way that satisfies the following two requirements:

(1) The sample is representative, i.e., each individual in the population has an equal chance to be selected, which means that each sample x_i has the same distribution as the total X_i.

(2) The sample should be independent, i.e., the value of each sample should not affect the value of the other samples, which means that x_1, x_2, …, x_n are independent of each other.

5.5.1 Other Sampling Distributions

1. χ^2 Distribution

If X_1, X_2, …, X_n are independent, following standard normal distribution $N(0, 1)$, then the distribution $\chi^2 = X_1^2 + X_2^2 + \cdots + X_n^2$ follows a χ^2 distribution with n degrees of freedom, denoted as $\chi^2(n)$.

The probability density function (PDF) of the chi-square of the distribution is given by the formula:

$$f(y)=\begin{cases} \dfrac{y^{\frac{n}{2}-1} e^{-\frac{y}{2}}}{2^{\frac{n}{2}}\Gamma\left(\frac{n}{2}\right)}, & y>0 \\ 0, & \text{Others} \end{cases} \tag{5.36}$$

The χ^2 distribution is a skewed distribution that takes only non-negative values, and the graph of its density function is shown in the Figure 5. 3.

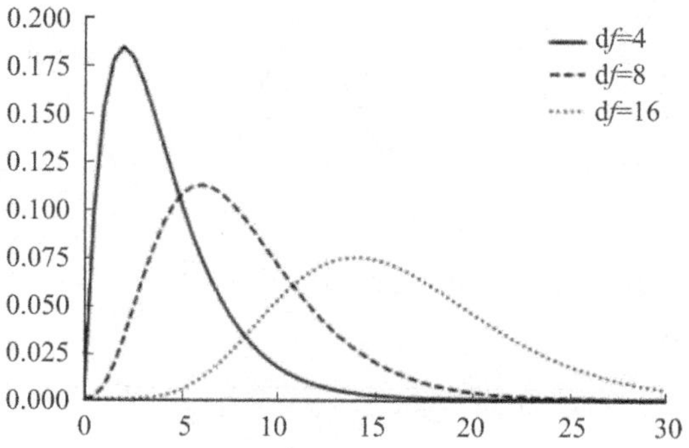

Figure 5.3 Probability density diagram of χ^2 distribution with different $df=4, 8, 16$

The expected value of χ^2 distribution is equal to its degrees of freedom, and the variance is equal to twice the degrees of freedom, i. e. $E(\chi^2)=n$, $\mathrm{Var}(\chi^2)=2n$.

The χ^2 distributions are additive: if χ_1^2, χ_2^2 are independent, following $\chi_1^2 \sim \chi^2(n_1)$, $\chi_2^2 \sim \chi^2(n_2)$, with n_1 and n_2 degrees of freedom, respectively, then we have $\chi_1^2+\chi_2^2 \sim \chi^2(n_1+n_2)$.

Suppose $x_1, x_2, \cdots, x_n$ is a sample from $N(\mu, \sigma^2)$ with a sample mean of $\bar{x} = \frac{1}{n}\sum_{i=1}^{n} x_i$, and a sample variance of $s^2 = \frac{1}{n-1}\sum_{i=1}^{n}(x_i - \bar{x})^2$.

Then we have,

(1) $\bar{x}$ and s^2 are independent of each other;

(2) $\bar{x} \sim N(\mu, \frac{\sigma^2}{n})$;

(3) $\frac{(n-1)s^2}{\sigma^2} \sim \chi^2(n-1)$.

2. student-*t* Distribution

Let the random variables X_1 and X_2 be independent and follow $X_1 \sim N(\mu, \sigma^2)$, $X_2 \sim \chi^2(n)$, then the random variables $t = X_1/\sqrt{\frac{X_2}{n}}$ follows the student-t distribution (also known as t-distribution) with n degrees of freedom, denoted as $t \sim t(n)$.

The probability density function of the t-distribution with n degrees of freedom, also known as the student-t distribution, is

$$h(t)=\frac{\Gamma[(n+1)/2]}{\sqrt{\pi n}\,\Gamma(n/2)}\left(1+\frac{t^2}{n}\right)^{-(n+1)/2}, \quad -\infty<t<\infty \tag{5.37}$$

The comparison of student-t distribution and standard normal distribution is shown in Figure 5.4. It can be seen that the function image of t-distribution is about $x=0$ symmetric distribution, similar to the density function image of standard normal distribution, but the peak is a little lower than the standard normal distribution, and the probability of the tail is a little larger than that of the standard normal distribution.

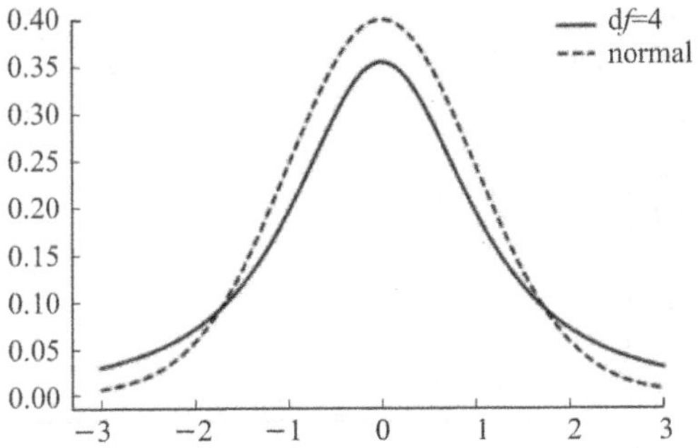

Figure 5.4 Comparison of student-t distribution and standard normal distribution

(1) When $n=1$, the student-t distribution is the standard Cauchy distribution, and the mean does not exist.

(2) When $n>1$, the mathematical expectation of the student-t distribution exists and is 0.

(3) When $n>2$, the variance of the student-t distribution exists and is $\frac{n}{(n-2)}$.

(4) When the degrees of freedom are large (typically $n \geqslant 30$), the student-t distribution approximates to the standard normal distribution.

Corollary 5.1 Let $x_1, x_2, \cdots, x_n$ be a sample from a normal distribution $N(\mu, \sigma^2)$, and $\bar{x}$ and s^2 is the sample mean and sample variance of the sample, respectively, then we have

$$t=\frac{\sqrt{n}(\bar{x}-\mu)}{s}\sim t(n-1) \tag{5.38}$$

Proof: Because $\bar{x}\sim N(\mu, \sigma^2/n)$, there are $\frac{\bar{x}-\mu}{\sigma/\sqrt{n}}\sim N(0, 1)$

$$t=\frac{\sqrt{n}(\bar{x}-\mu)}{s}=\frac{\frac{\bar{x}-\mu}{\sigma/\sqrt{n}}}{\sqrt{\frac{(n-1)s^2/\sigma^2}{n-1}}}$$

Since the numerator is a standard normal distribution, the equation in the root of the denominator obeys χ^2 distribution with degrees of freedom $(n-1)$, so according to the definition of t-distribution, $t\sim t(n-1)$.

3. *F* Distribution

If the random variables X_1 and X_2 are independent random variables with $X_1\sim\chi^2(m)$, $X_2\sim\chi^2(n)$, then the distribution

$$F=\frac{X_1/m}{X_2/n}$$

is said to be an F distribution with degrees of freedom m and n, denoted as $F\sim F(m,n)$.

The probability density function of the $F(m, n)$ is given by

$$\varphi(y)=\begin{cases}\dfrac{\Gamma\left(\frac{m+n}{2}\right)\left(\frac{m}{n}\right)^{\frac{m}{2}}}{\Gamma\left(\frac{m}{2}\right)\Gamma\left(\frac{n}{2}\right)}y^{\frac{m}{2}-1}\left(1+\frac{m}{n}y\right)^{-\frac{m+n}{2}}, & y>0 \\ 0, & \text{Others}\end{cases} \tag{5.39}$$

The image of the probability density function of the F distribution is a skewed distribution that takes only non-negative values, as shown in the Figure 5.5.

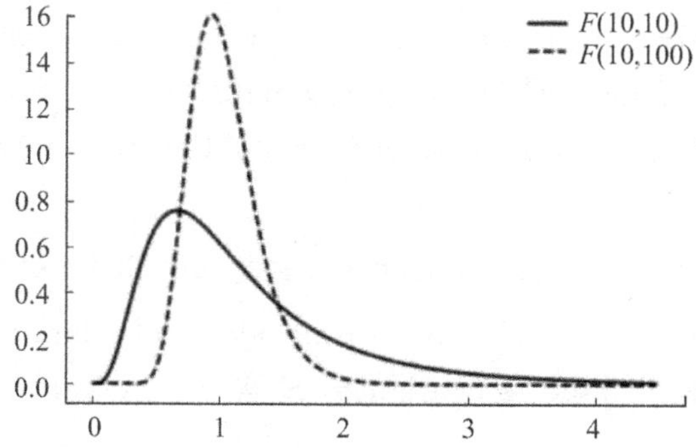

Figure 5.5 Probability density diagram of F distribution with different degrees of freedom

From the construction of the F distribution, we know that if $F \sim F(m, n)$, then we have $\frac{1}{F} \sim F(n, m)$.

So, for a given $\alpha(0<\alpha<1)$, we have

$$\alpha=\left(\frac{1}{F}\leqslant F_\alpha(n, m)\right)=\left(F\geqslant\frac{1}{F_\alpha(n, m)}\right)$$

It can be known

$$P\left(F\leqslant\frac{1}{F_\alpha(n, m)}\right)=1-\alpha$$

i. e.

$$F_\alpha(n, m)=\frac{1}{F_{1-\alpha}(m, n)} \tag{5.40}$$

Corollary 5.2 Let $x_1, x_2, \cdots, x_m$ be from the sample $N(\mu_1, \sigma_1^2)$, $y_1, y_2, \cdots, y_n$ is from the sample $N(\mu_2, \sigma_2^2)$, the two samples are independent of each other, write $s_x^2=\frac{1}{m-1}\sum_{i=1}^{m}(x_i-\bar{x})^2$, $s_y^2=\frac{1}{n-1}\sum_{i=1}^{n}(y_i-\bar{y})^2$, where $\bar{x}=\frac{1}{m}\sum_{i=1}^{m}x_i$, $\bar{y}=\frac{1}{n}\sum_{i=1}^{n}y_i$, We have

$$F=\frac{\frac{s_x^2}{\sigma_1^2}}{\frac{s_y^2}{\sigma_2^2}}\sim F(m-1, n-1) \tag{5.41}$$

If $\sigma_1^2=\sigma_2^2$, then $F=\frac{s_x^2}{s_y^2}\sim F(m-1, n-1)$.

5.5.2 Central Limit Theorem

In production activities, some phenomena are affected by many mutually independent random factors, and if the effect produced by each factor is small, the total effect can be regarded as obeying the normal distribution. The central limit theorem, as a class of theorems in probability theory that discusses the sequence of random variables whose parts, distributions are asymptotically normally distributed. This set of theorems is the theoretical basis for mathematical statistics and error analysis, and states the conditions that a large number of random variables approximately obey the normal distribution. As the most important class of theorems in probability theory, central limit theorem has a wide practical applications.

1. Central Limit Theorem Under Independent Identical Distribution

Let $\{X_n\}$ be a sequence of independent and identically-distributed random variables with mathematical expected value and variance, $E(X_i)=\mu$, $\mathrm{Var}(X_i)=\sigma^2>0$, $(i=1, 2, 3, \cdots)$. Then the distribution function $F_n(x)$ of the standardized variables $Y_n=\frac{\sum_{i=1}^{n} X_i - n\mu}{\sqrt{n}\sigma}$ of the sum of random variables $\sum_{i=1}^{n} X_i$ for any x has

$$\lim_{n\to\infty} F_n(x)=\lim_{n\to\infty} P\left(\frac{\sum_{i=1}^{n} X_i - n\mu}{\sqrt{n}\sigma}\right)=\int_{-\infty}^{x}\frac{1}{\sqrt{2\pi}}e^{-\frac{t^2}{2}}dt=\Phi(x) \tag{5.42}$$

[Example 5.18] An object consists of 2000 parts, each of which is a random variable that is independent of each other and follows the same distribution, with a mean of 200 g and a standard deviation of 10 g. Find the probability that the weight of the object exceeds 400.5 kg.

[Solution] Let X_i as the weight of the i-th part, because $E(X_i)=0.2$, $\mathrm{Var}(X_i)=0.0001$, there are

$$E\left(\sum_{i=1}^{2000} X_i\right)=400,\quad \mathrm{Var}\left(\sum_{i=1}^{2000} X_i\right)=0.2$$

By the central limit theorem, we have

$$P\left(\sum_{i=1}^{2000} X_i > 400.5\right)=1-\Phi\left(\frac{400.5-400}{\sqrt{0.2}}\right)=1-\Phi(1.118)\approx 0.1314$$

So, the probability of the object exceeding 400.5 kg is about 0.1314.

2. Normal Approximation of The Binomial Distribution (De Moivre-Laplace Theorem)

Let the probability of event A occurring in each of the n-fold Bernoulli trials be p $(0<p<1)$, denoted S_n as the number of times for event A occurs in n trials, and denote Y_n as

$$Y_n=\frac{S_n-np}{\sqrt{npq}}$$

Then for any real number y, we have

$$\lim_{n\to\infty} P(Y_n \leqslant y) = \int_{-\infty}^{y} \frac{1}{\sqrt{2\pi}} e^{-\frac{t^2}{2}} dt = \Phi(y) \tag{5.43}$$

[**Example 5.19**] A product has a pass rate of 90%. Ask how many pieces of each batch can be produced with 95% certainty (at least 100 pieces of each batch are qualified).

[**Solution**] Let each batch produce n products, of which the number of qualified is recorded as X, then there are $X \sim b(n, 0.9)$, and from the question we know: $E(X) = 0.9n$, $\mathrm{Var}(X) = 0.09n$.

The normal approximation of the binomial distribution yields

$$P(X < 100) = \Phi\left(\frac{100 + 0.5 - 0.9n}{\sqrt{0.09n}}\right) \leqslant 0.05$$

Check the table, it shows that

$$\frac{100 + 0.5 - 0.9n}{\sqrt{0.09n}} \leqslant -1.645$$

Solve $n > 117.613$, that is, each batch of 118 pieces can be produced with 95% certainty, so that each batch of products has at least 100 qualified products.

Chapter Review

This chapter first introduces some basic concepts of probability, such as random experiments, events, set theory and the definitions of three kinds of probability: classical probability, statistical probability and subjective probability. Secondly, the basic arithmetic of probability is introduced: addition rule, multiplication rule and conditional probability. The method of how to judge independent events is also given. Thirdly, the distribution functions and common distributions of discrete random variables and continuous random variables are discussed respectively, including binomial distribution, geometric distribution, Poisson distribution and normal distribution. Besides, χ^2 distribution, student-t distribution and F distribution in sampling distribution are introduced. Finally, the central limit theorem is introduced. Through the study of this chapter, you can have a basic understanding of probability theory and lay a foundation for later learning of inference statistics.

Exercise

1. Rolling 2 six-sides dice and getting a sum of 6. Identify the sample space of the random experiment and determine the outcomes in the event.

2. Describe the three types of probability briefly.

3. Write down the formula for addition rule, conditional probability and multiplication rule.

4. Give an example of two events that are independent.

5. Make a brief introduction to the concept of random variable.

6. There are two red balls and a bunch of white balls in a box. Given that the probability of selecting a white ball by random drawing is 0.75, find the number of white balls in the box.

7. A random sample of 250 families found that 74% have boys, 88% have girls, and 72% have boys and girls. Find the probability that a family in this sample selected at random have boys or girls.

8. Two students participate in the English speech contest. Their probability of winning the prize is 0.6 and 0.85 respectively. Calculate:

(1) The probability that both students will win the prize.

(2) The probability that at least one student will win.

(3) The probability that exactly one student will win.

9. Given that the probability that an airplane flight departs on time is 0.89, a flight arrives on time is 0.85, a flight departs and arrives on time is 0.81. Find the probability that a flight departed on given that it arrives on time.

10. If a player takes part in a shooting competition, the probability of hitting the bull's eye is 0.7. When the number of hitting the bull's eye is not less than 5, the player can win the prize.

(1) Conduct 6 independent shots, find the probability of winning prizes.

(2) Conduct 8 independent shots, find the probability of winning prizes.

11. The unqualified rate of goods produced by a factory is 0.05. Now, 5 pieces are sampled to find the probability of at most 3 unqualified goods.

12. Set random variable $X \sim b(n, p)$, if $\mu = 2.4$, $\sigma^2 = 1.44$, find the values of two parameters n and p.

13. Write the mean and standard deviation of the following normal distribution.

$$f_1(x)=\frac{1}{\sqrt{\pi}}e^{-(x^2-2x+1)},\ f_2(x)=\frac{1}{\sqrt{3\pi}}e^{-\frac{1}{3}(x^2+6x+9)},\ f_3(x)=\sqrt{\frac{2}{\pi}}e^{-2x^2}$$

14. The proportion of people who are known to have a special genetic disease in a certain area is 2.5%. Find:

(1) In order to detect a patient with the disease, the probability of detecting at least 10 times is required.

(2) In order to detect a patient with the disease with a probability of not less than 0.9, how many people in the region should be detected at least?

15. Based on the survey of the sales data of a large shopping mall, it is found that the monthly sales volume of a certain commodity follows the Poisson distribution with a parameter of $\lambda = 10$. In order to ensure that more than 90% of the goods are not out of

stock, how many pieces of such commodities must be purchased at the end of the month to ensure that they are not out of stock?

16. Set random variable $X \sim N(3,4)$

(1) calculate $P(|X|>2)$, $P(-4<X\leqslant 10)$.

(2) Determine the value of c to make: $P(X>c)=P(X<c)$.

17. In the production of a certain product, the product quality is subject to $N(130, 4^2)$. Now, five independent measurements have been made to try to determine the probability that two values fall outside the range [126, 134].

18. When the length of a product is measured, the random error of measurement X (unit: cm) has a density function

$$f(x)=\frac{1}{\sqrt{32\pi}}\mathrm{e}^{-\frac{(x-10)^2}{32}}, -\infty<x<\infty$$

Find the probability that the absolute value of at least one error in the three measurements does not exceed 14 cm.

Chapter 6

Parameter Estimation

As we all know, statistics can be divided into descriptive statistics and inferential statistics according to the different research methods. Descriptive statistics focuses on how to collect, organize, summarize, display, generalize, and analyze data, etc., see Chapters 2 to 4 for details; while inferential statistics focuses on how to use sample data to make certain reliable quantitative characteristics of the population. The estimation and judgment of degree of dispersion of the population distribution mainly include parameter estimation and hypothesis testing. This chapter introduces parameter estimation, that is, estimating unknown parameters in the population distribution from sample statistics. The next chapter covers hypothesis testing.

6.1 Sampling Distribution

Sampling distribution refers to the distribution of a particular statistic (such as the mean, proportion, or standard deviation) calculated from multiple random samples taken from the same population. It provides insights into the behavior and variability of the statistic when repeatedly sampled from the population.

When in conducting statistical analysis, it is often impractical or impossible to collect data from the entire population. Instead, the sample is taken from the population, and statistical inferences are made based on the sample data. The sampling distribution helps us understand the properties of sample statistics and the relationship and the properties of sample statistics to population parameters.

Since sample is random variable, the result of sampling cannot be determined in advance, it is necessary to study the probability distribution of statistics. Sampling distribution reflects the distribution characteristics of samples and is an important basis for statistical inference. In statistical inference, the most widely used four major sampling distributions are normal distribution, χ^2 distribution, t-distribution, and F distribution.

6.1.1 Basic Concepts of Sampling

The basic concepts of sampling include: population and sample, sample size and sample number, population parameters and sample statistics, sampling with replacement and sampling without replacement. Among them, we have already introduced the first three parts in Section 1.4.1 and Section 1.4.2. Here, we will focus on introducing commonly used population parameters and sample statistics.

1. Population Parameters and Sample Statistics

Population parameter is a numerical measurement describing some characteristics of a population, and is the object of sampling inference. The value of population parameter is unique, deterministic, but usually unknown. A population can have multiple parameters, which describe the comprehensive quantitative characteristics of the population from different aspects.

Common population parameters include: population mean, population variance, population standard deviation, population proportion (also known as population ratio), etc. Among them, population mean is to describe the central tendency of the population distribution, and population variance and standard deviation are to describe the degree of dispersion of the population distribution.

Let X represent the population variable under study, X_1, X_2, $\cdots$, X_N represent the variable values of each unit of the population, then we have

$$\text{Population mean } \bar{X} = \frac{\sum_{i=1}^{N} X_i}{N} \tag{6.1}$$

$$\text{Population variance } \sigma^2 = \frac{\sum_{i=1}^{N} (X_i - \bar{X})^2}{N} \tag{6.2}$$

$$\text{Population standard deviation } \sigma = \sqrt{\frac{\sum_{i=1}^{N} (X_i - \bar{X})^2}{N}} \tag{6.3}$$

Population proportion refers to the proportion of units with certain attributes in the population, reflecting the structural characteristics of the population. Let the number of population units with a certain attribute be N_1, then we have

$$\text{Population proportion } P = \frac{N_1}{N} \tag{6.4}$$

$$\text{Variance of population proportion } \sigma^2 = P(1-P) \tag{6.5}$$

$$\text{Standard deviation of population proportion } \sigma = \sqrt{P(1-P)} \tag{6.6}$$

Sample statistic is a comprehensive index calculated according to the variable attribute of each unit of the sample, and it is a function of the sample to infer the population parameters. The calculation method of sample statistic is definite, but the values of it vary with different samples, so sample statistic is a random variable. Corresponding to the population parameters, the population sample statistics are

$$\text{Sample mean } \bar{x} = \frac{\sum x}{n} \tag{6.7}$$

$$\text{Sample variance } s^2 = \frac{\sum (x-\bar{x})^2}{n-1} \tag{6.8}$$

$$\text{Sample standard deviation } s = \sqrt{\frac{\sum (x-\bar{x})^2}{n-1}} \tag{6.9}$$

$$\text{Sample proportion } p = \frac{n_1}{n} \tag{6.10}$$

$$\text{Standard deviation of sample proportion } s = \sqrt{p(1-p)} \tag{6.11}$$

2. Repeated Sampling and Non-repeated Sampling

Repeated sampling (or called sampling with replacement) and non-repeated sampling (or called sampling without replacement) are two sampling methods.

Repeated sampling refers to randomly selecting a unit from the population of N units, recording its value, putting it back into the population and continuing to participate in the next round of unit selection until the sample size n is enough. Therefore, the sample of repeated sampling is composed of n independent consecutive trials, each trial is carried out under exactly the same conditions, and the probability of each unit being selected in multiple trials is the same. Under repeated sampling conditions, the possible number of samples is N^n.

Non-repeated sampling means that a unit is randomly selected from the N units of the population, and after its variable value is recorded, it will not be returned to the population and will not participate in the next round of sampling. Therefore, the sample not with repeated sampling is also composed of the results of n consecutive extractions, but since each extraction is not repeated, it is essentially equivalent to simultaneously sampling n sample units from the population.

The results of n consecutive selections are not independent of each other, the results of each selection will affect the next selection, and the probability of each unit being selected in multiple trials is not equal. Under the condition of non-repeated sampling, if the order of sampling is considered, the possible number of samples is $\frac{N!}{(N-n)!}$; if the order of sampling is not considered, the possible number of samples is $\frac{N!}{(N-n)!\,n!}$.

6.1.2 Sampling Distribution

1. Repeated Sampling Distribution

1) The distribution of the Sample Mean

Let $x_i (i=1, 2, \cdots, n)$ be a sample drawn from the population. Due to repeated sampling, each x_i is a random variable with the same distribution as the population and independent of each other. Assuming the population mean is $\bar{X}$, and the variance is σ^2, then

$$E(x_i)=\bar{X},\ \sigma^2(x_i)=\sigma^2,\ (i=1, 2, \cdots, n) \tag{6.12}$$

The expected value and variance of the sample mean are:

$$E(\bar{x})=E\left(\frac{x_1+x_2+\cdots+x_n}{n}\right)=\frac{1}{n}[E(x_1)+E(x_2)+\cdots+E(x_n)]=\bar{X} \tag{6.13}$$

$$\sigma^2(\bar{x})=\sigma^2\left(\frac{x_1+x_2+\cdots+x_n}{n}\right)=\frac{1}{n^2}[\sigma^2(x_1)+\sigma^2(x_2)+\cdots+\sigma^2(x_n)]=\frac{\sigma^2}{n} \tag{6.14}$$

That is to say, the center of the distribution of sample mean is exactly the same as the center of the population distribution, and the variance of the sample mean is $\frac{1}{n}$ of the variance of the population. Since the sample mean can be concentrated around the population mean, we can use the sample mean to estimate the population mean. But since the population mean is an unknown constant and the sample mean is a random variable, we also need to consider the degree of dispersion of this random variable. Therefore, we use the standard deviation of the sample mean to reflect the average error degree between the sample mean and the population mean, which is called the sampling mean error of the sample mean, which is

$$\sigma_{\bar{x}}=\frac{\sigma}{\sqrt{n}} \tag{6.15}$$

The sampling mean error is the $\frac{1}{\sqrt{n}}$ of population standard deviation, which is much smaller than the population standard deviation.

[**Example 6.1**] An advertising company has a total of 500 employees, the average working age of service is 9 years, and the standard deviation is 3 years. Randomly select 60 people to form a sample by repeated sampling method, and try to calculate the sampling mean error of the average working age of the sample.

[**Solution**] According to the question, $\sigma=3$, $n=60$, we have:

$$\sigma_{\bar{x}}=\frac{\sigma}{\sqrt{n}}=\frac{3}{\sqrt{60}}=0.3873 \text{ year}$$

Therefore, the sampling mean error of the average working age of the sample is 0.3873 year.

2) Percentage Distribution

The population proportion P refers to the proportion of units with certain attributes in the population, which is actually the average of two-point distribution. Let the total number of units in the population be N, and the number of units with a certain attribute is N_1. Suppose X is a random variable that follows two-point distribution, that is, X takes value 1, or it takes value 0, then there is

$$P=\frac{N_1}{N}=\bar{X} \tag{6.16}$$

n sample units are randomly selected from the population X, and the number of units with a certain attribute is n_1, then the number of samples p is $p=\frac{n_1}{n}$, which is also a special average. According to the nature of the distribution of sample mean, we have

$$E(p)=E(\bar{x})=\bar{X}=P \tag{6.17}$$

$$\sigma_p=\frac{\sigma(X)}{\sqrt{n}}=\frac{\sqrt{P(1-P)}}{\sqrt{n}}=\sqrt{\frac{P(1-P)}{n}} \tag{6.18}$$

[**Example 6.2**] It is known that there are 15000 light bulbs produced in a certain batch, with a first-class quality rate of 85%. Now use repeated sampling method to select 150 light bulbs from it, and try to calculate the sampling mean error of the rate of first-class quality of the samples.

[**Solution**] According to the question, $P=0.85$, $n=150$, we have:

$$\sigma_p=\sqrt{\frac{p(1-p)}{n}}=\sqrt{\frac{0.85(1-0.85)}{150}}=2.92\%$$

Therefore, the sampling mean error of the first-class rate of the sample is 2.92%.

2. Sampling Distribution without Repetition

1) The Distribution of the Sample Mean

Under the condition of non-repeated sampling, the center of the distribution of the sample mean is still the center of the population distribution, that is, the formula still holds.

The sampling mean error with non-repeated sampling is

$$\sigma_{\bar{x}}=\sqrt{\frac{\sigma^2}{n}\cdot\frac{N-n}{N-1}} \tag{6.19}$$

Compared with the Formula (6.15), the sampling mean error of non-repeated sampling has one coefficient $\sqrt{\frac{N-n}{N-1}}$, which is called the correction factor of non-repeated sampling. In the case of large N, the correction factor $\sqrt{\frac{N-n}{N-1}}\approx\sqrt{1-\frac{n}{N}}$. Since the value of the correction factor is between 0 and 1, the sampling mean error of non-repeated sampling is smaller than that of repeated sampling.

However, when N is much larger than n, the correction factor is close to 1. At this time, the correction factor has almost no effect on the sampling mean error, and the difference brought by the sampling method can be ignored, that is, it is processed according to the repeated sampling method.

[Example 6.3] In Example 6.1, a sample of 60 people is randomly selected by non-repeated sampling method, and the sampling mean error of the average working age of the sample is calculated.

[Solution] According to the question, $N=500$, $\sigma=3$, $n=60$, according to the above formula:

$$\sigma_{\bar{x}}=\sqrt{\frac{\sigma^2}{n}\left(1-\frac{n}{N}\right)}=\sqrt{\frac{3^2}{60}\left(1-\frac{60}{500}\right)}=0.3633 \text{ year}$$

Therefore, the sampling average error of the average working age of the sample is 0.3633 year.

2) Sample Proportion Distribution

The sample proportion is the average number under two-point distribution, so under the condition of non-repeated sampling, there are

$$E(p)=P \tag{6.20}$$

$$\sigma_p=\sqrt{\frac{P(1-P)}{n}\cdot\left(1-\frac{n}{N}\right)} \tag{6.21}$$

[Example 6.4] In Example 6.2, 150 light bulbs were selected by non-repeated sampling method, and try to calculate the sampling mean error of the first-class product rate of the sample.

[Solution] According to the question, $N=15000$, $P=0.85$, $n=150$, we have:

$$\sigma_p=\sqrt{\frac{p(1-p)}{n}\left(1-\frac{n}{N}\right)}=\sqrt{\frac{0.85\times0.15}{150}\left(1-\frac{150}{15000}\right)}=2.9\%$$

Therefore, the sampling mean error of the sample rate of first-class product is 2.9%.

6.2 Point Estimation and Evaluation Criteria

Parameter estimation is to estimate the population parameters by sample statistics, for example, use the sample mean to estimate the population mean, use the sample proportion to estimate the population proportion, and so on. In parameter estimation, the estimator is the sample statistics $\hat{\theta}$ used to estimate the population parameters θ. Similarly, sample mean, sample proportion, sample variance, etc. are all estimators. The specific value of the estimator calculated when estimating the population parameter is called the estimated value. For example, when estimate the average score of a class test, a random sample is drawn from the scores, and the average score of the sample is calculated to be 80 points, then this 80 points is the estimated value. The methods of parameter estimation include point estimation and interval estimation.

6.2.1 Point Estimation

Point estimation is a method that directly uses sample statistics as the population parameter, also known as fixed value estimation. For example, take the sample mean, sample number, and sample variance as the estimators of the corresponding population parameters, there are

$$\begin{cases} \hat{X} = \bar{x} \\ \hat{P} = p \\ \hat{\sigma}^2 = s^2 = \dfrac{\sum (x - \bar{x})^2}{n - 1} \end{cases} \tag{6.22}$$

[**Example 6.5**] Assume that the service life of a certain type of battery $X \sim N(\bar{X}, 120)$, $\bar{X}$ is unknown, and now 4 batteries are randomly selected , and the measured service life (in hours) is 1532, 1375, 1461, 1610, try to estimate the average life time of this type of battery $\bar{X}$.

[**Solution**] Since $\bar{X}$ is the average life of a certain type of battery, $\bar{x}$ is the average life of the sample, it can be obtained according to the average point estimation formula:

$$\hat{\bar{X}} = \bar{x} = \frac{1}{4}(1532 + 1375 + 1461 + 1610) = 1494.5 \text{ hours}$$

Therefore, the estimated value of $\bar{X}$ is 1494.5 hours.

As we all know, point estimation can provide the specific estimated values of population parameters as quantitative basis for action decision-making, which is the advantage of point estimation. However, point estimation also has shortcomings, it cannot provide error information of the estimator. Therefore, as the selection criterion of the estimator, it is necessary for us to study the goodness of the point estimation.

6.2.2 Evaluation Criteria for Estimates

1. Unbiased

Let $\hat{\theta}$ be the sample statistic for θ, if the following conditions are satisfied as

$$E(\hat{\theta}) = \theta \tag{6.23}$$

$\hat{\theta}$ is said to be an unbiased estimate of θ. The accuracy of the estimator can be represented by the absolute distance $|E(\hat{\theta}) - \theta|$, and when $|E(\hat{\theta}) - \theta| = 0$, $\hat{\theta}$ is a completely accurate and unbiased estimator of θ. Unbiasedness requires that there is no systematic error in the constructed statistics $\hat{\theta}$. Although the estimated value of each possible sample is not necessarily exactly equal to the unknown population parameter, if multiple samples are taken, the average of each estimated value should be required to be equal to the population parameter, that is, in the average sense, this estimation is not biased.

In fact, since $E(\bar{x})=\bar{X}$, the sample mean is an unbiased estimate of the population mean. Similarly, the sample proportion is an unbiased estimate of the population proportion.

2. Effectiveness

Assume $\hat{\theta}_1$, $\hat{\theta}_2$ both are unbiased estimates of the population parameters θ, if

$$\sigma^2(\hat{\theta}_1)<\sigma^2(\hat{\theta}_2) \tag{6.24}$$

Then the estimator $\hat{\theta}_1$ is more efficient than $\hat{\theta}_2$. If the variance of $\hat{\theta}_1$ is the smallest among all unbiased estimators, it is called the minimum variance unbiased estimator. In fact, the smaller the variance of an estimator, the greater the chance that the estimated value given by this estimator is close to the population parameter.

3. Consistency

Let $\hat{\theta}$ be the sample statistic for estimating the population parameter θ, ε is an arbitrary small positive number, if

$$\lim_{n\to\infty} P\{|\hat{\theta}-\theta|<\varepsilon\}=1 \tag{6.25}$$

$\hat{\theta}$ is said to be a consistent estimate of θ. If the estimator $\hat{\theta}$ satisfies consistency, then when the sample size n continues to increase, $\hat{\theta}$ can be increasingly closer to θ. It can be explained that as the sample size n increases, the amount of information contained in the sample is also increasing, and the estimator obtained is more and more accurate.

In practical problems, we may not always be able to find an estimator that fully meets the above three criteria, but we always hope that the estimator used goes close to these criteria as for as possible. An estimator that satisfies the above three criteria at the same time is called a consistent minimum unbiased estimator variance. It can be shown that the sample mean and sample proportion are consistent minimum unbiased estimator variance of the population mean and that of the population proportion, respectively.

6.3 Interval Estimation

Interval estimation refers to the method of estimating the interval range of the population parameter with sample statistics under a certain confidence level. Let $\hat{\theta}_1$ and $\hat{\theta}_2$ be two estimators of the population parameter θ ($\hat{\theta}_1<\hat{\theta}_2$), for a given α $(0<\alpha<1)$, we have

$$P(\hat{\theta}_1\leqslant\theta\leqslant\hat{\theta}_2)=1-\alpha \tag{6.26}$$

We call $(\hat{\theta}_1, \hat{\theta}_2)$ the confidence interval of θ, where α is the significance level, usually 1%, 5% and 10%. Confidence $1-\alpha$, also known as confidence level or confidence probability, reflects the reliability of interval estimation. If there is $1-\alpha=95\%$, it can be explained as follows: in the process of sampling for 100 times, 100 confidence intervals can be obtained, of which 95 confidence intervals contain the true value of the population parameter θ.

In fact, the smaller the confidence interval, the higher the accuracy of the interval estimation; the larger the confidence level, the greater the reliability of the interval estimation. Generally speaking, under the premise of a certain sample size, precision and confidence level are often contradictory, that is, if the confidence level increases, the confidence interval will inevitably increase, reducing the accuracy; if the accuracy increases, the confidence interval will shrink, and the confidence level will decrease. If we increase the sample size, both the confidence level and the precision of interval estimation will increase.

For interval estimation, population mean and population proportion are issues to be discussed below.

6.3.1 Relations of Interval Estimation to Population Mean

1. Calculation to Population Mean for Interval Estimation When the Variance is Known

If the population obeys a normal distribution, then the sample mean is $\bar{x} \sim N(\bar{X}, \mu_{\bar{x}}^2)$; if the population does not obey a normal distribution, but when the sample size n is large enough, then the sample mean is $\bar{x} \overset{\cdot}{\sim} N(\bar{X}, \sigma_{\bar{x}}^2)$. Furthermore:

$$z = \frac{\bar{x} - \bar{X}}{\sigma_{\bar{x}}} \sim N(0, 1) \tag{6.27}$$

Given a significance level α, the critical value can be obtained by checking the standard normal distribution table $z_{\frac{\alpha}{2}}$, and it satisfies:

$$P(-z_{\frac{\alpha}{2}} \leqslant z \leqslant z_{\frac{\alpha}{2}}) = 1 - \alpha \tag{6.28}$$

Then under the confidence level $1-\alpha$, the population mean for interval estimation is

$$\bar{x} \pm z_{\frac{\alpha}{2}} \mu_{\bar{x}} \tag{6.29}$$

Conversely, assuming that the sampling error of the population mean is Δ, that is $|\bar{x} - \bar{X}| \leqslant \Delta$, and the confidence level of the interval estimation is $1-\alpha$ when there is $\bar{x} - \Delta \leqslant \bar{X} \leqslant \bar{x} + \Delta$, then we have

$$P(\bar{x} - \Delta \leqslant \bar{X} \leqslant \bar{x} + \Delta) = P(|\bar{x} - \bar{X}| \leqslant \Delta) = P\left(\left|\frac{\bar{x} - \bar{X}}{\sigma_{\bar{x}}}\right| \leqslant \frac{\Delta}{\sigma_{\bar{x}}}\right) = P\left(|z| \leqslant \frac{\Delta}{\sigma_{\bar{x}}}\right) = 1 - \alpha \tag{6.30}$$

The critical value $z_{\frac{\alpha}{2}}$ and the confidence level $1-\alpha$. Given a confidence level $1-\alpha$, the critical value $z_{\frac{\alpha}{2}}$ can be determined by looking up the standard normal distribution table in Appendix A. If the confidence level increases, that is, the reliability of the interval estimation increases, α must decrease, that is, the critical value $z_{\frac{\alpha}{2}}$ increases. Conversely, if the confidence level decreases, the critical value should also decrease. We can call the critical value $z_{\frac{\alpha}{2}}$ as the probability degree, expressed in symbols z, to indirectly measure the probability of interval estimation.

There is the following relationship among the sampling allowance error Δ, the sampling mean error $\sigma_{\bar{x}}$ and the probability degree z.

$$z=\frac{\Delta}{\sigma_{\bar{x}}},\ \Delta=z\cdot\sigma_{\bar{x}} \tag{6.31}$$

where $\sigma_{\bar{x}}=\frac{\sigma}{\sqrt{n}}$.

Given a confidence level $1-\alpha$, the confidence interval for the population mean under repeated sampling conditions is

$$\bar{x}\pm z_{\frac{\alpha}{2}}\frac{\sigma}{\sqrt{n}} \tag{6.32}$$

The confidence interval for the population mean with non-repeated sampling is

$$\bar{x}\pm z_{\frac{\alpha}{2}}\frac{\sigma}{\sqrt{n}}\sqrt{1-\frac{n}{N}} \tag{6.33}$$

[**Example 6.6**] The length of a certain type of mechanical handle $X\sim N(\bar{X},0.05^2)$. 6 mechanical handles were randomly selected by repeated sampling, and the measured length were 15.1, 14.4, 15.2, 15.4, 14.6, 15.3 (cm). Try to estimate the mean value of the length of the mechanical handles in the lot with 95% confidence.

[**Solution**] Since the population $X\sim N(\bar{X},0.05^2)$, so the sample mean is $\bar{x}\sim N\left(\bar{X},\frac{0.05^2}{6}\right)$.

First, calculate the sample mean:

$$\bar{x}=\frac{\sum x}{n}=\frac{15.1+14.4+15.2+15.4+14.6+15.3}{6}=15\ \text{cm}$$

Then, according to $F(z)=1-\alpha=95\%$, we have $z=1.96$;

Again, the sampling allowance error can be calculated as:

$$\Delta_{\bar{x}}=z\sigma_{\bar{x}}=1.96\times0.02=0.04\ \text{cm}$$

Finally, the confidence interval can be expressed as:

$$\bar{x}\pm\Delta=15\pm0.04\ \text{cm}$$

Therefore, at the 95% confidence level, the confidence interval forthe mean length of the batch of mechanical handles is (14.96, 15.04).

2. Calculate Population Mean for Interval Estimation When the Variance is Unknown

If the population obeys a normal distribution but the population variance is unknown, the sample standard deviation can be s instead of the population standard deviation σ to construct statistics, that is

$$t=\frac{\bar{x}-\bar{X}}{\frac{s}{\sqrt{n}}}\sim t(n-1) \tag{6.34}$$

Given a confidence level $1-\alpha$, the confidence interval for the population mean under repeated sampling conditions is

$$\bar{x} \pm t_{\frac{\alpha}{2}, n-1} \frac{s}{\sqrt{n}} \tag{6.35}$$

Similarly, the confidence interval for the population mean with non-repeated resampling is

$$\bar{x} \pm t_{\frac{\alpha}{2}, n-1} \frac{s}{\sqrt{n}} \sqrt{1-\frac{n}{N}} \tag{6.36}$$

Check the student-t distribution in Appendix B to get the critical value $t_{\frac{\alpha}{2}, n-1}$. In the case of large samples, the student-t distribution approximates the standard normal distribution. Therefore, at this time, the standard normal distribution critical value can also be $z_{\frac{\alpha}{2}}$ instead of $t_{\frac{\alpha}{2}, n-1}$.

[**Example 6.7**] It is known that there are 10,000 production line workers in a manufacturing enterprise, and the output of workers X follows a normal distribution. Now use non-repeated sampling to randomly select 1,000 people to investigate the output of the day, and find out that the per capita sample output is 35 pieces, and the sample standard deviation is 4.8 pieces. Try to estimate the average daily output of all workers with a 95.45% confidence level.

[**Solution**] It can be seen from question, $\bar{x}=35$(pieces), $s=4.8$(pieces). Because the population follows a normal distribution and the variance is unknown, the sample standard deviation can be used s instead of the population standard deviation σ for interval estimation.

First, calculate the sampling mean error:

$$\sigma_{\bar{x}} = \frac{s}{\sqrt{n}} \sqrt{1-\frac{n}{N}} = \frac{4.8}{\sqrt{1000}} \sqrt{1-\frac{1000}{10000}} = 0.144 \text{ piece}$$

Secondly, according to $F(z)=1-\alpha=95.45\%$, available $z=2$;

Again, the sampling allowance error can be calculated as:

$$\Delta_{\bar{x}} = z\sigma_{\bar{x}} = 2\times 0.144 = 0.288 \text{ piece}$$

Finally, the confidence interval can be expressed as:

$$\bar{x} \pm \Delta = 35 \pm 0.288 \text{ pieces}$$

Therefore, at the confidence level 95.45%, the confidence interval for the average daily output of all workers in the manufacturing enterprise is (34.712, 35.288).

6.3.2 Relations of Interval Estimation to Population Proportion

Let P be the population proportion, and p be the sample proportion. When the sample size n is large enough, and there is $p \overset{\cdot}{\sim} N(P, \sigma_p^2)$, then there is

$$z = \frac{p-P}{\sigma_p} \overset{d}{\sim} N(0, 1) \tag{6.37}$$

Given the confidence level $1-\alpha$, the confidence interval for the population proportion is

$$p \pm z_{\frac{\alpha}{2}} \sigma_p \tag{6.38}$$

Among them, σ_p is the sampling mean error of the number of samples, under repeated sampling conditions, it is

$$\sigma_p=\sqrt{\frac{P(1-P)}{n}} \tag{6.39}$$

Under the condition of non-repeated sampling, that is

$$\sigma_p=\sqrt{\frac{P(1-P)}{n}}=\sqrt{1-\frac{n}{N}} \tag{6.40}$$

Since the population number P is unknown, P in the formula and can be replaced by the sample number p in the formula.

[**Example 6.8**] In a follow-up investigation of the effectiveness of a certain health product, 700 people were randomly selected by repeated sampling, and 420 of them believed that the health product was effective. Try to estimate a confidence interval for the proportion of people who believe that the health product is effective at a 95.45% confidence level.

[**Solution**] Since $n=700$ (people) and $n_1=420$ (people), the number of samples and the sampling mean error are respectively

$$p=\frac{n_1}{n}=\frac{420}{700}=60\%,\ \sigma_p=\sqrt{\frac{p(1-p)}{n}}=\sqrt{\frac{0.6\times0.4}{800}}=0.0173$$

Secondly, according to $F(z)=1-\alpha=95.45\%$, available $z=2$;

Again, the sampling allowance error can be calculated as:

$$\Delta_p=z\sigma_p=2\times0.0173=3.46\%$$

Finally, the confidence interval can be expressed as:

$$p\pm\Delta_p=60\%\pm3.46\%$$

Therefore, at the95.45% confidence level, the confidence interval of the population proportion of people who believe that the health product is effective is (56.54%, 63.46%).

6.4 Determination of Sample Size

In the actual sampling survey, the selection of sample size is particularly important. Because the sample size is too large, it will inevitably increase the expenditure of manpower, financial resources, material resources, etc., resulting in unnecessary waste. However, if the sample size is too small, the sampling error will increase and the accuracy required by the sampling will not be reached. Therefore, it is necessary for us to study the influencing factors of sample size.

It is easy to see that there exists relationship among the sampling allowance error, probability degree, and sampling mean error as follows:

$$\Delta=z\sigma \tag{6.41}$$

When the sampling mean error σ remains unchanged, the sampling allowance error Δ increases, and the probability degree z also increases; and vice versa. Therefore, under constant conditions if σ is unchanged, there is an irreconcilable contradiction between the accuracy and reliability of sampling estimates.

To improve accuracy, the cost of reliability is sacrificed, and to improve reliability, the cost of estimation accuracy is sacrificed. However, once the sampling mean error σ is reduced (for example, by increasing the sample size n), the accuracy and reliability of the estimating can be improved at the same time. Therefore, the formula (6.41) further demonstrates the importance of determining the sample size from a mathematical point of view.

6.4.1 Determination of Sample Size When Estimating Population Mean

Under the condition that population variance is known, apply the method of repeated sampling, we have

$$\Delta = z_{\frac{\alpha}{2}} \frac{\sigma}{\sqrt{n_0}} \tag{6.42}$$

Given the sampling mean error and probability degree, the sample size should be drawn at least as

$$n_0 = \frac{z_{\frac{\alpha}{2}}^2 \sigma^2}{\Delta^2} \tag{6.43}$$

Under the condition that population variance is known, apply the method of non-repeated sampling, we have

$$\Delta = z_{\frac{\alpha}{2}} \frac{\sigma}{\sqrt{n_1}} \sqrt{1 - \frac{n_1}{N}} \tag{6.44}$$

Given the sampling average error and probability degree, the sample size should be drawn at least as

$$n_1 = \frac{N z_{\frac{\alpha}{2}}^2 \sigma^2}{N\Delta^2 + z_{\frac{\alpha}{2}}^2 \sigma^2} \tag{6.45}$$

Divide the numerator and denominator by $N\Delta^2$ of the above formula at the same time, we can get

$$n_1 = \frac{\dfrac{z_{\frac{\alpha}{2}}^2 \sigma^2}{\Delta^2}}{1 + \dfrac{z_{\frac{\alpha}{2}}^2 \sigma^2}{N\Delta^2}} = \frac{n_0}{1 + \dfrac{n_0}{N}} \tag{6.46}$$

Seen from above derivation process, the sample size by non-repeated sampling can be obtained by calculating the sample size by repeated sampling. The sample size of non-repeated sampling is smaller than that of repeated sampling, other things being equal.

6.4.2 Determination of Sample Size When Estimating Population Proportion

Similarly, under the condition of applying the method of repeated sampling, the sample size that should be drawn as

$$n_0=\frac{z_{\frac{\alpha}{2}}^2 P(1-P)}{\Delta_p^2} \tag{6.47}$$

Under the condition of applying the method of non-repeated sampling, the sample size that should be drawn as

$$n_1=\frac{Nz_{\frac{\alpha}{2}}^2 P(1-P)}{N\Delta_p^2+z_{\frac{\alpha}{2}}^2 P(1-P)}=\frac{n_0}{1+\frac{n_0}{N}} \tag{6.48}$$

When using the above formula to determine sample size, the following should be kept in mind. First of all, since the calculated result is the minimum sample size required to meet the given accuracy and reliability, the calculated result should be rounded up rather than be rounded. In practice, more units are usually drawn to meet the needs. Secondly, since the population variance and population proportion are usually unknown, the variance and proportion of trial sample can be used instead, and the variance and proportion data of similar historical surveys can also be used instead. If there are multiple variance data, the largest one should be selected; for the proportion, if there is no historical data, the most conservative value can be taken, that is, the maximum value of the variance of the proportion is 0.25 instead. Finally, when multiple variables are involved in the research question, and each variable has different requirements for accuracy and reliability, so the necessary sample size suitable for different requirements of each variable is also changeable. At this time, the largest sample size value should be taken to meet the requirements of all variables.

[**Example 6.9**] A pharmaceutical factory wants to check the dosage accuracy of 1500 bottles of drugs produced this month. According to last month's data, the standard deviation of the dosage for each bottle of this drug is 50 milligrams. At a confidence level of 95.45%, the error range of the average dose of each bottle of drugs should not exceed 10 milligrams. How many bottles of drugs should be extracted at least?

[**Solution**] According to the problem, $N=1500$, $\sigma=50$, $\Delta=10$. Because $F(z)=1-\alpha=95.45\%$, so $z=2$.

If repeated sampling is used, a sample size at least

$$n_0=\frac{z^2\sigma^2}{\Delta^2}=\frac{2^2\times 50^2}{10^2}=100 \text{ bottles}$$

If non-repeated sampling is used, the sample size should be drawn at least as

$$n_1=\frac{n_0}{1+\frac{n_0}{N}}=\frac{100}{1+\frac{100}{1500}}=93.75=94 \text{ bottles}$$

[**Example 6. 10**] The factory conducts quality inspection on a batch of tires. The total number of tires in this batch is 6000. The qualified rate of the tires obtained in the past several similar investigations was 92%, 94%, and 95%. Determine the sample size required to achieve a maximum allowable error of 3% for a qualification rate with a confidence level of 99. 73%.

[**Solution**] According to the question, $N=6000$, $\Delta_P=3\%$. Take the maximum variance value, that is, $P=92\%$. Because $F(z)=1-\alpha=99.73\%$, so $z=3$.

If repeated sampling is used, a sample size at least of

$$n_o=\frac{z^2P(1-P)}{\Delta_P}=\frac{3^2\times 92\%(1-92\%)}{0.03^2}=736$$

If non-repeated sampling is used, at least the sample size should be drawn as

$$n_1=\frac{n_0}{1+\frac{n_0}{N}}=\frac{736}{1+\frac{736}{6000}}=655.582=656$$

[**Example 6. 11**] Test the photoelectric conversion efficiency of a certain type of solar panel. According to the empirical data of normal production in the past, the standard deviation $\sigma=0.5$ of photoelectric conversion efficiency and the qualified rate $P=95\%$. Using the repeated sampling method, it is required that under the 99. 73% confidence level, the error range of the sampling average photoelectric conversion efficiency is not more than 0. 05, and the error range of the sampling pass rate is not more than 3%. Try to find the necessary sample size.

[**Solution**] According to the problem, $\sigma=0.5$, $P=95\%$, $\Delta=0.05$, $\Delta_P=3\%$. because $F(z)=1-\alpha=99.73\%$, so $z=3$.

The necessary sample size to sample the average photoelectric conversion efficiency is

$$n_{01}=\frac{z^2\sigma^2}{\Delta^2}=\frac{3^2\times 0.5^2}{0.05^2}=900$$

The necessary sample size for the sampling pass rate is

$$n_{02}=\frac{z^2P(1-P)}{\Delta_P{}^2}=\frac{3^2\times 95\%(1-95\%)}{0.03^2}=475$$

Take the larger value among the above calculation results, i. e. $n_0=900$. Therefore, 900 solar panels should be taken as samples.

Chapter Review

This chapter first introduces sampling distribution concepts such as population and sample, sample size and sample number, population parameter and sample statistics, repeated sampling and non-repeated sampling, and then discusses the sampling distribution of sample mean and sample proportion. Secondly, the point estimation method and its evaluation criteria are given, including unbiasedness, validity, consistency and so on. Thirdly, for the cases of known variance and unknown variance, the problem of interval estimation of population mean and population proportion is discussed. Finally, when estimating the population mean and population proportion, the calculation formulas of the sample size are given respectively.

Through the study of the content of this chapter, firstly, one must understand the four pairs of basic concepts of sampling distribution, and on this basis, master the formulas for calculating the sampling mean error of the sample mean and sample proportion. Secondly, master the point estimation and interval estimation methods of the population parameters, and compare the respective advantages and disadvantages of these two methods. Finally, master the calculation formulas of the sample size to estimate the population mean and population proportion under the conditions of repeated sampling and non-repeated sampling, and compare the differences.

Exercise

1. What is point estimation and explains the advantages and disadvantages of point estimation.

2. What are the criteria for evaluating good estimates?

3. What are confidence levels and confidence intervals and what do they mean?

4. What are the factors that affect sample size?

5. A random sample of the amount paid (in dollars) for taxi fare from downtown to the airport was obtained:

15 19 17 23 21 17 16 18 12 18 20 22 15 18 20

Use the data to find a point estimate for each of the following parameters.

(1) mean;

(2) variance;

(3) standard deviation.

6. A sample of 60 night-school students' ages is obtained in order to estimate the mean age of night-school students. $\bar{x}=25.5$ years. The population variance is 16.

(1) Give a point estimate for $\bar{x}$.

(2) Find the 95% confidence interval for $\bar{x}$.

(3) Find the 99% confidence interval for $\bar{x}$.

7. The following data set represents the repair costs (in dollars) for a random sample of 30 dishwashers.

41.82	52.81	57.80	68.16	73.48	78.88	88.13	88.79
90.07	90.35	91.68	91.72	93.01	95.21	95.34	96.50
100.05	101.32	103.59	104.19	105.62	111.32	117.14	118.42
118.77	119.01	120.70	140.52	141.84	147.06		

(1) Find the point estimate of the population mean.

(2) Find the maximum error of estimate for a 95% level of confidence.

(3) Construct a 95% confidence interval for the population mean and interpret the results.

8. The following data set represents the time (in minutes) for a random sample of phone calls made by employees at a company.

7.5 2.0 12.1 8.8 9.4 7.3 1.9 2.8 7.0 7.3

(1) Find the sample mean.

(2) Find the sample standard deviation.

(3) Use the student-t distribution to construct a 90% confidence interval for the population mean and interpret the result. Assume the population of the data set is normally distributed.

(4) Repeat Part (3), assuming $\sigma=3.5$ minutes. Compare the results.

9. In a random sample of eight people with advanced degrees in biology, the mean monthly income was \$3800 and the standard deviation was \$566. Assume the monthly incomes are normally distributed and use a student-t distribution to construct a 95% confidence interval for the population mean monthly income for people with advanced degrees in biology.

10. The new mini-laptop computers can deliver computing-power several times compared to machine size at least, but the weight no more than 1.36 kg. How large a sample would be needed to estimate the population mean weight if the maximum error of estimate is to be 0.4 of 1 standard deviation with 95% confidence?

11. In a survey of 2000 adults from the U. S. aged 65 and over 1400 people received a flu shot.

(1) Find the point estimation for the population proportion p of those receiving flu shots.

(2) Construct a 90% confidence interval for the population proportion.

(3) Find the minimum sample size needed to estimate the population proportion at the 99% confidence level in order to ensure that the estimate is accurate within 4% of the population proportion.

12. How large a sample should be taken if the population mean is to be estimated with 99% confidence to within \$75? The population has a standard deviation of \$900.

13. In a survey of 474 women, 365 of them said that the media have a negative effect on women's health because they set unattainable standards for appearance.

(1) Find a point estimate for p. Construct a 95% confidence interval for the population proportion p.

(2) Find the minimum sample size needed to estimate the population proportion p with 99% confidence. The estimate must be accurate within 2% of p.

Chapter 7

Hypothesis Testing

A hypothesis test, also known as a statistical hypothesis test or significance test, is a statistical procedure used to make inferences or draw conclusions about a population based on sample data. It is a fundamental tool in statistical analysis and helps determine whether a claim or hypothesis about a population is supported by the evidence provided by the sample.

This chapter will introduce the process and method of hypothesis testing in detail.

7.1 Basic Questions about Hypothesis Testing

7.1.1 The Concept of Hypothesis Testing

Hypothesis testing must first have a hypothesis problem, that is, some kind of guess or judgment about the population. Below we use two specific examples to illustrate how to raise hypothesis testing questions.

[**Example 7.1**] In 2010, the average visual acuity of middle school students in a certain region was 1.1. In 2013, 100 middle school students were randomly selected and their average visual acuity was measured to be 0.8. Can we say that the average visual acuity of middle school students in this region in 2013 has decreased compared with that in 2010?

[**Example 7.2**] The Consumer Association received complaints from consumers that the net content of a certain brand of bagged snacks was insufficient. Therefore, they randomly selected 100 bags of bagged snacks from the market and found that the average net content was 495 grams, which is lower than the 500 grams marked on the packaging. Based on this, can it be judged that the manufacturer has cheated consumers?

For example, in Example 7.1 we can make an assumption: the average visual acuity of middle school students in 2013 was 1.1. However, it cannot be assumed that the average visual acuity of middle school students in 2013 is 0.8, because 0.8 is the average visual acuity of middle school students in the sample, not the whole population. Similarly, in Example 7.2, we can make a hypothesis: the average net content of the population is 500 grams as marked on the package. After setting up the hypothesis, use the method of statistical inference to test the authenticity of the hypothesis and then make a decision, that is, if the hypothesis is true, accept it, and if it is false, reject it.

As we all know, logically speaking, it is difficult to affirm something, but it is relatively easy to deny it. Likewise, accepting a hypothesis is much more difficult than rejecting one. Therefore, hypothesis testing is a statistical inference method that utilizes the principle of small probability and aims to deny the hypothesis, and the basis for the denial comes from the information provided by the random sample. For example, in Example 7.1, it is very difficult for us to affirm the hypothesis that the average visual acuity of middle school students in 2013 was 1.1, but it is much easier to deny this hypothesis based on the sample information. The same is true in Example 7.2. However, is the basis for denying the hypothesis sufficient, is the evidence sufficient, and to what extent can the hypothesis of the whole be denied? This is related to the basic principle of hypothesis testing—the principle of small probability events.

Small probability events refer to events that have a low likelihood of occurring. In statistics and probability theory, probabilities are assigned to events ranging from 0 (impossible) to 1 (certain). When an event has a probability close to 0, it is considered a small probability event. If a small probability event happens, how should people think and make decisions? For example, if a manufacturer claims that its product qualification rate is very high, reaching 99%, then randomly select 1 piece from a batch of products (such as 100 pieces), the probability that this 1 piece happens to be a defective product is 1%, which is a small probability event. If this small probability event happens, we have reason to deny the manufacturer's claim and make a judgment that the manufacturer's claim is false. Similarly, in Example 7.2, assuming in advance that the average net content of a certain brand of bagged snacks is 500 grams marked on the package, and then randomly select a few samples, if a small probability event occurs, we can deny the assumption that population average net content is 500 grams. That is to say, when a small probability event occurs, the assumptions made in advance are rejected.

For example, in Example 7.1, $H_0: \bar{X}=1.1$, there are three types of possible H_1:

(1) If investigators want to know whether the average visual acuity of middle school students in the region is 1.1 in 2010, the alternative hypothesis can be determined as: H_0: $\bar{X}\neq 1.1$, which is a two-sided test.

(2) If investigators want to know whether the average visual acuity of middle school students in the region is less than 1.1 in 2010, the alternative hypothesis can be determined

as: $H_0: \bar{X} < 1.1$, which is a left one-sided test.

(3) If investigators want to know whether the average visual acuity of middle school students in the region is greater than 1. 1 in 2010, the alternative hypothesis can be determined as: $H_0: \bar{X} > 1.1$, which is a right one-sided test.

7. 1. 2 Steps of Hypothesis Testing

1. Establishment of Hypothesis

The hypothesis consists of two parts: the null hypothesis and the alternative hypothesis. For a hypothesis testing problem, the hypothesis that the researcher hopes to collect evidence to deny is called the null hypothesis, usually denoted by H_0. The alternative hypothesis is opposite to the null hypothesis. It is another possible conclusion when the null hypothesis is denied. It is the hypothesis that the researcher hopes to collect evidence to support. It is also called the research hypothesis and is usually expressed in H_1.

If the alternative hypothesis has no specific direction and contains the symbol "$\neq$", such hypothesis test is called a two-sided test, also known as a two-tailed test. If the alternative hypothesis has a specific direction and contains the symbol "$>$" or "$<$", such a hypothesis test is called a one-sided test, also known as a one-tailed test or a one-sided test. If the direction of the alternative hypothesis is "$<$", it is called a left one-sided test. If the direction of the alternative hypothesis is "$>$", it is called a right one-sided test.

Whether a hypothesis test uses a two-sided test or a one-sided test, and whether a one-sided test uses a left one-sided test or a right one-sided test depends on the problem of the alternative hypothesis.

For example, in Example 7. 1, H_0: $\bar{X} = 4.2$, there are three types of possible H_1:

(1) If investigators want to know whether the average weight of newborns in the province is 4. 2 kg in 2010, the alternative hypothesis can be determined as: H_1: $\bar{X} \neq 4.2$, which is a two-sided test.

(2) If investigators want to know whether the average weight of newborns in this province is less than 4. 2 kg in 2010, the alternative hypothesis can be determined as: H_1: $\bar{X} < 4.2$ which is a left one-sided test.

(3) If investigators want to know whether the average weight of newborns in this province is greater than 4. 2 kg in 2010, the alternative hypothesis can be determined as: H_1: $\bar{X} > 4.2$ which is a right one-sided test.

2. Selection of Test Statistics methods

After the null hypothesis and the alternative hypothesis are established, we need to select appropriate test statistic based on the nature of the data and the research question.

Based on the test statistics, we need to make decisions on "accept the null hypothesis and reject the alternative hypothesis" or "reject the null hypothesis and accept the alternative hypothesis". For a specific problem, factors to be considered in statistic test are basically the same as that in parameter estimation. For example, whether the sample is a large sample or a small sample, whether the population obeys a normal distribution, whether the population variance is known, and so on. Different test statistics should be chosen in different situations. They include t-statistic, z-statistic, chi-square statistic, or another relevant statistic.

3. Significance Level

The significance level determined by the actual problem further determines the value range for the test statistic to accept or reject the null hypothesis. Among them, the significance level refers to the probability of rejecting the null hypothesis when the null hypothesis is true, that is, the risk of rejecting the null hypothesis, generally expressed by $\alpha(0<\alpha<1)$. Once the significance level α is given, the critical values of the acceptance domain and rejection domain of the null hypothesis are uniquely determined. For the same significance level α, different test statistics are selected to obtain different critical values; for the same significance level α and the same test statistic, the critical values of two-sided test and one-sided test are also different.

4. Calculate the Value of the Test Statistic and Make Statistical Decisions

Under the condition of a given significance level α, the value range of the test statistic can be divided into two parts according to the probability: the small probability area and the high probability area. The small probability area is the area where the probability does not exceed α, which is the rejection area of the null hypothesis; the high probability area is the area where the probability is $1-\alpha$, and it is the acceptance area of the null hypothesis. The junction point of these two areas is the critical value. For example, taking $\alpha=0.05$ means that when H_0 is true, the test statistic has only a 5% chance of falling in the rejection area, and a 95% chance of falling in the acceptance area. If the value of the test statistic falls into the rejection area, the null hypothesis is rejected and the alternative hypothesis is accepted, so the sample data is considered to support the conclusion of the alternative hypothesis; if the value of the test statistic falls into the acceptance area, the null hypothesis is accepted and it is considered that there is no sufficient evidence show that the alternative hypothesis is true.

As we all know, the rejection area is a small probability area, and the null hypothesis should be rejected according to the small probability principle, but small probability events are not zero probability events after all, and may still happen. The acceptance area is a high probability area, but high probability events are not inevitable events after all. Therefore, whether a decision is made to accept or reject the null hypothesis, there is a possibility of misjudgment.

7.1.3 p-value

The classic significance test method is based on the domain of rejection, that is, first determine a significance level α, check the statistical distribution table to determine the critical value, then compare the critical value and the value of the statistic test, and finally make a judgement. However, in the age of computers, we can also make judgments about the null hypothesis based on p-value. The term p-value represents the probability of observing a test statistic as extreme as the one obtained, assuming the null hypothesis is true. In hypothesis testing, the p-value test involves comparing this p-value to a predefined significance level. When the p-value is smaller than the chosen significance level, we reject the null hypothesis; otherwise, we accept it.

Compared with the classic critical value test, the p-value test can provide more information. That is because the p-value reflects the probability of a discrepancy between the observed actual data and the null hypothesis. If the p-value is smaller, it means that the sample observation value is less likely to occur, and if it occurs, then according to the principle of small probability events, we have the more reasons to reject the null hypothesis. Of course, if the p-value is calculated by manual calculation, it will appear more complicated. Therefore, we usually use statistical software to calculate p-value, for example, SPSS, MATLAB, R, etc. For convenience, we summarize the steps of the p-value test as follows:

(1) Formulate a hypothesis.

(2) Identify the relevant test statistics and their distribution.

(3) Utilize the observed sample values to compute the test statistic.

(4) Calculate the p-value.

(5) Compare the obtained p-value with the chosen significance level α to make a decision.

7.1.4 Comparison of Two-tailed Test to One-tailed Test

After determining the test statistic and given the significance level, a critical value can be determined, which divides the value range of the test statistic into two parts: the rejection area and the acceptance area.

The rejection area is a small probability area for the value of the test statistic. The small probability area can be arranged at both ends of the test statistic distribution, or on one side of the test statistic distribution, which are called two-tailed test and one-tailed test respectively.

One-tailed test can be divided into left-tailed test and right-tailed test according to whether the rejection area is on the left or right. When the question we care about is to test whether the population mean or the population proportion has changed, regardless of whether the direction of change is positive or negative, whether it is large or small, a two-tailed test should be used.

When the question we are concerned about is whether the population mean or the population percentage not exceeds the assumption, the left one-tailed test should be used. When the question we care about is whether the population mean or the population proportion exceeds the assumption, the right one-tailed test should be used.

Below we use the test statistics that obey the normal distribution to demonstrate the two-sided test, the left one-sided test and the right one-sided test. The specific graphics are shown as Figure 7. 1 and Figure 7. 2.

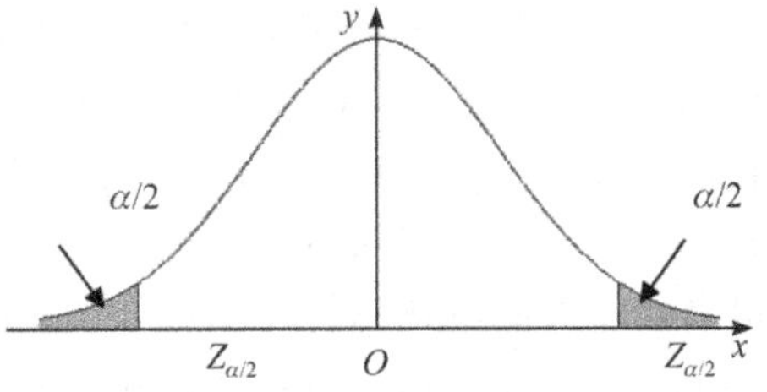

Figure 7. 1 Two-tailed test

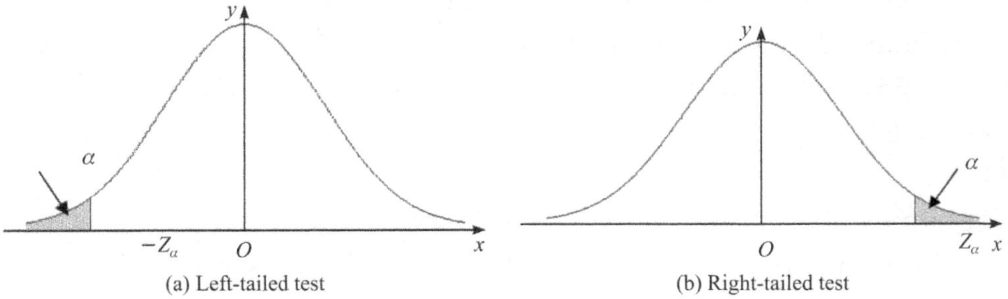

Figure 7. 2 One-tailed test

7. 1. 5 Two Types of Errors

Hypothesis testing involves comparing sample statistics to make decisions. As the test statistic is a random variable, judgments based on it aren't always guaranteed to be correct. There are four possible outcomes:

① If the null hypothesis is true, and we accept the null hypothesis, which is a correct judgment.

② If the null hypothesis is false, and we reject the null hypothesis, which is also a correct judgment.

③ If the null hypothesis is true, and we reject the null hypothesis. This is a judgment of "abandoning the truth and making mistakes", which is called the Type Ⅰ error and is represented by α.

④ If the null hypothesis is false, and we accept the null hypothesis. This is a judgment of "false-taking error", which is called the Type Ⅱ error and is represented by β.

These four cases form the following statistical decision table as Table 7.1:

Table 7.1 Statistical decision table

Situations	Accept H_0	Reject H_0
H_0 true	correct	Type Ⅰ Error α
H_0 false	Type Ⅱ Error β	correct

The Type Ⅰ error or the Type Ⅱ error is a manifestation of the distortion of the test conclusion and should be avoided as much as possible. Even if it cannot be completely avoided, the probability of its occurrence should be controlled. The reason for the Type Ⅰ error is that when the null hypothesis is true, the test statistic accidentally falls into the area of a small probability event, so we come to the conclusion that the null hypothesis is rejected. Obviously, the probability of making a Type Ⅰ error is equal to the significance level α. We can control the probability of making the Type Ⅰ error by controlling α. In order to avoid the Type Ⅰ error, the significance level should be controlled very small, usually 1%, 5% and 10%.

However, under certain sample size, shrinking α expands the possibility of the Type Ⅱ error. The Type Ⅱ error is "false-taking error", and the probability of making the Type Ⅱ error is recorded as β. We hope that the probability of making these two types of errors is as small as possible, but under certain sample size, this contradiction is difficult to resolve, that is to say, if we reduce both α and β, the sample size must be increased. Meantime, increasing the sample size will inevitably increase the survey cost (or test cost), so factors such as two types of errors, sample size and cost should be considered comprehensively.

Generally speaking, if the consequences of making the Type Ⅰ error are more serious than that of making the Type Ⅱ error, we should try to reduce the probability of making the Type Ⅰ error, and the value of α should be smaller; If the consequences of making the Type Ⅱ error are more serious than that of making the Type Ⅰ error, so we should try to reduce the Type Ⅱ error, and the value of α should be larger .

For example, in medical testing, Type Ⅰ error could result in wrongly diagnosing a healthy individual as having a disease, leading to unnecessary treatments or interventions. In order to minimize the risk of Type Ⅰ error, researchers should choose a more conservative significance level, conduct larger sample size to increase the power of test statistic, or employ additional methods such as confidence intervals to provide a more comprehensive assessment of the data.

[**Example 7.3**] Regarding the inspection of medical devices, compared to rejecting a qualified product as a non-conforming product by mistake (type I error), if a non-conforming product is mistakenly accepted as a qualified product (type II error), it may cause much greater damage to patient health. In this case, we should focus on reducing the type II error, but make α larger.

[**Example 7.4**] According to Anglo-American law system, the defendant is assumed to be innocent before being proven guilty, that is, the null hypothesis H_0: The defendant is not guilty; and the alternative hypothesis H_1: The defendant is guilty.

For cases in Example 7.4, the Type Ⅰ error: the jury may commit that it is falsely accusing innocent people, the defendant is innocent but found guilty; the Type Ⅱ error: the people who commit offense but not been punished by law, the defendant is guilty but found not guilty. In order to reduce the probability of wronging the good people, it should be accepted as much as possible H_0, and the defendant is acquitted, which may increase the conversely of letting the offender cheat the law; conversely, this may increase the probability of wronging good people.

However, this relationship between α and β is only a dilemma under certain circumstances of evidence. If further evidence is collected, with sufficient evidence, it is possible to neither wronging the good people nor letting the offender cheat the law. Under the condition of insufficient evidence, the jury's practice of controlling the probability of two types of errors is usually as follow: according to the nature of the case, it is decided which type of error should be controlled first. If the case is very harmful, the Type Ⅱ error should be controlled. The probability of making a mistake is to prevent the victim from continuing to do evil; on the contrary, decrease the probability of Type Ⅰ error will lead the results: acts of not wronging the good people make the jury have a higher tendency of letting the offender cheat the law.

7.1.6 The Power of the Statistical Test

The power of a statistical test quantifies the probability that the test will accurately reject the null hypothesis when it is indeed false. In essence, it gauges the test's capability to detect a genuine effect or difference, or to correctly identify the presence of the alternative hypothesis.

A higher power indicates a better ability to detect a true effect, reducing the risk of a Type Ⅱ error, where a lower power implies a greater chance of failing to detect a true effect, leading to a higher probability of a Type Ⅱ error (failing to reject the null hypothesis when it is false).

Several factors influence the power of the statistical test:

(1) Effect Size. It refers to the magnitude of the true effect or difference being investigated. A larger effect size generally results in higher power.

(2) Sample Size. A larger sample size generally leads to higher power, as it provides more information and reduces sampling variability.

(3) Significance Level. The significance level (alpha) affects the power. A more

stringent significance level reduces the power, while a less stringent significance level increases the power.

(4) Variability. It refers to the amount of variability or dispersion within the data. Higher variability tends to lower the power of the statistical test.

Power analysis is often conducted to achieve a desired level of power for detecting a specific effect size prior to conducting a study to determine the required sample size. It helps researchers plan studies and assess the likelihood of detecting meaningful effects.

7.2 Tests for the Population Mean

7.2.1 When the Variance is Known

As we all know, if the population variance σ^2 is known, and the sample comes from a normal population, or in the case of a large sample, the test method of the population mean can use the z-test. That is, construct the test statistic as

$$z=\frac{\bar{x}-\bar{X}_0}{\frac{\sigma}{\sqrt{n}}}\sim N(0,1) \tag{7.1}$$

Given the significance level α, there are three conclusions as follows:

(1) H_0: $\bar{X}=\bar{X}_0$, H_1: $\bar{X}\neq\bar{X}_0$

When $|z|\geqslant z_{\frac{\alpha}{2}}$, reject H_0; otherwise, H_0 cannot be rejected.

p-value test : If the observed value of the test statistic is z_0, then the $p=2P(z>|z_0|)$, if the $p<\alpha$, then reject H_0; otherwise, H_0 cannot be rejected .

(2) H_0: $\bar{X}\leqslant\bar{X}_0$, H_1: $\bar{X}>\bar{X}_0$

When $z\geqslant z_\alpha$, reject H_0; otherwise, H_0 cannot be rejected.

Furthermore, we can calculate $p=P(z>z_0)$ to perform the p-value test.

(3) H_0: $\bar{X}\geqslant\bar{X}_0$, H_1: $\bar{X}<\bar{X}_0$

When $z\leqslant -z_\alpha$, reject H_0; otherwise, H_0 cannot be rejected.

Furthermore, we can calculate $p=P(z<z_0)$ to perform p-value test.

【**Example 7.5**】 A manufacturing factory produces mechanical equipments. According to the statistical results of historical data, the average service life is 25000 hours, and the standard deviation is 1800 hours. Now randomly select 360 equipments from the new batch of mechanical equipments for testing, and obtain the average service life of the samples $\bar{x}=25200$ km.

Try to judge whether there is a significant difference between the average service life of the new batch of mechanical equipments and the usual service life at a significance level of 5%.

[**Solution**] Because the problem only considers whether there is a significant difference between the average service life of the new batch of mechanical equipments and the usual one, regardless of whether it is positive or negative, it is a two-tailed test problem and belongs to the large sample situation.

First, establish a hypothesis

$$H_0: \bar{X}=25000$$

$$H_1: \bar{X}\neq 25000$$

the critical value corresponding to the significance level α is $z_{0.025}=1.96$;

Then, the test statistic is calculated $z=\dfrac{\bar{x}-\bar{X}_0}{\sigma/\sqrt{n}}=\dfrac{25200-25000}{1800/\sqrt{360}}=2.108$.

Because $z>z_{0.025}=1.96$, we reject H_0 at a significance level of 5%, that is, the average service life of the new batch of mechanical equipments is considered to be significantly different from the usual service life.

In addition, $p=2P(z>2.108)=0.0348<0.05$, so it was rejected H_0 at the significance level of 5%.

[**Example 7.6**] The plane of a airline has a total of 500 seats, with a ticket price of \$150 per seat and the average reservation rate of 70%. Now, in order to promote sales, the airline is implementing promotional measures to reduce the ticket price by 10%. After 36 days, an average of 375 seats are sold every day, with a standard deviation of 72 seats. Try to evaluate whether the preferential measures have a significant effect at a significance level of 5%.

[**Solution**] This problem requires testing whether the population mean is significantly exceeded, so it is a right-tailed test problem. According to the problem, $\bar{X}_0=500\times 70\%=350$.

First, establish a hypothesis

$$H_0: \bar{X}\leqslant 350$$

$$H_1: \bar{X}>350$$

the critical value corresponding to the significance levelα is $z_{0.05}=1.645$.

Then, the test statistic is calculated $z=\dfrac{\bar{x}-\bar{X}_0}{\sigma/\sqrt{N}}=\dfrac{375-350}{72/\sqrt{36}}=2.083$.

Because $z>z_{0.05}=1.645$, we reject H_0 at a significance level of 5%, that is to say, the airline's preferential measures have significantly increased the reservation rate.

In addition, calculated $p=P(z>2.083)=0.019<0.05$, so we reject H_0 at the significance level 5%.

7.2.2 When the Variance is Unknown

If the population variance σ^2 is unknown, and the sample comes from a normal population, the t-test can be used to test the population mean. That is, construct the test statistic as

$$t=\frac{\bar{x}-\bar{X}_0}{\frac{s}{\sqrt{n}}}\sim t(n-1) \tag{7.2}$$

where s is the standard deviation of sample.

At the significance level α, there are three conclusions as follows:

(1) H_0: $\bar{X}=\bar{X}_0$, H_1: $\bar{X}\neq\bar{X}_0$

When $|t|\geqslant t_{\frac{\alpha}{2}}$, reject H_0; otherwise, H_0 cannot be rejected.

(2) H_0: $\bar{X}\leqslant\bar{X}_0$, H_1: $\bar{X}>\bar{X}_0$

When $t\geqslant t_\alpha$, reject H_0; otherwise, H_0 cannot be rejected.

(3) H_0: $\bar{X}\geqslant\bar{X}_0$, H_1: $\bar{X}<\bar{X}_0$

When $t\leqslant -t_\alpha$, reject H_0; otherwise, H_0 cannot be rejected.

In addition, the t-test can also perform p-value test, and the calculation method of p-value is the same as the previous section. The difference is that the p-value of the t-test is not from the standard normal distribution table, but from the t-distribution table. It is not difficult to see that the t-test is very similar to the z-test, except that the distribution table checked for determining the critical value is different. However, in the case of large samples, the t-statistic is similar to the standard normal statistic, so the z-test instead of the t-test can be used.

【**Example 7.7**】 A beverage manufacturing factory, according to regulations, has a standard bottled beverage net content of 600 milliliters for automatic filling machines. Now, take out 10 bottles from the first production shift to measure the net content of the beverage. The average value of the sample is 603.4 milliliters, and the standard deviation of the sample is 7.86 milliliters. At a significance level of 1%, is workshop production normal?

【**Solution**】 This problem requires checking whether the net content of the beverage meets the net content of 600 milliliters, so it is a two-tailed test problem, so the t-test method can be used.

First, establish a hypothesis

$$H_0:\ \bar{X}=600,\ H_1:\ \bar{X}\neq 600$$

the critical value corresponding to the significance level α is $t_{0.005}(9)=3.25$.

Then, the test statistic is calculated $t=\dfrac{\bar{x}-\bar{X}_0}{s/\sqrt{n}}=\dfrac{603.4-600}{7.86/\sqrt{10}}=1.368$.

Because $t<t_{0.005}(9)=3.25$, we cannot reject H_0 at the significance level of 1%, that is, the production in the beverage manufacturing factory is considered to be normal.

In addition, we can calculate $p=2P(t>1.368)=0.204>0.01$, so we cannot reject H_0 at the significance level of 1%.

7.3 Hypothesis Testing of Population Proportion

When the sample size n and the number of samples p meet the conditions $n \geqslant 30$, $np > 5$, $n(1-p) > 5$, it can be known from the central limit theorem that $p \overset{d}{\sim} N\left(P,\ P\left(\frac{1-P}{n}\right)\right)$. Therefore, under above conditions, the following test statistics can be constructed for the population proportion P:

$$z = \frac{p - P_0}{\sqrt{\frac{P_0(1-P_0)}{n}}} \overset{d}{\sim} N(0,\ 1) \tag{7.3}$$

At the significance level α, there are three conclusions as follows:

(1) H_0: $P = P_0$, H_1: $P \neq P_0$

When $|z| \geqslant z_{\frac{\alpha}{2}}$, reject H_0; otherwise, H_0 cannot be rejected.

(2) H_0: $P \leqslant P_0$, H_1: $P > P_0$

When $z \geqslant z_\alpha$, reject H_0; otherwise, H_0 cannot be rejected.

(3) H_0: $P \geqslant P_0$, H_1: $P < P_0$

When $z \leqslant -z_\alpha$, reject H_0; otherwise, H_0 cannot be rejected.

In addition, for the above hypothesis testing problem, we can use p-value test. The calculation method of p-value is similar to Section 7.1.3.

[**Example 7.8**] The food processing factory produces chocolate containing 80% cocoa solids according to regulations. Now take 60 kg per hour and take a total of 7 hours for inspection. The average cocoa solids content is 86%, at the significance level of 5%. Whether there is a significant difference in the cocoa solids content of this chocolate.

[**Solution**] Since the problem is to consider whether the cocoa solids content in chocolate is 80%, it is a two-tailed test problem. In addition, according to the problem, $P_0 = 0.8$, $p = 0.86$, $n = 60 \times 7 = 420$, $np = 361.2 > 5$, $n(1-p) = 58.8 > 5$.

First, establish a hypothesis

$$H_0: P = 0.8, H_1: P \neq 0.8$$

the critical value corresponding to the significance level α is $z_{0.025} = 1.96$.

Then, the test statistic is calculated

$$z = \frac{p - P_0}{\sqrt{\frac{P_0(1-P_0)}{n}}} = \frac{0.86 - 0.8}{\sqrt{\frac{0.8 \times 0.2}{420}}} = 3.074$$

Because $z > z_{0.025} = 1.96$, we reject H_0 at the 5% significance level, that is, there is a significant difference between the cocoa solids content in chocolate and the standard content.

In addition, we can calculate $p=2P(z>3.074)=0.0022<0.05$, so we reject H_0 at the 5% significance level.

[**Example 7.9**] A head of a research institution noticed that there were many errors in the experimental results recorded in the laboratory. Based on past experience, it can be concluded that incorrect experimental records account for over 30% of these records. For the sake of prudence, the head randomly selected 360 experimental result records and found that 35% of the records were incorrect. Try to test whether the judgment of the head of the research institution is correct at a significance level of 5%.

[**Solution**] Because the problem is to consider whether incorrect experimental records account for more than 30% of all records, it is a right-tailed test problem. In addition, according to the problem, $P_0=0.3$, $p=0.35$, $n=360$, $np=126>5$, $n(1-p)=234>5$.

First, establish a hypothesis

$$H_0: P\leqslant 0.3,\ H_1: P>0.3$$

the critical value corresponding to the significance level α is $z_{0.05}=1.645$.

Then, the test statistic is calculated $z=\dfrac{p-P_0}{\sqrt{\dfrac{P_0(1-P_0)}{n}}}=\dfrac{0.35-0.3}{\sqrt{\dfrac{0.3\times 0.7}{360}}}=2.07$.

Because $z>z_{0.025}=1.645$, so we reject H_0 at a significance level of 5%, it means the judgment of the head of the research institution is correct.

In addition, we can calculate $p=P(z>2.07)=0.0192<0.05$, so we reject H_0 at the significance level of 5%.

7.4 Hypothesis Testing of Two Population Parameters

The previous sections have introduced the testing method of the population parameter and its applications. However, in many cases, we need to compare whether there is a significant difference between two population parameters.

For example, in the same age group, whether there is a significant difference in the income of highly educated workers and low-educated workers; whether the same teaching method has different effects on different grades or different courses; whether the operation on the product has different effects, and so on. For this kind of question, the answer can be sought through the test of two population parameters.

7.4.1 Test for Difference Between Two Population Means

1. Two Population Variances are Known

When both populations follow a normal distribution or when neither population follows a normal distribution but the sample sizes are sufficiently large, the variances of the two populations are known as σ_1^2 and σ_2^2, we have

$$z=\frac{(\bar{x}_1-\bar{x}_2)-(\mu_1-\mu_2)}{\sqrt{\frac{\sigma_1^2}{n_1}+\frac{\sigma_2^2}{n_2}}}\sim N(0,1) \tag{7.4}$$

where, μ_1 and μ_2 are the means of the two populations, respectively. For the null hypcthesis $H_0: \mu_1=\mu_2$, the test statistic can be defined based on Formula (7.4)

$$z=\frac{\bar{x}_1-\bar{x}_2}{\sqrt{\frac{\sigma_1^2}{n_1}+\frac{\sigma_2^2}{n_2}}} \tag{7.5}$$

[**Example 7.10**] Assume that the nutrient content in the soil of a certain crop obeys a normal distribution, and the variance before and after sowing is 36. 8 samples were taken before sowing, and the average nutrient content was 25.36, and 10 samples were taken after sowing, and the average nutrient content was 18.95. At the 5% significance level, test if there is significant change in the nutrient content in the soil before and after sowing.

[**Solution**] Because the problem is to consider whether the soil nutrient content is the same before and after sowing, it is a two-tailed test problem.

According to the meaning of the title, $\bar{X}_1=25.36$, $\bar{X}_2=18.95$; $n_1=8$, $n_2=10$, $\sigma_1^2=\sigma_2^2=36$.

First, establish a hypothesis

$$H_0: \mu_1=\mu_2,\ H_1: \mu_1\neq\mu_2$$

Then, the critical value corresponding to the significance level α is $z_{0.025}=1.96$;

Finally, the test statistic is calculated as $z=\frac{\bar{x}_1-\bar{x}_2}{\sqrt{\frac{\sigma_1^2}{n_1}+\frac{\sigma_2^2}{n_2}}}=\frac{25.36-18.95}{\sqrt{\frac{36}{8}+\frac{36}{10}}}=2.2522$.

Because $z>z_{0.025}=1.96$, we reject H_0 at a significance level of 5%, that is, there is a significant change in the nutrient content in the soil before and after sowing.

In addition, we can calculate $p=2P(z>2.2522)=0.0243<0.05$, so H_0 was rejected at the significance level of 5%.

2. Two Population Variances are Unknown

Considering the null hypothesis $H_0: \mu_1=\mu_2$, when σ_1^2 and σ_2^2 are unknown, and $\sigma_1^2=\sigma_2^2$, construct the test statistic:

$$t=\left.\frac{\bar{x}_1-\bar{x}_2}{s_p\sqrt{\frac{1}{n_1}+\frac{1}{n_2}}}\right|_{H_0}\sim t(n_1+n_2-2) \tag{7.6}$$

where

$$s_p=\sqrt{\frac{(n_1-1)s_1^2+(n_2-1)s_2^2}{n_1+n_2-2}}$$

When the σ_1^2 and σ_2^2 are unknown, and $\sigma_1^2 \neq \sigma_2^2$

$$t = \left.\frac{\bar{x}_1 - \bar{x}_2}{\sqrt{\frac{s_1^2}{n_1} + \frac{s_2^2}{n_2}}}\right|_{H_0} \overset{d}{\sim} t(f) \tag{7.7}$$

where f is the degree of freedom, its expression is

$$f = \frac{\left(\frac{s_1^2}{n_1} + \frac{s_2^2}{n_2}\right)^2}{\frac{\left(\frac{s_1^2}{n_1}\right)^2}{n_1 - 1} + \frac{\left(\frac{s_2^2}{n_2}\right)^2}{n_2 - 1}}$$

[**Example 7.11**] The sulfur dioxide content in a certain industrial emission gas obeys the normal distribution. The current standard method and the new method are used to determine the sulfur dioxide content in the emitted gases at the same time, assuming that the variance of the two methods is the same. Among them, the new method was measured 11 times, with an average result of 5.19 ppm and a standard deviation of 1.05 ppm; the standard method was tested 10 times, with an average result of 4.06 ppm and a standard deviation of 1.12 ppm. At the 5% significance level, is there significant difference in the results of these two determinations?

[**Solution**] Because the question is to consider whether there is a significant difference between the two measurement results, it is a two-tailed test problem.

According to the problem, $\bar{x}_1 = 5.19$, $\bar{x}_2 = 4.06$; $s_1 = 1.05$, $s_2 = 1.12$; $n_1 = 11$, $n_2 = 10$.

First, establish a hypothesis

$$H_0: \mu_1 = \mu_2, \ H_1: \mu_1 \neq \mu_2$$

Then, the critical value corresponding to the significance level α is $t_{0.025}(19) = 2.09$;

Finally, calculate the standard deviation and test statistic after combining the two samples as

$$s_p = \sqrt{\frac{(n-1)s_1^{\ 2} + (n-1)s_2^{\ 2}}{n_1 + n_2 - 2}} = \sqrt{\frac{10 \times 1.05^2 + 9 \times 1.12^2}{11 + 10 - 2}} = 1.08$$

$$t = \frac{\bar{x}_1 - \bar{x}_2}{s_p\sqrt{\frac{1}{n_1} + \frac{1}{n_2}}} = \frac{5.19 - 4.06}{1.08\sqrt{\frac{1}{11} + \frac{1}{10}}} = 2.39$$

Because $t > t_{0.025}(19) = 2.09$, we reject H_0 at the significance level of 5%, that is to say, there is a significant difference between the two measurement results.

In addition, we can calculate $p = 2P(t > 2.39) = 0.027 < 0.05$, so H_0 is rejected at the 5% significance level.

7.4.2 Hypothesis Testing for the Difference Between Two Population Proportions

1. Null Hypothesis H_0: $P_1 - P_2 = 0$

In the case of large samples, construct the test statistic:

$$z=\left.\frac{p_1-p_2}{\sqrt{p(1-p)(\frac{1}{n_1}+\frac{1}{n_2})}}\right|_{H_0} \overset{d}{\sim} N(0, 1) \tag{7.8}$$

where, p is the number estimator obtained after combining the two samples, that is:

$$p=\frac{x_1+x_2}{n_1+n_2}=\frac{p_1n_1+p_2n_2}{n_1+n_2} \tag{7.9}$$

x_1 and x_2 are the number of units with a certain characteristic in the two samples.

2. Null Hypothesis H_0: $P_1-P_2\neq 0$

When H_0: $P_1-P_2=P_0(P_0\neq 0)$, construct the test statistic:

$$z=\left.\frac{(p_1-p_2)-(P_1-P_2)}{\sqrt{\frac{p_1(1-p_1)}{n_1}+\frac{p_2(1-p_2)}{n_2}}}\right|_{H_0}=\left.\frac{(p_1-p_2)-P_0}{\sqrt{\frac{p_1(1-p_1)}{n_1}+\frac{p_2(1-p_2)}{n_2}}}\right|_{H_0} \overset{d}{\sim} N(0, 1) \tag{7.10}$$

[**Example 7.12**] In order to study the effect of light conditions on chlorophyll content in certain plant leaves, 380 plant leaves under low light conditions were investigated, among them, 351 leaves had chlorophyll content below normal levels. 395 plant leaves under high light conditions were investigated, among them, 309 leaves had chlorophyll content below normal levels. If the significance level is 1%, compare whether there is a significant difference in chlorophyll content of plant leaves under two lighting conditions.

[**Solution**] Because the problem is to consider whether there is a significant difference in chlorophyll content of plant leaves under two lighting conditions, it is a two-tailed test problem. According to the problem, $p_1=351/380=0.924$, $p_2=309/395=0.782$, $n_1=380$, $n_2=395$,

$$p=\frac{n_1p_1+n_2p_2}{n_1+n_2}=\frac{351+309}{380+395}=0.852$$

First, establish a hypothesis

$$H_0: P_1=P_2, \quad H_1: P_1\neq P_2$$

Then, the critical value corresponding to the significance level α is $z_{0.005}=2.58$;

Finally, calculate the test statistic

$$z=\frac{p_1-p_2}{\sqrt{p(1-p)\left(\frac{1}{n_1}+\frac{1}{n_2}\right)}}=\frac{0.924-0.782}{\sqrt{0.852(1-0.852)\left(\frac{1}{380}+\frac{1}{395}\right)}}=5.565$$

Because $z>z_{0.005}=2.58$, we reject H_0 at the significance level of 1% , that is, there is a significant difference in chlorophyll content of plant leaves under two lighting conditions.

In addition, we can calculate the $p=2P(z>5.418)=2.622\times 10^{-8}<0.01$, so H_0 is rejected at the significance level 1%.

7.4.3 Tests for the Ratio of Two Population Variances

In many practical applications, we need to compare whether the two population variances are equal, that is, whether the ratio of the two population variances is equal to 1. For example, compare the risks of two investment scenarios; compare the stability of two production processes, etc.

In Section 7.4.1, when we do the hypothesis test between two population means, we should assume that the variances of the two populations are equal, but in fact whether the variances of the two populations are equal is often unknown in advance. Therefore, before we can test the difference between two population means, we need to test whether the two population variances are equal or not.

The null hypothesis is $H_0: \sigma_1^2=\sigma_2^2$, the test statistic:

$$F=\left.\frac{s_1^2}{s_2^2}\right|_{H_0} \sim F(n_1-1, n_2-1) \qquad (7.11)$$

where, s_1 and s_2 are the standard deviations of two samples respectively, n_1-1 are the degrees of freedom of the numerator, and n_2-1 are the degrees of freedom of the denominator.

In the two-tailed test, the rejection area of the null hypothesis located on both sides of the F distribution, and the two critical values are $F_{\alpha/2}(n_1-1, n_2-1)$ and $F_{1-\alpha/2}(n_1-1, n_2-1)$.

In a one-tailed test, the rejection area is located on only one side of the F distribution, either in the upper tail or the lower tail, depending on the direction of interest. This allows us to be more sensitive to detecting the effect in the specified direction. If the null hypothesis is $H_0: \sigma_1^2\leqslant\sigma_2^2$, and the alternative hypothesis is $H_0: \sigma_1^2>\sigma_2^2$, then the rejection area is on the right side of the F distribution, and critical value is $F_{1-\alpha}(n_1-1,n_2-1)$.

[**Example 7.13**] In order to compare the differences in fruit yield fluctuations between two different kinds of fruit trees, A and B, we investigated the fruit yield data of these two kinds of fruit trees in 7 and 8 different orchards respectively as Table 7.2.

Table 7.2 Fruit yield of each kind of fruit tree **Unit: ton**

A	300	700	650	730	800	900	1100	—
B	600	1500	1250	1800	1150	1850	1600	1500

Ask whether the fluctuation of fruit yield of fruit tree A is smaller than that of fruit tree B (significant level $\alpha=5\%$).

[**Solution**] Because the problem is to consider whether the imbalance of fruit yield of fruit tree A is greater than that of fruit tree B, it is a left-tailed test problem. According to the problem, $n_1=7$, $n_2=8$, $s_1=245.7$, $s_2=404.8$.

First, establish a hypothesis

$$H_0: \sigma_1^2\geqslant\sigma_2^2, \ H_1: \sigma_1^2<\sigma_2^2$$

Secondly, the critical value corresponding to the significance level α is $F_{0.95}(6,7)=3.87$;

Finally, compute the test statistic as $F=\frac{s_1{}^2}{s_2{}^2}=\frac{245.7^2}{404.8^2}=0.3684$.

Because $F<F_{0.95}(6,7)=3.87$, H_0 cannot be rejected at the 5% significance level, that is to say, it cannot be considered that the fruit yield of fruit tree A fluctuates less.

In addition, we can calculate $p=P(F>0.3684)=0.88>0.05$, so H_0 cannot be rejected at the 5% significance level.

Chapter Review

This chapter first introduces the basic issues of hypothesis test, including the basic concepts and steps of hypothesis test, p-value test methods, two-tailed test method and one-tailed test method, two types of errors, power, etc. Secondly, for the cases where the population variance is known and unknown, discuss the test methods of the population mean, including z-test and t-test. Thirdly, discuss the test problem of the population proportion, and gives out z-test method. Finally, for two population parameters, three types of hypothesis testing problems are discussed, including the test of the difference between two population means, the test of the difference between two population proportion, and the test of the ratio of two population variances.

Through the study of this chapter, you must understand the basic concepts of small probability events, two types of errors, and test power, and master the five steps of hypothesis testing, two-tailed test method and one-tailed test method, critical value test and p-value test. Secondly, aiming at the problem of hypothesis testing of the population mean and the population proportion, focus on mastering the z-test and t-test methods and their applicable conditions. Finally, for the three types of hypothesis testing problems of two population parameters, focus on mastering z-test, t-test, F-test and other test methods.

Exercise

1. Briefly describe the definition of hypothesis testing, and introduce the meaning of null hypothesis and alternative hypothesis.

2. Please introduce two types of errors in hypothesis testing and their control methods.

3. What are the similarities and differences between hypothesis testing and parameter estimation?

4. What is the rationale behind hypothesis testing?

5. Please briefly describe the concept of p-value, the principle of using p-value to make decisions and the three determinants of p-value size.

6. What is the significance of significance level α in hypothesis testing?

7. Please briefly describe the advantages of using p-values for hypothesis testing over traditional methods and the steps of using p-values for hypothesis testing.

8. Make the claim about the population mean μ at the given significance level by using the given sample statistics.

Claim: $\mu=40$; $\alpha=0.05$. Sample statistics: $\bar{x}=39.5$, $s=3.25$, $n=65$

9. The number of years it takes a random sample of 32 former smokers to quit smoking permanently is listed. At $\alpha=0.05$, test the claim that the mean time it takes smokers to quit smoking permanently is 15 years.

15.7	13.2	22.6	14.0	10.5	18.5	14.6	7.0
11.9	16.9	21.6	13.2	16.5	15.3	9.8	20.3
12.8	9.0	11.5	18.4	8.4	19.8	10.7	11.6
15.6	17.4	21.6	19.5	11.2	12.3	8.9	14.6

10. A tea drinker's society estimates that the mean consumption of tea by a person in the U. S. is more than 26 L per year. In a sample of 100 people, you find that the mean consumption of tea is 30 L per year with a standard deviation of 10 L. At $\alpha=0.05$, can you support the society's claim?

11. An environmentalist estimates that the mean waste recycled by adults in the U. S. is more than 1 pound per person per day. You find that the mean waste recycled per person per day for a random sample of 16 adults in the U. S. is 1.2 pounds and the standard deviation is 0.3 pound. At $\alpha=0.05$, can you support the claim?

12. You receive a brochure from a university. The brochure indicates that the mean class size for full-time faculty is less than 35. You want to test this claim. You randomly select 16 classes taught by full-time faculty and determine the class size of each. The results are listed below. At $\alpha=0.01$, can you support the university's claim?

35 38 28 27 32 36 29 40 27 25 28 26 27 25 28 29

13. A medical researcher estimates that no more than 55% of U. S. adults eat breakfast every day. In a random sample of 250 U. S. adults, 56% say that they eat breakfast. At $\alpha=0.01$, is there enough evidence to reject the researcher's claim?

14. At a trade show, you interview a random sample of 50 attendees. The results of the survey show that 48% of the attendees said they were more likely to visit an exhibit when there is a giveaway. At $\alpha=0.05$, test the claim that at least 52% of the attendees at trade shows are more likely to visit an exhibit when there is a giveaway.

15. In your work for a business regulatory agency, you find that in a sample of 1500 people in the U. S., 950 of them believe that government regulation of business does more harm than good. At $\alpha=0.01$, can you reject the claim that 60% of people in the U. S. have this view?

Chapter 8

Correlation Analysis and Regression Analysis

Is there a relationship between personal height and weight? Is personal income level related to education level? Is the sales revenue of commodities related to advertising investment? When we are studying similar practical problems, many variables are often involved. For relationship analysis between variables based on experience, it is correlation analysis. For relationship analysis between variables to build a model so as to predict the value of a variable, it is regression analysis. Correlation analysis and regression analysis are very important content in modern statistics, which have been widely used in many research fields such as enterprise management, business decision-making, financial analysis, natural science and social science. This chapter will introduce the theories and methods of correlation analysis and regression analysis in detail.

8.1 Correlation Analysis

8.1.1 Relationship Between Variables

Objective things are always interrelated and interdependent. The quantitative relationship between them is generally divided into two types: one is deterministic relationship, also know as functional relationship, such as the radius of a circle determines the area of a circle. The other is uncertain relationship, which is called correlation, such as the relationship between sales and advertising expenses.

1. Functional Relationship

Functional relationship refers to the strict, definite and one-to-one dependency between variables, which can be expressed by mathematical expressions. Assuming that there are two variables x and y, y changes with the change of x, and completely depends on x. For each x, there is only a certain y value corresponding to it, then y is called a function of x, where x is called the independent variable and y is called the dependent variable. For example, in the sales activity of a product, the sales of the product is y, the sales volume is x, and the sales price is p. Then the relationship between x and y can be expressed as $y=px$, which is a functional relationship. Under the condition that the sales price p is constant, the sales y is completely determined by the sales volume x.

2. Correlation

Correlation refers to the dependence between variables that is not strict, uncertain and has no one-to-one correspondence, which cannot be expressed by mathematical expressions. For example, personal income level y is related to his education level x to some extent, but it is not a one-to-one relationship, because education level x is not the only factor that affects income level y. Other factors such as working years, occupation type, etc. will also affect income level. Therefore, there is a correlation between income level y and education level x.

8.1.2 Description and Measurement of Correlation

Correlation analysis is the description and measurement of the linear relationship between two variables. When conducting correlation analysis, we usually first judge the relationship between variables by scatter plot. If the relationship is linear, we can use correlation coefficient to measure the strength of the relationship between variables. Then, we can judge whether the relationship reflected by the sample can represent the relationship between two populations through the significance test of the correlation coefficient.

1. Scatter Plot

Scatter plot can be used to describe the relationship between variables, from which we can intuitively see the relationship between variables. For the two variables x and y, a scatter plot is formed by plotting the paired data corresponding to the two variables in the form of coordinate points. These scatter plots are drawn with x as the abscissa and y as the ordinate.

As shown in Figures 8.1(a) and Figure 8.1(b), the scattered points approximately fall on a straight line. It is considered that there is a linear relationship between the two variables, and the former shows a positive linear correlation (As x increases, y tends to increase). The latter shows a negative linear correlation (As x increases, y tend to decrease). While the scattered points shown in Figure 8.1(c) approximately fall on a curve, indicating that there is a nonlinear correlation between the two variables. Scatter distribution in Figure 8.1(d) is scattered and irregular, which means that the two variables are completely irrelevant.

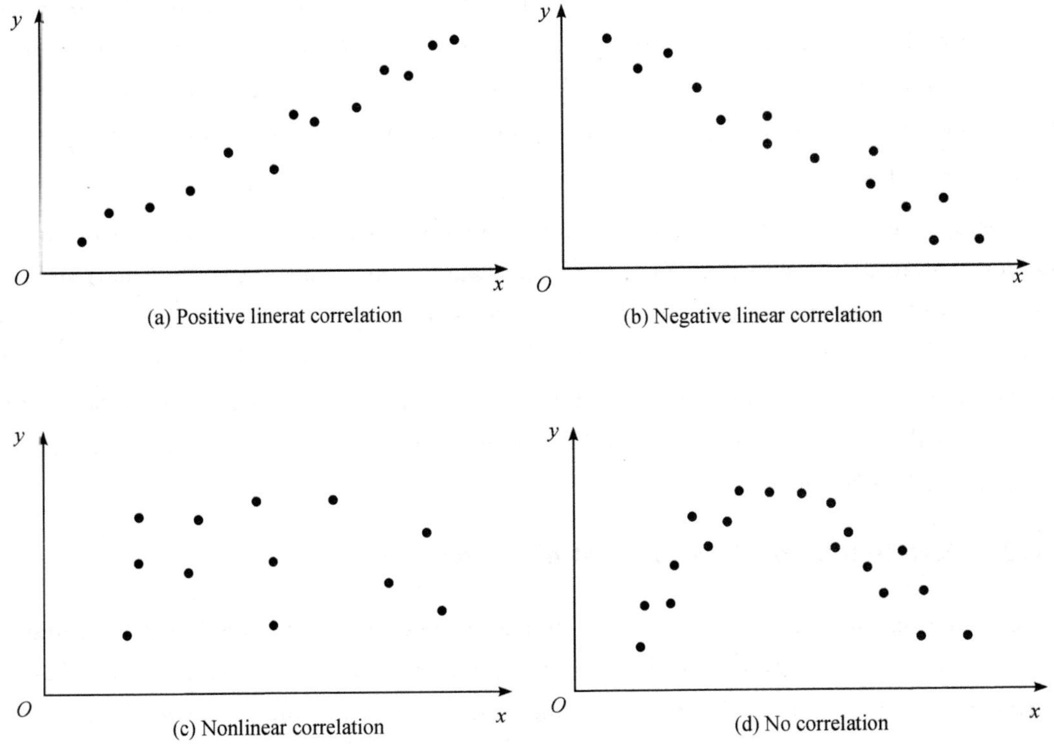

Figure 8.1 Correlation plot

2. Correlation Coefficient

The shape of the correlation between the two variables can be intuitively judged by the scatter plot. However, it can't accurately reflect the relationship strength between variables. Therefore, in order to describe the relationship strength between variables more accurately, it is necessary to calculate the correlation coefficient.

The correlation coefficient is a measure of the strength and the direction of a linear relationship between two variables. The symbol r represents the sample correlation coefficient. A formula for r is

$$r=\frac{n\sum xy-\sum x\sum y}{\sqrt{n\sum x^2-(\sum x)^2}\cdot\sqrt{n\sum y^2-(\sum y)^2}} \tag{8.1}$$

where n is the number of pairs of data.

Sample correlation coefficient is a statistic that measures the intensity of linear correlation between two variables calculated from sample data. If the correlation coefficient is calculated from all the data of the population, it is called the population correlation coefficient, which is represented by ρ.

The range of correlation coefficient (r) is -1 to 1. When $0<r\leqslant 1$, it indicates that there is a positive linear correlation between two variables; when $-1\leqslant r<0$, it indicates that there is a negative linear correlation between the two variables. The closer r goes to

1, the stronger the positive correlation between two variables is; the closer r goes to -1, the stronger the negative correlation between two variables is. When the two variables have perfect positive linear correlation or perfect negative linear correlation, r is equal to 1 or -1. If $r=0$, it means that there is no linear correlation between the two variables, but it does not mean that there is no relationship between them, because there may be a nonlinear correlation.

Here is an example to show the calculation of correlation coefficient.

[Example 8.1] Calculate the correlation coefficient between the height of the tree (y) and the diameter of the trunk (x) according to the data in Table 8.1.

Table 8.1 The dataset of the height of the tree (y) and the diameter of the trunk (x)

y	35	49	27	33	60	21	45	51
x	8	9	7	6	13	7	11	12

[Solution] First, calculate to get results as Table 8.2 data.

Table 8.2 Calculation results

y	x	xy	y^2	x^2
35	8	280	1225	64
49	9	441	2401	81
27	7	189	729	49
33	6	198	1089	36
60	13	780	3600	169
21	7	147	441	49
45	11	495	2025	121
51	12	612	2601	144
$\sum y = 321$	$\sum x = 73$	$\sum xy = 3142$	$\sum y^2 = 14111$	$\sum x^2 = 713$

Then calculate the correlation coefficient r

$$r = \frac{n\sum xy - \sum x \sum y}{\sqrt{n\sum x^2 - (\sum x)^2} \cdot \sqrt{n\sum y^2 - (\sum y)^2}}$$

$$= \frac{8\times 3142 - 73\times 321}{\sqrt{8\times 713 - (73)^2} \times \sqrt{8\times 14111 - (321)^2}}$$

$$= 0.886$$

Therefore, in this example, the correlation coefficient between the height of the tree and the diameter of the trunk is equal to 0.886.

8.1.3 Significant Test of Correlation Coefficient

The population correlation coefficient ρ is generally unknown, so we usually use the sample correlation coefficient r as the approximate estimate of ρ. However, the value of r

will be affected by the sampling fluctuation. Therefore, if we want to estimate the population correlation coefficient according to the sample correlation coefficient, we need to carry out the significance test first. We can use a hypothesis testing to determine whether the sample correlation coefficient r provides enough evidence, so we can finally make the conclusion that the population correlation coefficient ρ is significant.

The steps of hypothesis testing are as follows:

Step 1: Propose the null hypothesis and alternative hypothesis.

$$H_0: \rho=0; \ H_1: \rho\neq 0$$

Step 2: Calculate the t test statistic.

$$t=|r|\sqrt{\frac{n-2}{1-r^2}} \tag{8.2}$$

where n is the number of pairs of data.

The t-test statistic follows a t-distribution with $n-2$ degrees of freedom.

Step 3: Identify α and make decision.

Determine the critical value ($t_{\alpha/2}$) from the t-distribution according to the significance level (α) and the degrees of freedom ($n-2$). Then make the decision to reject or fail to reject the null hypothesis:

If the absolute value of the t-test statistic is greater than the critical value, then reject the null hypothesis, which means that there is a significant linear correlation between the two variables; otherwise, fail to reject the null hypothesis, which means that there is no significant linear correlation between the two variables.

In mathematical language, it is expressed as follows:

If $|t|>t_{\alpha/2}$, reject H_0; otherwise, fail to reject H_0.

Here is an example:

[**Example 8.2**] According to the data in Example 8.1, can we think that there is a linear correlation between the height of the tree and the diameter of the trunk at the significance level of 5%?

[**Solution**]

Step 1: Propose the null hypothesis and alternative hypothesis.

$$H_0: \rho=0; \ H_1: \rho\neq 0$$

Step 2: Calculate the t test statistic.

$$t=|r|\sqrt{\frac{n-2}{1-r^2}}=0.886\times\sqrt{\frac{8-2}{1-0.886^2}}=4.68$$

Step 3: Identify α and make decision.

According to the t-distribution table, at 5% significance level, when the degrees of freedom are $n-2=6$, $t_{\alpha/2}=2.4469$.

$$t=4.68>t_{\alpha/2}=2.4469$$

thus, reject H_0, which means there is a linear correlation between the height of the tree and the diameter of the trunk.

8.2 Simple Linear Regression Analysis

8.2.1 Definition of Regression

What is regression analysis? In Section 8.1, we explored initially about correlation analysis, and know that it is an analytical method and focuses on examining the direction and degree of correlation between variables and using the correlation coefficient as a metric. Regression analysis, in contrast, focuses on examining the quantitative relationships between variables and describing them by mathematical expressions which are used to determine the degree of influence of the independent variables on the dependent variables. Specifically, correlation analysis and regression analysis have certain connections and differences.

For the connections, the two analyses both study the statistical dependence between non-deterministic variables and measure the strength of this relationship. In addition, when there is a certain degree of correlation between variables, it is practically meaningful to seek the specific mathematical form of correlation between variables by regression analysis.

For the differences, ① from the perspective of research, correlation analysis uses the correlation coefficient to measure the direction and degree of interconnection between variables, and the independent and dependent variables are equal. In contrast, regression analysis is to estimate and predict the mean value of the dependent variable based on the given value of the independent variable, and the role of the independent variable is different from that of the dependent variable. ② From the perspective of the variable treatment, correlation analysis does not distinguish independent variables from dependent variables, and considers them as random variables without considering whether there is a causal relationship between them. In contrast, regression analysis clearly delineate the independent variable from the dependent variable, and it is based on the analysis of the causal relationship between variables and used to study the specific effects of changes of the independent variable on the dependent variable.

Moreover, the main problems solved by regression analysis include the followings. First, it is essential to determine the mathematical relationship equations between variables from a set of sample data. Second, it is necessary to conduct various statistical tests on the credibility of these equations so as to find out which independent variables are significant and which are insignificant according to many independent variables (the independent variables affect the dependent variables). Third, the equations can be used to estimate or predict the values of the dependent variable based on the values of the independent variables, giving the degree of reliability for estimates or predictions.

8.2.2 Simple Linear Regression Model

1. Population Regression Model

In the regression analysis, different regression models should be built depending on the data obtained from statistical survey. Based on the number of independent variables, we can build a univariate regression model or a multivariate regression model; based on the specific form of variable changes, we can build a linear regression model or a non-linear regression model.

A univariate linear regression model, also known as a simple linear regression model, assumes that the dependent variable (explained variable) Y is only affected in some way by the independent variable (explanatory variable) X and that there is a certain linear relationship between them, it can be expressed in the following form:

$$Y_i = \beta_0 + \beta_1 X_i + \varepsilon_i \tag{8.3}$$

In statistical studies, we usually also consider the above equation as the *population regression model*, where β_0 and β_1 are called the parameters of the model, and Y_i and X_i are the i-th observations of the population random variables Y and X, respectively. ε_i is the i-th observations of the random variable ε, which is the variability that cannot be explained by the linear relationship between X and Y, because ε_i reflects the influence of random factors on the linear relationship between X and Y rather than the influence of X on Y.

For such a model, the following five assumptions usually need to be satisfied.

Linearity: there is a linear relationship between the dependent variable Y and the independent variable X.

Independence: the values of the independent variable X are non-random.

Unbiasedness: for all i, the expected value of ε_i is zero: $E(\varepsilon_i)=0$.

Homoscedasticity: for all i, the variance of ε_i is a constant σ^2: $\mathrm{Var}(\varepsilon_i)=\sigma^2$.

Normality: the error terms obey normal distribution and are independent of each other: $\varepsilon_i \sim N(0, \sigma^2)$.

2. Sample Regression Function

Based on the assumptions in the regression model above, we know that the expected value of ε_i is equal to zero. Therefore, the expected value of Y satisfies:

$$E(Y) = \beta_0 + \beta_1 X \tag{8.4}$$

which means that the expected value of Y is a linear function of X. At this point, we could define the Equation(8.4) as the *regression function*, which describes how the expectation of the dependent variable Y depends on the independent variable X. In the Equation (8.4), β_0 is referred to as the *intercept*, β_1 is referred to as the *slope*.

It is often difficult to investigate the population unit completely in practice. In general, we can take a sample from the population and use the information contained in the sample to build a sample regression function to estimate the population regression function. The *sample regression function* takes the following form:

$$y_i=\hat{\beta}_0+\hat{\beta}_1 x_i+e_i \tag{8.5}$$

Similarly, where both $\hat{\beta}_0$ and $\hat{\beta}_1$ in Equation (8.5) are parameters, the former is the intercept and the latter is the slope; y_i and x_i are the i-th observation of the sample variables y and x separately; and e_i is called the *residual* of the function.

As we know from previous chapters, the sample is randomly selected from the population, so it is not unique. To summarize, the population regression function is deterministic but unknown, while the sample regression function, on the other hand, can be built differently depending on different samples selected each time, so it is not unique.

If the parameters β_0 and β_1 in the population regression function are known, for a given value of X, the expected value of Y can be calculated using the equation $E(Y)=\beta_0+\beta_1 X$. However, β_0 and β_1 are unknown, so we must use the sample statistics $\hat{\beta}_0$ and $\hat{\beta}_1$, which imply known sample data, to estimate β_0 and β_1. The *estimated simple regression function* has the following form:

$$\hat{y}_i=\hat{\beta}_0+\hat{\beta}_1 x_i \tag{8.6}$$

where, $\hat{\beta}_1$ is not only the slope of the equation, but also called the *regression coefficient*, which represents the average change in y_i for each unit change in x_i (Obviously, the slope $\hat{\beta}_1$ is positive when there is a linear positive correlation between two variables). Thus, $\hat{y}_i$ is also an estimate of the expectation $E(y_i)$ of y_i. Furthermore, it is not difficult to find that following equation holds:

$$e_i=y_i-\hat{y}_i \tag{8.7}$$

This also explains the meaning of the term "residual", which is the difference between the actual observed value y_i and the estimated value $\hat{y}_i$.

8.2.3 Estimates of Simple Regression Function

1. Estimates of Parameters by Method of Least Squares

When building the regression function, we certainly hope that the fitted line can adequately represent each sample observation, that is, we hope that the estimated value $\hat{y}_i$ can be as close as possible to the observed value y_i. This also means that the smaller the sum $\sum e_i$ of the values of the residuals e_i, the better. However, the value of y_i may be greater or lesser than the value of $\hat{y}_i$, so e_i may be positive or negative, and the values of $\sum e_i$ are likely to counteract each other, leading to an underestimation of error.

To avoid above situation, we need to use the *method of least squares* to calculate the sum of squares of the deviations between the observed value of the dependent variable y_i and the estimated value $\hat{y}_i$, in a hope that the sum of squares of the deviations should reach the minimum value and be used to estimate $\hat{\beta}_0$ and $\hat{\beta}_1$. Here we don't calculate the residual sum $\sum e_i$, but the residual sum of squares $\sum e_i^2$, which reflects the actual size of error. The method of least squares is illustrated as Figure 8. 2.

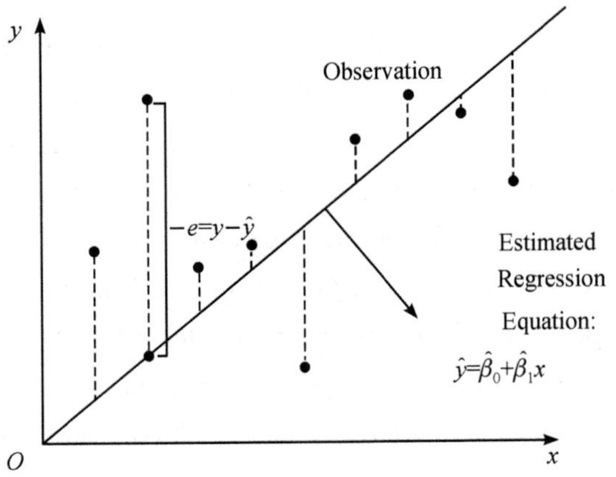

Figure 8. 2 The method of least squares

According to the least squares method, we write Q as if it were $\sum_{i=1}^{n} e_i^2$ and want to minimize

$$Q=\sum_{i=1}^{n} e_i^2=\sum_{i=1}^{n}(y_i-\hat{y}_i)^2=\sum_{i=1}^{n}(y_i-\hat{\beta}_0-\hat{\beta}_1 x_i)^2 \tag{8.8}$$

From the *Extreme Value Theorem* in mathematics, the above equation must satisfy that the first order partial derivative of each of $\hat{\beta}_0$ and $\hat{\beta}_1$ is equal to zero in order to minimize the value of Q. Next, we find the first-order partial derivatives of Q corresponding to $\hat{\beta}_0$ and $\hat{\beta}_1$, and let them be zero to obtain the set of equations as follows:

$$\begin{cases} \left.\dfrac{\partial Q}{\partial \beta_0}\right|_{\beta_0=\hat{\beta}_0}=-2\sum_{i=1}^{n}(y_i-\hat{\beta}_0-\hat{\beta}_1 x_i)=0 \\ \left.\dfrac{\partial Q}{\partial \beta_1}\right|_{\beta_1=\hat{\beta}_1}=-2\sum_{i=1}^{n}x_i(y_i-\hat{\beta}_0-\hat{\beta}_1 x_i)=0 \end{cases} \tag{8.9}$$

Organizing the set of equations, we obtain:

$$\begin{cases} n\hat{\beta}_0+\hat{\beta}_1\sum x_i=\sum y_i \\ \hat{\beta}_0\sum x_i+\hat{\beta}_1\sum x_i^2=\sum x_i y_i \end{cases} \tag{8.10}$$

Finally, solve the above set of equations and get the equations as follows:

$$\begin{cases} \hat{\beta}_1=\dfrac{n\sum_{i=1}^{n}x_i y_i-\sum_{i=1}^{n}x_i\sum_{i=1}^{n}y_i}{n\sum_{i=1}^{n}x_i^2-(\sum_{i=1}^{n}x_i)^2}=\dfrac{\sum(x_i-\bar{x})(y_i-\bar{y})}{\sum(x_i-\bar{x})^2} \\ \hat{\beta}_0=\bar{y}-\hat{\beta}_1\bar{x} \end{cases} \tag{8.11}$$

At this point, we have obtained the estimates of the overall parameters $\hat{\beta}_0$ and $\hat{\beta}_1$, and it is easy to see that the sample regression line passes through the point $(\bar{x}, \bar{y})$, which is one of the important features of the regression line.

[Example 8.3] Final exams are one of the most important concerns in college students' academic life, and there seems to be a relationship between revision time and exam score. A researcher randomly selected a sample of 10 students from a major in a university and investigated their average daily revision time and statistical exam score as shown in the Table 8.3. Please establish a regression function between revision time (x) and exam score (y).

Table 8.3 Average daily revision time and scores of 10 students

No.	1	2	3	4	5	6	7	8	9	10
Revision time x/min	20	30	33	40	15	13	26	38	35	43
Exam score y/point	64	80	78	79	59	57	68	85	82	89

[Solution] First, we should establish the regression equation

$$\hat{y}=\hat{\beta}_0+\hat{\beta}_1 x$$

According to the method of least squares, we need to calculate the following statistics: $\bar{x}$, $\bar{y}$, $\sum x$, $\sum y$, $\sum x^2$, $\sum y^2$, $\sum xy$, and the results are shown in Table 8.4.

Table 8.4 Calculation results of statistics

Statistics	$\bar{x}$	$\bar{y}$	$\sum x$	$\sum y$	$\sum x^2$	$\sum y^2$	$\sum xy$
Value	29.3	74.1	293	741	9577	56045	22735

Thus, substituting the above calculation results into the least squares estimator, we can obtain

$$\begin{cases} \hat{\beta}_1=\dfrac{n\sum\limits_{i=1}^{n}x_iy_i-\sum\limits_{i=1}^{n}x_i\sum\limits_{i=1}^{n}y_i}{n\sum\limits_{i=1}^{n}x_i^2-(\sum\limits_{i=1}^{n}x_i)^2}=\dfrac{10\times 22735-293\times 741}{10\times 9577-293^2}=\dfrac{10237}{9921}=1.0319 \\ \hat{\beta}_0=74.1-1.0319\times 29.3=43.8667 \end{cases}$$

Therefore, the regression equation for the average daily revision time on test scores is

$$\hat{y}=43.8667+1.0319x$$

2. Estimates of the Error Variance

After obtaining the estimates of the overall parameters $\hat{\beta}_0$ and $\hat{\beta}_1$, do not forget to consider the error term in the five assumptions of the simple regression function. In the assumptions, we know that the variance of the population random error term ε_i is a certain constant σ^2, which reflects the theoretical value of the model error. But this constant is unknown and again, we need to estimate it. In addition, the random error term ε_i is unobservable, so we must estimate it from the residual e_i obtained by the method of least squares.

The residuals in a simple linear regression model need to satisfy the following two conditions:

$$\sum e_i = 0; \ \sum e_i x_i = 0 \tag{8.12}$$

So the degrees of freedom of the unbiased estimator of σ^2 should be $n-2$. In this way, the unbiased estimate $\hat{\sigma}^2$ of σ^2 should be

$$\hat{\sigma}^2 = \frac{\sum e_i^2}{n-2} = \frac{\sum (y_i - \hat{y}_i)^2}{n-2} \tag{8.13}$$

Here, we define the square root of $\hat{\sigma}^2$ as the *standard error of estimate*, whose expression is

$$s_e = \sqrt{\hat{\sigma}^2} = \hat{\sigma} = \sqrt{\frac{\sum e_i^2}{n-2}} = \sqrt{\frac{\sum (y_i - \hat{y}_i)^2}{n-2}} \tag{8.14}$$

which can be further simplified as

$$\begin{aligned} s_e &= \sqrt{\frac{\sum (y_i - \hat{y}_i)^2}{n-2}} = \sqrt{\frac{\sum (y_i - \hat{\beta}_0 - \hat{\beta}_1 x_i)^2}{n-2}} \\ &= \sqrt{\frac{\sum y_i^2 - \hat{\beta}_0 \sum y_i - \hat{\beta}_1 \sum x_i y_i}{n-2}} \end{aligned} \tag{8.15}$$

The standard error of estimate s_e is an estimate of the standard deviation σ of the random error term ε_i, which can be considered as an estimate of the degree of the random fluctuations of y_i when the linear effect of x_i on y_i is excluded. It also illustrates the status of each actual observation point scattered around the regression line from the side: the closer the observation points to the line go, the smaller s_e is, and the more representative the regression line for each point is. Moreover, we can easily see from the simplified results in Formula(8.14) that the regression line has the smallest value of $\sum e_i^2$ among all the lines created for n pairs of observations, and therefore, *Se* is the one with the smallest standard error of estimate.

[**Example 8.4**] Continue the discussion in Example 8.3, we can also calculate the estimated standard error of the regression equation as well as the regression residuals.

[**Solution**] Substituting the calculated statistics into the Formula (8.15) for the standard error of estimate, we can obtain that

$$\begin{aligned} s_e &= \sqrt{\frac{\sum (y_i - \hat{y}_i)^2}{n-2}} = \sqrt{\frac{\sum y_i^2 - \hat{\beta}_0 \sum y_i - \hat{\beta}_1 \sum x_i y_i}{n-2}} \\ &= \sqrt{\frac{56045 - 43.8667 \times 741 - 1.0319 \times 22735}{10-2}} = 3.1740 \end{aligned}$$

Meanwhile, we were able to calculate the residual values based on the equations that has been established and display the calculated results as shown in Table 8.5 below.

Table 8.5 The residual values

No.	1	2	3	4	5	6	7	8	9	10
y_i	64	80	78	79	59	57	68	85	82	89
$\hat{y}_i$	64.50	74.82	77.92	85.14	59.34	57.28	70.69	83.08	79.98	88.24
e_i	−0.5	5.18	0.08	−6.14	−0.34	−0.28	−2.69	1.92	2.02	0.76

The distribution of residuals can be seen by plotting residuals as shown in Figure 8.3. Obviously, the residual values are distributed on both sides of the horizontal axis and are close to it, which can satisfy the assumption that the mean is zero and the variance is the same.

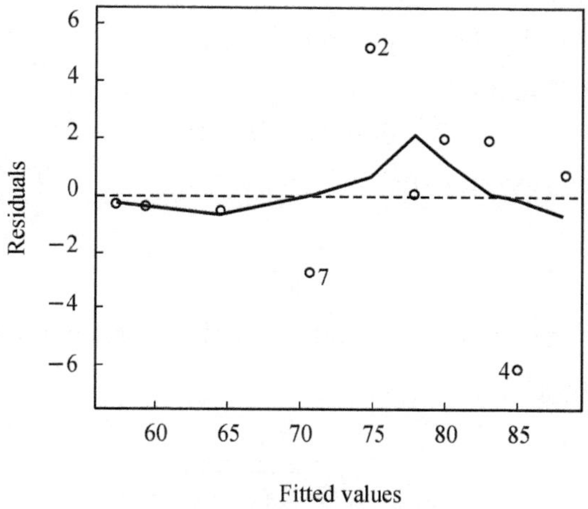

Figure 8.3 Residuals and fitted values

With the R software, we can also plot the scatter plot of the exam score and the fitted regression line, from which we can roughly see the fitting effect of the regression line as shown in Figure 8.4.

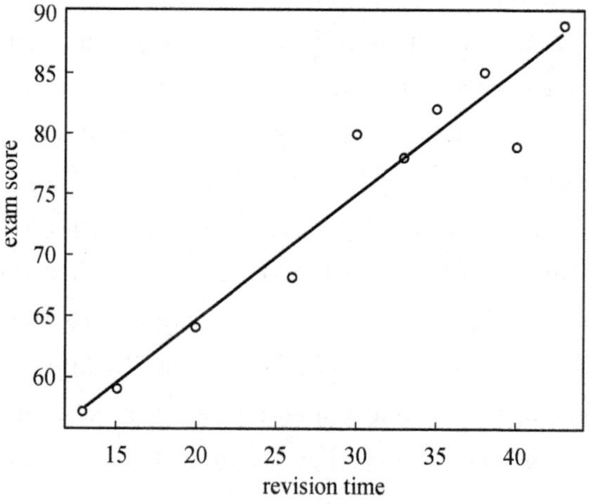

Figure 8.4 Fitting effect of the regression line

Intuitively, more than half of the observations are close to the regression line, and also the value of the standard error of estimate is small, so the fitting effect of the regression line is good.

8.2.4 Significance Test for a Single Population Parameter

In the regression analysis, we have obtained the estimates of each unknown parameter, followingly, we will make certain tests to determine whether the estimates are significant or not, that is, to make inferences about the simple regression function.

In the simple regression function, the test of the regression coefficient is also a test of whether β_1 equal to zero. If $\beta_1=0$, then the regression line is a horizontal line parallel to the x-axis with zero slope, in other words, there is no effect of the change in the independent variable x_i on the dependent variable y_i.

Step 1: Formulate the hypothesis:

$$H_0: \beta_1=0; \quad H_1: \beta_1 \neq 0$$

Step 2: Establish the test statistic

$$t=\frac{\hat{\beta}_1}{s_{\hat{\beta}_1}} \tag{8.16}$$

where, we define $s_{\hat{\beta}_1}$ as the standard deviation of the regression coefficient $\hat{\beta}_1$, which can be obtained from the following equation

$$s_{\hat{\beta}_1}=\frac{s_e}{\sqrt{\sum(x_i-\bar{x})^2}} \tag{8.17}$$

Following the mathematical knowledge, we can know that the statistic t obeys a t-distribution with degrees of freedom $n-2$, and the specific process is not proved here.

Step 3: Determine the significance level α, and check the t distribution table according to the degrees of freedom $df=n-2$ to find the corresponding critical value t.

Step 4: Make a decision: if $|t|>t_{\alpha/2}$, the null hypothesis is rejected and the probability that the regression coefficient is less than α, indicating that the population parameter β_1 is significant; in other words, there is a significant linear relationship between the two variables. If $|t|<t_{\alpha/2}$, the null hypothesis cannot be rejected and there is no evidence that the population parameter β_1 is significant.

It is worth noting that there is only one single regression coefficient in the simple regression function, so the hypotheses testing is about whether the linear combination of parameters is significant at this point, which is equivalent to the t-test (the hypotheses testing is about whether the regression coefficient is significant).

[**Example 8.5**] During the second collective learning session of the Political Bureau of the Central Committee of the Communist Party of China in February, 2023, Chinese President Xi Jinping emphasized "Focus on expanding income-supported consumer demand". Residents' income and expenditures are throughout their daily life, and they are closely related to each other. Through the website of National Bureau of Statistics, the data of per capita disposable income (x) and per capita consumption expenditure (y) of Chinese residents in the past 20 years is shown as in Table 8.6 below. Please:

(1) Establish a regression equation between income and expenditure and explain the economic significance of the regression coefficient;

(2) Plot a scatter plot and a regression line between per capita disposable income and consumption expenditure, calculate the standard error of estimate to show the effect of the fit;

(3) Test the significance of the regression equation and the regression coefficient at a significance level of 0.05.

Table 8.6 Per capita disposable income and consumption expenditure

Year	2002	2003	2004	2005	2006	2007	2008	2009	2010
Income(x)/yuan	4532	5007	5661	6385	7229	8584	9957	10977	12520
Expenditure(y)/yuan	3548	3889	4395	5035	5634	6592	7548	8377	9378

Year	2011	2012	2013	2014	2015	2016	2017	2018
Income(x)/yuan	14551	16510	18311	20167	21966	23821	25974	28228
Expenditure(y)/yuan	10820	12054	13220	14491	15712	17111	18322	19853

Year	2019	2020	2021
Income(x)/yuan	30733	32189	35128
Expenditure(y)/yuan	21559	21210	24100

[**Solution**]

(1) Establish the regression equation

$$\hat{y}=\hat{\beta}_0+\hat{\beta}_1 x$$

According to the method of least squares, we need to calculate the following statistics: $\bar{x}$, $\bar{y}$, $\sum x$, $\sum y$, $\sum x^2$, $\sum y^2$, $\sum xy$, and list the calculated results in Table 8.7.

Table 8.7 Calculation results of statistics

Statistics	$\bar{x}$	$\bar{y}$	$\sum x$	$\sum y$	$\sum x^2$	$\sum y^2$	$\sum xy$
Value	16 921.5	12 142.4	338 430	242 848	7 583 106 056	3 774 753 548	5 346 104 617

By substituting the above calculation results into the least squares estimator, we can obtain

$$\hat{\beta}_0=868.9022,\ \hat{\beta}_1=0.6662$$

Therefore, the regression equation for the average daily revision time on test score is

$$\hat{y}=868.9022+0.6662x$$

$\hat{\beta}_0=868.9022$ is the intercept of the regression equation and $\hat{\beta}_1=0.6662$ is the slope of the regression equation, which indicates that for every one unit increase in per capita disposable income, per capita consumption expenditure increases by 0.6662 units.

(2) We can also plot the scatter plot and the fitted regression line as shown in Figure 8.5, from which we can roughly see the fitting effect.

$$\hat{y}=868.9022+0.6662x$$

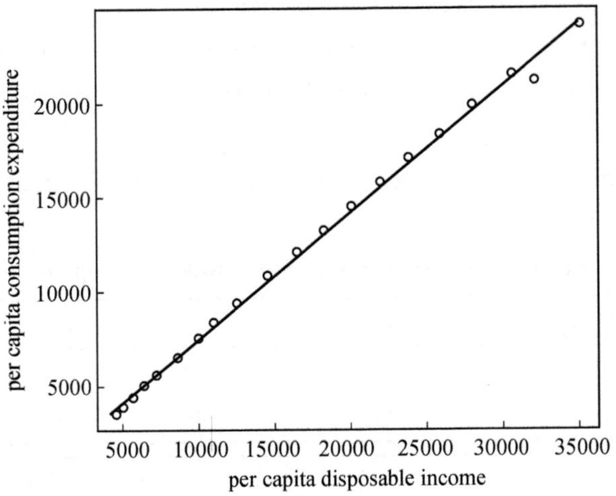

Figure 8.5 Fitting effect of the regression line

Substituting the calculated statistics into the Formula(8.15) for the standard error of estimate, we can obtain that $s_e=336.8855$.

We should test the significance of the regression coefficient.

Step 1: Formulate the hypothesis: $H_0: \beta_1=0$; $H_1: \beta_1 \neq 0$.

Step 2: Calculate the standard deviation

$$s_{\hat{\beta}_1}=\frac{s_e}{\sqrt{\sum(x_i-\bar{x})^2}}=\frac{336.8855}{43085.5290}=0.0078$$

Then establish the test statistic

$$t=\frac{\hat{\beta}_1}{s_{\hat{\beta}_1}}=\frac{0.6662}{0.0078}=85.4103$$

which shows the t-test obeys a $t(18)$ distribution.

Step 3: Check the t-distribution table, it shows that at the significance level of 0.05, $t_{0.025}(18)=-2.1010$.

Step 4: Make a decision. Apparently $|t|>t_{0.025}(18)$, so the null hypothesis is rejected which means that the regression coefficient β_1 is considered significant.

3. Goodness-of-Fit

After estimating and testing the unknown parameters, the regression line can be used to estimate and predict the problem we are interested in. However, the accuracy of the estimation and prediction depends largely on how well the regression line fits the actual observed data.

We have already learned about the concept of the standard error of estimate, which describes how close the regression line goes to the actual observation, and now, we give a new definition for this degree, which we call the *goodness-of-fit* of the regression line to the data. In the following, we need to calculate the *coefficient of determination* to interpret the mystery of the goodness-of-fit.

The observed values of the dependent variable y are different from each other according to the actual situation, and we call this difference "*deviation*". And the reason for such deviation is divided into two parts: on the one hand, the deviation is caused by the different values of the independent variable x, and on the other hand, besides influenced by x, the deviation is also caused by other factors. The decomposition diagram of the deviation is shown in Figure 8.6.

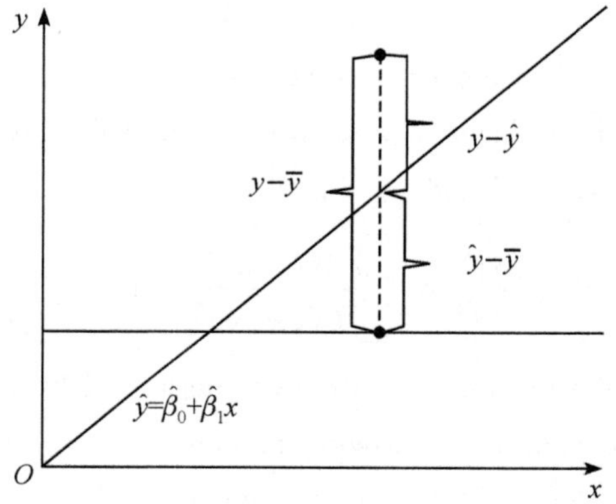

Figure 8.6 Decomposition diagram of the deviation

For a specific observation of the dependent variable, the deviation can be expressed as the difference $y_i - \bar{y}_i$ between the actual observation y_i and the sample mean $\bar{y}$. It can also be decomposed into two parts as follows:

$$y_i - \bar{y} = (\hat{y}_i - \bar{y}) + (y_i - \hat{y}_i)$$

The first part $\hat{y}_i - \bar{y}$ is the deviation of the theoretical regression value of the dependent variable from its sample mean, which is the part that can be explained by the regression line, and the second part $y_i - \hat{y}_i$ is the deviation of the actual observed value y_i from the regression value $\bar{y}$ which is actually the residual part of the regression line and cannot be explained by the regression line.

Squaring both sides of the above equation and summing over all n points, we have:

$$\sum (y_i - \bar{y})^2 = \sum (\hat{y}_i - \bar{y})^2 + \sum (y_i - \hat{y}_i)^2 + 2\sum (\hat{y}_i - \bar{y})(y_i - \hat{y}_i)$$

Here, we can prove that

$$\sum (\hat{y}_i - \bar{y})(y_i - \hat{y}_i) = 0$$

So, there is

$$\sum (y_i - \bar{y})^2 = \sum (\hat{y}_i - \bar{y})^2 + \sum (y_i - \hat{y}_i)^2$$

The left side $\sum (y_i - \bar{y})^2$ of the above equation is called the SST (Sum of Squares in Total), which can be decomposed into two parts: the first part $\sum (\hat{y}_i - \bar{y})^2$ is the sum of squares of the deviations of the theoretical regression value of the dependent variable from the mean, called the SSR (Sum of Squares of Regression value), which is the part of the change in the dependent variable caused by the change in the independent variable; the second part $\sum(y_i - \hat{y}_i)^2$ is called the SSE (Sum of Squares of Error), which is the part of the change in the dependent variable caused by factors other than the linear effect of the independent variable on the dependent variable. So, there is the following equation

$$\text{SST}=\text{SSR}+\text{SSE} \tag{8.18}$$

Dividing both the left and right sides of the above equation by SST, we get

$$1=\frac{\text{SSR}}{\text{SST}}+\frac{\text{SSE}}{\text{SST}} \tag{8.19}$$

If each observation point is closer to a straight line, then the SSR is larger and the proportion of SSR in SST is larger, and we define this ratio as the *coefficient of determination* R^2, which is calculated as

$$R^2=\frac{\text{SSR}}{\text{SST}}=1-\frac{\text{SSE}}{\text{SST}}=\frac{\sum(\hat{y}_i-\bar{y})^2}{\sum(y_i-\bar{y})^2}=1-\frac{\sum(y_i-\hat{y}_i)^2}{\sum(y_i-\bar{y})^2} \tag{8.20}$$

The coefficient of determination measures the degree of fit of the regression line to the actual observed data, which has the following properties:

(1) The coefficient of determination is non-negative;

(2) If all observed points fall on the regression line, then the SSE is zero and the line adequately represents each point, at this time, $R^2=1$;

(3) If the independent variable cannot cause a change in the dependent variable, then $\hat{y}=\bar{y}$, at this time, $R^2=0$;

(4) The range of values of the coefficient of determination is $[0, 1]$;

(5) In simple linear regression, the coefficient of determination of the sample is actually the square of the sample correlation coefficient.

[**Example 8.6**] Continue with Example 8.5, explain the goodness-of-fit of the regression line.

[**Solution**] According to the results calculated in Example 8.3, we can get that

$$\begin{cases}\text{SST}=\sum(y_i-\bar{y})^2=825995992.8\\ \text{SSR}=\sum(\hat{y}_i-\bar{y})^2=823953140.0\\ \text{SSE}=\sum(y_i-\hat{y}_i)^2=2042852.8\end{cases}$$

it is clear that SST=SSR+SSE holds, while the coefficient of determination

$$R^2=\frac{\text{SSR}}{\text{SST}}=0.9975$$

can be calculated. This indicates that 99.75% of the variation in per capita consumption expenditure can be explained by the regression equation, in other words, the goodness-of-fit is great. In fact, we can see from Figure 8.4 that the regression line has an excellent fitting effect.

8.2.5 Prediction

After the previous study, we have built a regression model that passes various tests and meets the requirements, and we are going to use the model to make predictions.

1. Point Estimation

Point estimation is to use the estimated regression function to find an estimate of the dependent variable y for a particular value x_0 of the independent variable x. It generally has two forms, one is the estimation of the mean and the other is the estimation of the individual values.

Point estimation of the mean is to find an estimate $E(y/x_0)$ of the mean of y for a particular value x_0. Point estimation of the individual values is to find an estimate $\hat{y}_0$, the individual values of y for a particular value x_0, when $x=x_0$, $\hat{y}_0=\hat{\beta}_0+\hat{\beta}_1 x_0$.

2. Interval Estimation

In contrast to point estimation, interval estimation is to use the estimated regression function to find an estimated interval of the dependent variable y for a specific value x_0 of the independent variable x, which generally has two forms: one is the estimation of the confidence interval and the other is the estimation of the prediction interval.

1) Confidence Interval

The estimation of confidence interval is an estimation interval for a particular value x_0 of the independent variable x to find an estimated mean value of the dependent variable y. For a given value of x_0, the statistician defines the formula for estimating the standard deviation s of $\hat{y}_0$, expressed by $s_{\hat{y}_0}$:

$$s_{\hat{y}_0}=s_e\sqrt{\frac{1}{n}+\frac{(x_0-\bar{x})^2}{\sum_{i=1}^{n}(x_i-\bar{x})^2}} \tag{8.21}$$

Then, for a given value of x_0, the confidence interval of $E(y_0)$ at a confidence level of $1-\alpha$ can be expressed as

$$\hat{y}_0 \pm t_{\alpha/2} s_e\sqrt{\frac{1}{n}+\frac{(x_0-\bar{x})^2}{\sum_{i=1}^{n}(x_i-\bar{x})^2}} \tag{8.22}$$

2) Prediction Interval

The estimation of prediction interval is an estimation interval for a particular value x_0 of the independent variable x to find an estimated individual value of the dependent variable y. For a given value of x_0, the statistician defines the formula for estimating the standard deviation s of y_0, expressed by s_{ind}:

$$s_{ind} = s_e \sqrt{1 + \frac{1}{n} + \frac{(x_0 - \bar{x})^2}{\sum_{i=1}^{n}(x_i - \bar{x})^2}} \tag{8.23}$$

So, for a given value of x_0, the confidence interval of y_0 of the individual values of y at a confidence level of $1-\alpha$ can be expressed as

$$\hat{y}_0 \pm t_{\alpha/2} s_e \sqrt{1 + \frac{1}{n} + \frac{(x_0 - \bar{x})^2}{\sum_{i=1}^{n}(x_i - \bar{x})^2}} \tag{8.24}$$

Obviously, the width of the prediction interval is larger than the confidence interval, which means that the estimated mean value of y is more accurate than the individual value.

[**Example 8.7**] The regression equation of income and expenditure is obtained as in Example 8.6, it is necessary to use the equation for forecasting purposes. Assuming that the national per capita disposable income in 2022 is $x_0 = 38500$, give the prediction interval for the national per capita consumption expenditure.

[**Solution**] First, the estimated value of y is calculated by substituting x_0 into the regression equation as $y = 868.9022 + 0.6662 \times 38500 = 26517.6022$.

Since $s_e = 336.8855$, $n = 20$, $x_0 = 38500$, we can first calculate

$$s_{ind} = s_e \sqrt{1 + \frac{1}{n} + \frac{(x_0 - \bar{x})^2}{\sum_{i=1}^{n}(x_i - \bar{x})^2}} = 384.2312$$

So, at a significance level of 0.05, $t_{0.025}(8) = -2.3060$, the prediction interval for the national per capita consumption expenditure is

$$\hat{y}_0 \pm t_{\alpha/2} s_e \sqrt{1 + \frac{1}{n} + \frac{(x_0 - \bar{x})^2}{\sum_{i=1}^{n}(x_i - \bar{x})^2}}$$

$$= 26517.6022 \pm 2.3060 \times 384.2312$$

$$= [25631.5651, 27403.6393]$$

8.3 Multiple Regression Analysis

8.3.1 Multiple Regression Model

In last section, the simple linear regression which studies the relationship between a dependent variable and an independent variable is introduced. However, the relationship between objective things is very complicated. In practical problems, there is often more than one factor that affects the dependent variable. Therefore, it is necessary to establish a multiple regression model for analysis.

Given a dependent variable y and k independent variables x_1, x_2, …, x_k, the general form of multiple regression model can be expressed as follows:

$$y=\beta_0+\beta_1 x_1+\beta_2 x_2+\cdots+\beta_k x_k+\varepsilon \tag{8.25}$$

where β_0, β_1, …, β_k are parameters in the model and ε is a random variable called error term, which reflects the influence of other factors not included in the equation on the dependent variable.

Similar to the simple linear regression model, in the multiple linear regression model, there are also three assumptions for the error term ε:

(1) $E(\varepsilon)=0$, that is, the error term is a random variable with an expected value of 0.

(2) $\mathrm{Var}(\varepsilon)=\sigma^2$, that is, for all x_i, the variance of error term is equal.

(3) $\varepsilon \sim N(0, \sigma^2)$, that is, the error term is a random variable that obeys normal distribution and is independent of each other for all ε_t.

8.3.2 Find A Multiple Regression Equation

Prediction on a multiple regression equation for independent variables x_1, x_2, …, x_k and a dependent variable y is as follows:

$$\hat{y}=b_0+b_1 x_1+b_2 x_2+\cdots+b_k x_k \tag{8.26}$$

where $\hat{y}$ is the predicted y-value for given x_i values, the coefficients b_1, b_2, …, b_k are chosen to minimize the sum of squared residuals between the predicted $\hat{y}$ values and the actual y responses in the sample.

Because the calculation of coefficients b_1, b_2, …, b_k is very complicated, we usually use a computer to get their values. The following example demonstrates how to use a computer to find a multiple regression equation.

[**Example 8.8**] The manager of a pie distributor wants to evaluate the factors that affect the pie sales. For this reason, he takes the pie sales as the dependent variable (y), the price and advertising investment as the independent variables (x_1, x_2), collects the data of the past 15 weeks as the sample shown in the Table 8.8. Use SPSS to establish a multiple regression equation.

Table 8.8 Dataset of dependent variable and independent variables

Week	Pie sales(y)	Price(x_1)/($)	Advertising investment (x_2)/(100 $)
1	350	5.50	3.3
2	460	7.50	3.3
3	350	8.00	3.0
4	430	8.00	4.5
5	350	6.80	3.0
6	380	7.50	4.0
7	430	4.50	3.0
8	470	6.40	3.7
9	450	7.00	3.5

Continued Table

Week	Pie sales(y)	Price(x_1)/($)	Advertising investment (x_2)/(100 $)
10	490	5.00	4.0
11	340	7.20	3.5
12	300	7.90	3.2
13	440	5.90	4.0
14	450	5.00	3.5
15	300	7.00	2.7

[**Solution**] As shown in Figure 8.7, import the data into SPSS for multiple regression analysis. And the output results are shown in Figure 8.8.

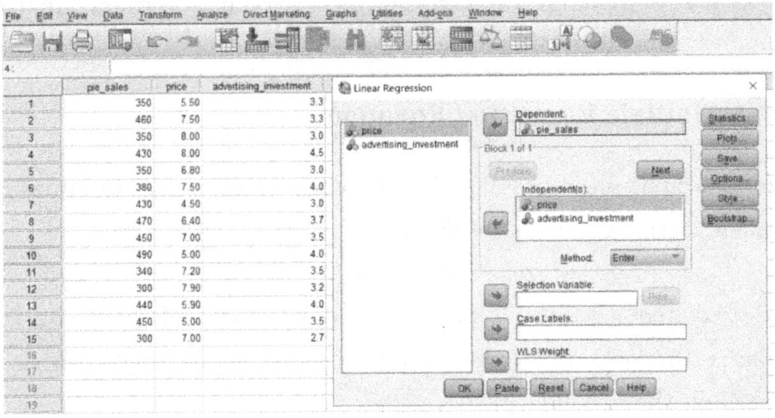

Figure 8.7 Data into SPSS

Model Summary

Model	R	R Square	Adjusted R Square	Std.Error of the Estimate
1	0.722[a]	0.521	0.442	47.463

a. PredictorsL:(Constant),advertisin_investment.price

ANOVA[a]

Model		Sum of Squares	df	Mean Square	F	Sig.
1	Regression	29460.027	2	14730.013	6.539	0.012[b]
	Residual	27033.306	12	2252.776		
	Total	56493.333	14			

a.Dependent Variable:pie_sales
b.Predictors:(Constant).advertising_investment.pric

Coefficients[a]

Model		Unstandardized Coefficients		Standardized Coefficients		
		B	Std.Error	Beta	t	Sig.
1	(Constant)	306.526	114.254		2.683	0.020
	price	−24.975	10.832	−0.461	−2.306	0.040
	advertising_investment	74.131	25.967	0.570	2.855	0.014

a.Dependent Variable:pie_sales

Figure 8.8 Output results

From output results in Figure 8.8, the computed values of the regression coefficients are

$$b_0=306.526,\ b_1=-24.975,\ b_2=74.131$$

Therefore, the multiple regression equation is

$$\hat{y}=306.526-24.975x_1+74.131x_2$$

where $\hat{y}$ is predicted pie sales, x_1 is price, x_2 is advertising investment.

The intercept ($b_0=306.526$) refers to the predicted value of the pie sales($\hat{y}$) when both the price(x_1) and the advertising investment(x_2) are zero.

The slope of price with pie sales ($b_1=-24.975$) indicates that, for a given amount of advertising investment (x_2), the predicted pie sales ($\hat{y}$) are estimated to decrease by 24.975 per week for each 1-dollar increase in the price.

The slope of advertising investment with pie sales ($b_2=74.131$) indicates that, for a given amount of price (x_1), the predicted pie sales ($\hat{y}$) are estimated to increase by 74.131 per week for each 100 dollar increase in the advertising investment.

8.3.3 Predict the Dependent Variable *y*

When a multiple regression equation is established, prediction on the value of dependent variable y according to the value of the given independent variable is very simple. We only need to substitute the values of independent variables into the equation to get the predicted values.

[**Example 8.9**] Use the regression equation found in Example 8.8 to predict the pie sales when the price is \$5.50 and the advertising investment is \$350.

[**Solution**] Since

$$\begin{aligned}\hat{y}&=306.526-24.975x_1+74.131x_2\\&=306.526-24.975\times 5.50+74.131\times 3.5\\&=428.62\end{aligned}$$

Therefore, the predicted sales volume is 428.62.

8.3.4 Coefficient of Multiple Determination

In this section, the coefficient of determination in simple linear regression equation is introduced. Similarly, in multiple regression equation, there are also coefficient of multiple determination. In multiple regression, the coefficient of multiple determination represents the proportion of the variation in y that is explained by the set of independent variables. Equation (8.27) defines the coefficient of multiple determination for a multiple regression model.

$$R^2=\frac{\text{SSR}}{\text{SST}} \tag{8.27}$$

where SSR represents the regression sum of squares, SST represents the total sum of squares.

However, in multiple regression analysis, we usually use adjusted coefficient of determination (R_a^2) to avoid over-estimating R^2 because of increasing independent variables.

$$R_a^2=1-(1-R^2)\left(\frac{n-1}{n-k-1}\right) \tag{8.28}$$

where k is the number of independent variables in the regression equation and n is sample size.

The closer R_a^2 to 1 goes, the better the regression equation fits.

[**Example 8.10**] According to the data in Example 8.8, calculate R_a^2 and explain its significance.

[**Solution**] According to the output results in Figure 8.8, we know that

$$\text{SSR}=29460.027$$

$$\text{SST}=56493.333$$

Then

$$R^2=\frac{\text{SSR}}{\text{SST}}=\frac{29460.027}{56493.333}=0.521$$

So

$$\begin{aligned} R_a^2 &=1-(1-R^2)\left(\frac{n-1}{n-k-1}\right) \\ &=1-(1-0.521)\times\frac{15-1}{15-2-1} \\ &=0.442 \end{aligned}$$

Actually, the output result in Figure 8.8 directly gives the value of R^2 and R_a^2. We can see that $R_a^2=0.442$, which means that in the variation of dependent variable, the proportion that can be explained by the regression equation is 44.2%.

8.3.5 Significance Test

The significance test in multiple regression analysis is divided into linear relationship test(F test) and regression coefficient test (t-test). In simple linear regression analysis, F test and t-test are equivalent. But in multiple regression analysis, they are no longer equivalent.

1. Linear Relationship Test (F test)

Linear relationship test is to test whether the relationship between dependent variables y and k independent variables is significant.

The specific steps of the test are as follows:

Step 1: Propose the null hypothesis and alternative hypothesis.

$$H_0: \beta_1=\beta_2=\cdots=\beta_k=0;$$

or

$$H_1: \text{At least one } \beta_j \neq 0,\ j=1, 2, \cdots, k$$

H_0: There is no linear relationship between the dependent variable and the independent variable.

H_1: There is a linear relationship between the dependent variable and at least one of the independent variables.

Step 2: Calculate the F test statistic.

$$F=\frac{\text{MSR}}{\text{MSE}}=\frac{\dfrac{\text{SSR}}{k}}{\dfrac{\text{SSE}}{n-k-1}} \tag{8.29}$$

where F statistic follows a F distribution with $(k, n-k-1)$ degrees of freedom, k is the number of independent variables and n is sample size.

Step 3: Identify α and make decisions.

Determine the critical value (F_α) from the F distribution according to the level of significance (α) and the degrees of freedom $(k, n-k-1)$. Then make a decision to reject or fail to reject the null hypothesis:

If the value of the F test statistic is greater than the critical value (F_α), then reject the null hypothesis, which means that there is a linear relationship between the dependent variable and at least one of the independent variables; otherwise, fail to reject the hypothesis, which means that there is no linear relationship between the dependent variable and the independent variable.

In mathematical language, it is:

If $F>F_\alpha$, reject H_0; otherwise, fail to reject H_0.

In addition, we can directly use the p value to make decisions according to the computer output results.

If $p<\alpha$, reject H_0; otherwise, fail to reject H_0.

2. Regression Coefficient Test (t-test)

When a regression equation passes the F-test, it doesn't mean that every independent variable has an influence on the dependent variable y. We are supposed to carry out t-test for each regression coefficient.

The steps are as follows:

Step 1: Propose the null hypothesis and alternative hypothesis.

$$H_0: \beta_i=0;\ H_1: \beta_i\neq 0 \quad i=1, 2, \cdots, k$$

Step 2: Calculate the t-test statistic.

$$t_i = \frac{\hat{\beta}_i}{S_{\hat{\beta}_i}} \tag{8.30}$$

where $S_{\hat{\beta}_i}$ is the standard deviation of the sampling distribution of the regression coefficient $\hat{\beta}_i$.

The t-test statistic follows a t-distribution with $n-k-1$ degrees of freedom.

Step 3: Identify α and make decisions.

Determine the critical value ($t_{\alpha/2}$) from the t-distribution according to the level of significance (α) and the degrees of freedom ($n-k-1$). Then make a decision to reject or fail to reject the null hypothesis:

If the absolute value of the t-test statistic is greater than the critical value ($t_{\alpha/2}$), then reject the null hypothesis, which means that the independent variable has a significant influence on the dependent variable; otherwise, fail to reject the hypothesis, which means that the independent variable has no significant influence on the dependent variable.

In mathematical language, it is:

If $|t| > t_{\alpha/2}$, reject H_0; otherwise, fail to reject H_0.

We can also directly use the p-value to make decisions according to the computer output results.

If $p < \alpha$, reject H_0; otherwise, fail to reject H_0.

The following example demonstrates the steps of significance test.

[**Example 8.11**] Perform F test on the regression equation in Example 8.8 and t-test on the regression coefficient.

[**Solution**]

1) F test

(1) Propose the null hypothesis and alternative hypothesis.

$$H_0: \beta_1 = \beta_2 = \cdots = \beta_k = 0;$$

or

$$H_1: \text{At least one } \beta_j \neq 0,\ j = 1, 2, \cdots, k$$

(2) Calculate the F test statistic.

$$\text{SSR} = 29460.027,\ \text{SSE} = 27033.306$$

$$F = \frac{\text{MSR}}{\text{MSE}} = \frac{\frac{\text{SSR}}{k}}{\frac{\text{SSE}}{n-k-1}} = \frac{\frac{29460.027}{2}}{\frac{27033.306}{15-2-1}} = 6.539$$

(3) Make a decision. According to the F distribution table, $F_\alpha = 3.885$, $F > F_\alpha$, so reject H_0, which means there is a linear relationship between the dependent variable and

at least one of the independent variables.

Also, we can directly compare the p-value in the ANOVA in SPSS output results with the given significance level α. As we can see, in the ANOVA table in Figure 8.8,

$$p\text{-value}=0.012<\alpha=0.05$$

So, reject H_0.

2) t-test

(1) Propose the null hypothesis and alternative hypothesis.

$$H_0: \beta_i=0; \ H_1: \beta_i \neq 0 \quad i=1, 2$$

(2) Calculate the t-test statistic.

$$t_i=\frac{\hat{\beta}_i}{S_{\hat{\beta}_i}}$$

(3) Make a decision. By looking up the t distribution table, we can know that with $n-2=6$ degrees of freedom, $t_{\alpha/2}=2.1788$. According to the output results in Figure 8.8, SPSS directly gives the t-value and p-value.

$$t_1|=|-2.306|>2.1788, \ p\text{-value}=0.04<\alpha=0.05$$

$$|t_2|=2.855>2.1788, \ p\text{-value}=0.014<\alpha=0.05$$

So, reject H_0, which means that price and advertising investment both have a significant influence on the pie sales.

Chapter Review

Correlation and regression analysis is an important analytical method in statistics. Deterministic relationships between variables are difficult to determine in practice, so the popular method is still to perform correlation analysis on variables. The main contents of this chapter are as follows: the relationship between variables, the basic concepts of correlation analysis and the methods of measuring the correlation between variables — using the correlation coefficient. Regression analysis, which includes both simple dimension and multiple dimension, is presented on the basis of correlation analysis. And the regression analysis is introduced to express the relationship between variables by establishing a regression equation, and one learns how to test the significance of the relationship and use the regression equation to make predictions about the problem under study.

Exercise

1. The data of hardness x and tensile strength y of the casting mold produced by the

aluminum smelter are shown in the following Table 8. 9. Calculate the correlation coefficient between x and y, and test its significance.

Table 8. 9

x	68	53	70	84	60	72	51	83	70	64
y	288	293	349	343	290	354	283	324	340	286

2. Please calculate the correlation coefficient between the number of newly issued insurance policies x and overtime hours y according to the data in the following Table 8. 10 and test its significance.

Table 8. 10

x	825	215	1070	550	480	920	1350	325	670	1215
y	3. 5	1	4	2	1	3	4. 5	1. 5	3	5

3. The data of output y and production cost x of 12 enterprises randomly selected from a certain industry are as Table 8. 11. Please calculate the correlation coefficient and test the significance.

Table 8. 11

x	130	150	155	140	150	154	165	170	167	180	175	185
y	40	42	50	55	65	78	84	100	116	125	130	140

4. Explain the following concepts:

regression coefficient　　residual　　total sum of squares

regression sum of squares　　error sum of squares　　coefficient of determination

5. What are the connections and differences between correlation analysis and regression analysis?

6. Briefly describe the assumptions of the simple linear regression model.

7. Perform two significance tests on the regression equation created in Example 8. 3 of Section 8. 2.

8. Studies have shown that human height is inextricably linked to shoe size. The height and shoe size (in cm) data of 16 adults are now collected as Table 8. 12.

Table 8. 12

No.	1	2	3	4	5	6	7	8
Shoe Size(x)	23	26	26. 75	26	24. 75	25. 5	25. 25	25
Height(y)	165	176	178	172	168	174	173	172. 5
No.	9	10	11	12	13	14	15	16
Shoe Size(x)	24	26. 5	27	24. 5	25	23. 5	27	26. 5
Height(y)	169	179	181	172. 5	173	166	175	180

(1) Draw a scatter plot and calculate the correlation coefficient between size and height;

(2) Use the method of least squares to find the regression equation for shoe size and height;

(3) Calculate the standard error of estimate and coefficient of determination;

(4) Perform significance tests on the regression equation and regression coefficient at a significant level of 0.05.

(5) If there is an adult male with a shoe size of 27 cm, try to find the predict interval of the height of the male. (Retain to two decimal places.)

9. The following Table 8.13 is the relevant data of similar products sold in 15 large shopping malls randomly selected. Please use SPSS to solve the following problems.

Table 8.13

Sale price (y)	Purchase price (x_1)	Sale expense (x_2)
1238	966	223
1266	894	257
1200	440	387
1193	664	310
1106	791	339
1303	852	283
1313	804	302
1144	905	214
1286	771	304
1084	511	326
1120	505	339
1156	851	235
1083	659	276
1263	490	390
1246	696	316

(1) Regression the data in above table and find the regression equation.

(2) Test the significance of regression model at the significance level of 5%.

(3) Explain the meaning of the adjusted coefficient of multiple determination.

10. A product sales company has sales branches in 25 regions. In order to study the relationship between product sales volume (y) and the sales price (x_1), the annual per capita income of each region (x_2) and advertising expenses (x_3), relevant data of 25 regions were collected as Table 8.14, and the following regression results were obtained by SPSS.

Table 8.14

ANOVA

Model	Sum of squares	df	Mean square	F	Significance F
Regression	98369.1	3	32789.7	48.33	0.00001
Residual	14248.5	21	678.5	—	—
Total	112617.6	24	—	—	—
	Standard Error	t		p-value	Sigifinance F
Constant	758.12	45.03		3.105	0.0045
x_1	−87.84	11.87		−3.096	0.0010
x_2	80.61	15.67		4.867	0.0000
x_3	0.51	0.19		2.583	0.0034

(1) Write the multiple regression equation and explain the significance of each regression coefficient.

(2) Test the significance of the linear relationship and regression coefficient of regression equation at the significance level of 5%.

(3) Explain the meaning of the adjusted coefficient of multiple determination.

11. The business problem for a consumer products company is to measure the effectiveness of different types of advertising media in sales promotion. Specifically, the company is interested in the effectiveness of radio advertising and newspaper advertising (including the cost of discount coupons). During a one month test period, data were collected from a sample of 22 cities with approximately equal populations. Each city is allocated a specific expenditure level for radio advertising and for newspaper advertising. The sales of the product (in thousands of dollars) and also the levels of media expenditure (in thousands of dollars) during the test month are recorded, with the following results shown as Table 8.15.

(1) State the multiple regression equation.

(2) Interpret the meaning of the slopes, b_1 and b_2, for this problem.

(3) Interpret the meaning of the regression coefficient, b_0.

(4) Which type of advertising is more effective? Explain your viewpoint.

Table 8.15

City	Sales (in $ Thousands)	Radio Advertising (in $ Thousands)	Newspaper Advertising (in $ Thousands)
1	973	0	40
2	1119	0	40
3	875	25	25
4	625	25	25
5	910	30	30
6	971	30	30
7	931	35	35
8	1177	35	35
9	882	40	25
10	982	40	25
11	1628	45	45
12	1577	45	45
13	1044	50	0
14	914	50	0
15	1329	55	25
16	1330	55	25
17	1405	60	30
18	1436	60	30
19	1521	65	35
20	1741	65	35
21	1866	70	40
22	1717	70	40

Appendix

Appendix A Standard Normal Distribution

$$\Phi(x) = \int_{-\infty}^{x} \frac{1}{\sqrt{2\pi}} e^{-\frac{t^2}{2}} dt = P(X \leqslant x)$$

x	0	1	2	3	4	5	6	7	8	9
0.0	0.5000	0.5040	0.5080	0.5120	0.5160	0.5199	0.5239	0.5279	0.5319	0.5359
0.1	0.5398	0.5438	0.5478	0.5517	0.5557	0.5596	0.5636	0.5675	0.5714	0.5753
0.2	0.5793	0.5832	0.5871	0.5910	0.5848	0.5987	0.6026	0.6064	0.6103	0.6141
0.3	0.6179	0.6217	0.6255	0.6293	0.6331	0.6368	0.6406	0.6443	0.6480	0.6517
0.4	0.6554	0.6591	0.6628	0.6664	0.6700	0.6736	0.6772	0.6808	0.6844	0.6879
0.5	0.6915	0.6950	0.6985	0.7019	0.7054	0.7088	0.7123	0.7157	0.7190	0.7224
0.6	0.7257	0.7219	0.7324	0.7357	0.7389	0.7422	0.7454	0.7486	0.7571	0.7549
0.7	0.7580	0.7611	0.7642	0.7673	0.7703	0.7734	0.7764	0.7794	0.7823	0.7852
0.8	0.7881	0.7910	0.7939	0.7967	0.7995	0.8023	0.8051	0.8087	0.8106	0.8133
0.9	0.8159	0.8186	0.8212	0.8283	0.8264	0.8289	0.8315	0.8340	0.8365	0.8389
1.0	0.8413	0.8438	0.8461	0.8485	0.8508	0.8531	0.8554	0.8577	0.8599	0.8621
1.1	0.8643	0.8665	0.8686	0.8708	0.8729	0.8749	0.8770	0.8790	0.8810	0.8830
1.2	0.8849	0.8869	0.8888	0.8907	0.8925	0.8944	0.8962	0.8980	0.8997	0.9015
1.3	0.9023	0.9049	0.9066	0.9082	0.9099	0.9115	0.9131	0.9147	0.9162	0.9177
1.4	0.9192	0.9207	0.9222	0.9236	0.9251	0.9265	0.9278	0.9292	0.9306	0.9319
1.5	0.9332	0.9345	0.9357	0.9370	0.9382	0.9394	0.9406	0.9418	0.9430	0.9441
1.6	0.9452	0.9463	0.9474	0.9484	0.9495	0.9505	0.9515	0.9525	0.9535	0.9545
1.7	0.9554	0.9564	0.9573	0.9582	0.9591	0.9599	0.9608	0.9616	0.9625	0.9633
1.8	0.9641	0.9648	0.9656	0.9664	0.9671	0.9678	0.9686	0.9693	0.9700	0.9706
1.9	0.9713	0.9719	0.9726	0.9732	0.9738	0.9744	0.9750	0.9756	0.9762	0.9767
2.0	0.9772	0.9778	0.9783	0.9788	0.9793	0.9798	0.9803	0.9808	0.9812	0.9817
2.1	0.9821	0.9826	0.9830	0.9834	0.9838	0.9842	0.9846	0.9850	0.9854	0.9857
2.2	0.9861	0.9864	0.9868	0.9871	0.9874	0.9878	0.9881	0.9884	0.9887	0.9890
2.3	0.9893	0.9896	0.9898	0.9901	0.9904	0.9906	0.9909	0.9911	0.9913	0.9916
2.4	0.9918	0.9920	0.9922	0.9925	0.9927	0.9929	0.9931	0.9932	0.9934	0.9936
2.5	0.9938	0.9940	0.9941	0.9943	0.9945	0.9946	0.9948	0.9949	0.9951	0.9952
2.6	0.9953	0.9955	0.9956	0.9957	0.9959	0.9960	0.9961	0.9962	0.9963	0.9964
2.7	0.9965	0.9966	0.9967	0.9968	0.9969	0.9970	0.9971	0.9972	0.9973	0.9974
2.8	0.9974	0.9975	0.9976	0.9977	0.9977	0.9978	0.9979	0.9979	0.9980	0.9981
2.9	0.9981	0.9982	0.9982	0.9983	0.9984	0.9984	0.9985	0.9985	0.9986	0.9986
3.0	0.9987	0.9990	0.9993	0.9995	0.9997	0.9998	0.9998	0.9999	0.9999	1.0000

Appendix B Student-t Distribution

$$p\{t(n)>t_{\alpha}(n)\}=\alpha$$

n	$\alpha=0.25$	0.10	0.05	0.025	0.01	0.005
1	1.0000	3.0777	6.3138	12.7062	31.8207	63.6574
2	0.8165	1.8856	2.9200	4.3037	6.9646	9.9248
3	0.7649	1.6377	2.3534	3.1824	2.5407	5.8409
4	0.7407	1.5332	2.1318	2.7764	3.7469	4.6014
5	0.7267	1.4759	2.0150	2.5706	3.3649	4.0322
6	0.7176	1.4398	1.9432	2.4469	3.1427	3.7074
7	0.7111	1.4149	1.8946	2.3634	2.9980	3.4995
8	0.7064	1.3968	1.8595	2.3060	2.8965	3.3554
9	0.7027	1.3830	1.8331	2.2622	2.8214	3.2498
10	0.6998	1.3722	1.8125	2.2281	2.7638	3.1693
11	0.6974	1.3634	1.7959	2.2010	2.7181	3.1058
12	0.6955	1.3562	1.7823	2.1788	2.6810	3.0545
13	0.6938	1.3502	1.7709	2.1604	2.6503	3.0123
14	0.6924	1.3450	1.7613	2.1448	2.6245	2.9768
15	0.6912	1.3406	1.7531	2.1315	2.6205	2.9467
16	0.6901	1.3368	1.7459	2.1199	2..5835	2.9208
17	0.6892	1.3334	1.7396	2.1098	2.5669	2.8982
18	0.6884	1.3304	1.7341	2.1009	2.5524	2.8784
19	0.6876	1.3277	1.7291	2.0930	2.5395	2.8609
20	0.9870	1.3253	1.7247	2.0860	2.5280	2.8453
21	0.6864	1.3232	1.7207	2.0796	2.5177	2.8314
22	0.6858	1.3212	1.7171	2.0739	2.5083	2.8188
23	0.6853	1.3195	1.7139	2.0687	2.4999	2.8073
24	0.6848	1.3178	1.7109	2.0639	2.4922	2.7969
25	0.6844	1.3163	1.7108	2.0595	2.4851	2.7874
26	0.6840	1.3150	1.7056	2.0555	2.4786	2.7787
27	0.6837	1.3137	1.7033	2.0518	2.4727	2.7707
28	0.6834	1.3125	1.7011	2.0484	2.4671	2.7664
29	0.6830	1.3114	1.6991	2.0452	2.4620	2.7564
30	0.6828	1.304	1.6973	2.0423	2.4573	2.7500
31	0.6825	1.3095	1.6599	2.0395	2.4528	2.7440
32	0.6822	1.3086	1.6939	2.0369	2.4487	2.7385
33	0.6820	1.3077	1.6924	2.0345	2.4448	2.7333
34	0.6818	1.3070	1.6909	2.0322	2.4411	2.7384
35	0.6816	1.3062	1.6896	2.0301	2.4377	2.7238
36	0.6814	1.3055	1.6883	2.0281	2.4345	2.7195
37	0.6812	1.3049	1.6871	2.0262	2.4314	2.7154
38	0.6810	1.3042	1.6860	2.0244	2.4286	2.7116
39	0.6808	1.3036	1.6849	2.0227	2.4258	2.7079
40	0.6807	1.3031	1.6839	2.0211	2.4223	2.7045
41	0.6805	1.3025	1.6829	2.0195	2.4208	2.7012
42	1.6804	1.3020	1.6820	2.0181	2.4185	2.6981
43	1.6802	1.3016	1.6811	2.0167	2.4163	2.6951
44	1.6801	1.3011	1.6802	2.0154	2.4141	2.6923
45	0.6800	1.3006	1.6794	2.0141	2.4121	2.6896

Appendix C *F* Distribution

$$P\{F(n_1, n_2) > F_\alpha(n_1, n_2)\} = \alpha$$

$\alpha = 0.10$

n_2	n_1								
	1	2	3	4	5	6	7	8	9
1	39.86	49.50	53.59	55.33	57.24	58.20	58.91	59.44	59.86
2	8.53	9.00	9.16	9.24	6.29	9.33	9.35	9.37	9.38
3	5.54	5.46	5.39	5.34	5.31	5.28	5.27	5.25	5.24
4	4.54	4.32	4.19	4.11	4.05	4.01	3.98	3.95	3.94
5	4.06	3.78	3.62	3.52	3.45	3.40	3.37	3.34	3.32
6	3.78	3.46	3.29	3.18	3.11	3.05	3.01	2.98	2.96
7	3.59	3.26	3.07	2.96	2.88	2.83	2.78	2.75	2.72
8	3.46	3.11	2.92	2.81	2.73	2.67	2.62	2.59	2.56
9	3.36	3.01	2.81	2.69	2.61	2.55	2.51	2.47	2.44
10	3.20	2.92	2.73	2.61	2.52	2.46	2.41	2.38	2.35
11	3.22	2.86	2.66	2.54	2.45	2.39	2.34	2.30	2.27
12	3.18	2.81	2.61	2.48	2.39	2.33	2.28	2.24	2.21
13	3.14	2.76	2.56	2.43	2.35	2.28	2.23	2.20	2.16
14	3.10	2.73	2.52	2.39	2.31	2.24	2.19	2.15	2.12
15	3.07	2.70	2.49	2.36	2.27	2.21	2.16	2.12	2.09
16	3.05	2.67	2.46	2.33	2.24	2.18	2.13	2.09	2.06
17	3.03	2.64	2.44	2.31	2.22	2.15	2.10	2.06	2.03
18	3.01	2.62	2.42	2.29	2.20	2.13	2.08	2.04	2.00
19	2.99	2.61	2.40	2.27	2.18	2.11	2.06	2.02	1.98
20	2.97	2.50	2.38	2.25	2.16	2.09	2.04	2.00	1.96
21	2.96	2.57	2.36	2.23	2.14	2.08	2.02	1.98	1.95
22	2.95	2.56	2.35	2.22	2.13	2.06	2.01	1.97	1.93
23	2.94	2.55	2.34	2.21	2.11	2.05	1.99	1.95	1.92
24	2.93	2.54	2.33	2.19	2.10	2.04	1.98	1.94	1.91
25	2.92	2.53	2.32	2.18	2.09	2.02	1.97	1.93	1.89
26	2.91	2.52	2.31	2.17	2.08	2.01	1.96	1.92	1.88
27	2.90	2.51	2.30	2.17	2.07	2.00	1.95	1.91	1.87
28	2.89	2.50	2.98	2.16	2.06	2.00	1.93	1.90	1.87
29	2.89	2.50	2.88	2.15	2.06	1.99	1.93	1.89	1.86
30	2.88	2.49	2.22	2.14	2.05	1.98	1.93	1.88	1.85
40	2.84	2.41	2.23	2.00	2.00	1.93	1.87	1.83	1.79
60	2.79	2.39	2.18	2.04	1.95	1.87	1.82	1.77	1.74
120	2.75	2.35	2.13	1.99	1.90	1.82	1.77	1.72	1.68
∞	2.71	2.30	2.08	1.94	1.85	1.77	1.72	1.67	1.63

$\alpha=0.10$

n_2	n_1									
	10	12	15	20	24	30	40	60	120	∞
1	60.19	60.71	61.22	61.74	62.06	62.26	62.53	62.79	63.06	63.33
2	9.39	9.41	9.42	9.44	9.45	9.46	9.47	9.47	9.48	9.49
3	5.23	5.22	5.20	5.18	5.18	5.17	5.16	5.15	5.14	5.13
4	3.92	3.90	3.87	3.84	3.83	3.82	3.80	3.79	3.78	3.76
5	3.30	3.27	3.24	3.21	3.19	3.17	3.16	3.14	3.12	3.10
6	2.94	2.90	2.87	2.84	2.82	2.80	2.78	2.76	2.74	2.72
7	2.70	2.67	2.63	2.59	2.58	2.56	2.54	2.51	2.49	2.47
8	2.54	2.50	2.46	2.42	2.40	2.38	2.36	2.34	2.32	2.29
9	2.42	2.38	2.34	2.30	2.28	2.25	2.23	2.21	2.18	2.16
10	2.32	2.28	2.24	2.20	2.18	2.16	2.13	2.11	2.08	2.06
11	2.25	2.21	2.17	2.12	2.10	2.08	2.05	2.03	2.00	1.97
12	2.19	2.15	2.10	2.06	2.04	2.01	1.99	1.96	1.93	1.90
13	2.14	2.10	2.05	2.01	1.98	1.96	1.93	1.90	1.88	1.85
14	2.10	2.05	2.01	1.96	1.94	1.91	1.89	1.82	1.83	1.80
15	2.06	2.02	1.97	1.92	1.90	1.87	1.85	1.82	1.79	1.76
16	2.03	1.99	1.94	1.89	1.87	1.84	1.81	1.78	1.75	1.72
17	2.00	1.96	1.91	1.86	1.84	1.81	1.78	1.75	1.72	1.69
18	1.98	1.93	1.89	1.84	1.81	1.78	1.75	1.72	1.69	1.66
19	1.96	1.91	1.86	1.81	1.79	1.76	1.73	1.70	1.67	1.63
20	1.94	1.89	1.84	1.79	1.77	1.74	1.71	1.68	1.64	1.61
21	1.92	1.87	1.83	1.78	1.75	1.72	1.69	1.66	1.62	1.59
22	1.90	1.86	1.81	1.76	1.73	1.70	1.69	1.64	1.60	1.57
23	1.89	1.84	1.80	1.74	1.72	1.69	1.66	1.62	1.59	1.55
24	1.88	1.83	1.78	1.73	1.70	1.67	1.64	1.60	1.57	1.53
25	1.87	1.82	1.77	1.72	1.69	1.66	1.63	1.59	1.56	1.52
26	1.86	1.81	1.76	1.71	1.68	1.65	1.61	1.58	1.54	1.50
27	1.85	1.80	1.75	1.70	1.67	1.64	1.60	1.57	1.53	1.49
28	1.84	1.79	1.74	1.69	1.66	1.63	1.59	1.56	1.52	1.48
29	1.83	1.78	1.73	1.68	1.65	1.62	1.58	1.55	1.51	1.47
30	1.82	1.77	1.72	1.67	1.64	1.61	1.57	1.54	1.50	1.46
40	1.76	1.71	1.71	1.61	1.57	1.54	1.51	1.47	1.42	1.38
60	1.71	1.66	1.66	1.54	1.51	1.48	1.44	1.40	1.35	1.29
120	1.65	1.60	1.60	1.48	1.45	1.41	1.37	1.32	1.36	1.19
∞	1.60	1.55	1.55	1.42	1.38	1.34	1.30	1.24	1.17	1.00

$\alpha=0.05$

n_2	n_1								
	1	2	3	4	5	6	7	8	9
1	161.4	199.5	215.7	224.6	230.2	234.0	236.8	238.9	240.5
2	18.51	19.00	19.25	19.25	19.30	19.33	19.35	19.37	19.38
3	10.13	9.55	9.12	9.12	9.90	8.94	8.89	8.85	8.81
4	7.71	6.94	6.39	6.39	6.26	6.16	6.09	6.04	6.00
5	6.61	5.79	5.41	5.19	5.05	4.95	4.88	4.82	4.77
6	5.99	5.14	4.76	4.53	4.39	4.28	4.21	1.15	4.10
7	5.59	4.74	4.35	4.12	3.97	3.87	3.79	3.73	3.68
8	5.32	4.46	4.07	3.84	3.69	3.58	3.50	3.44	3.69
9	5.12	4.26	3.86	3.63	3.48	3.37	3.29	3.23	3.18
10	4.96	4.10	3.71	3.48	3.33	3.22	3.14	3.07	3.02
11	4.84	3.98	3.59	3.36	3.20	3.09	3.01	2.95	2.90
12	4.75	3.89	3.49	3.26	3.11	3.00	2.91	2.85	2.80
13	4.67	3.81	3.41	3.18	3.03	2.92	2.83	2.77	2.71
14	4.60	3.74	3.34	3.11	2.96	2.85	2.76	2.70	2.65
15	4.54	3.68	3.29	3.06	2.90	2.79	2.71	2.64	2.59
16	4.49	3.63	3.24	3.01	2.85	2.74	2.66	2.59	2.54
17	4.45	3.59	3.20	2.96	2.81	2.70	2.61	2.55	2.49
18	4.41	3.55	3.16	2.93	2.77	2.66	2.58	2.51	2.46
19	4.38	3.52	3.13	2.90	2.74	2.63	2.54	2.48	2.42
20	4.35	3.49	3.10	2.87	2.71	2.60	2.51	2.45	2.39
21	4.32	3.47	3.07	2.84	2.68	2.57	2.49	2.42	2.37
22	4.30	3.44	3.05	2.82	2.66	2.55	2.46	2.40	2.34
23	4.28	3.42	3.03	2.80	2.64	2.53	2.44	2.37	2.32
24	4.26	3.40	3.01	2.78	2.62	2.51	2.42	2.36	2.30
25	4.24	3.39	2.99	2.76	2.60	2.49	2.40	2.34	2.28
26	4.23	3.37	2.98	2.74	2.59	2.47	2.39	2.32	2.27
27	4.21	3.35	2.96	2.73	2.57	2.46	2.37	2.31	2.25
28	4.20	3.34	2.95	2.71	2.56	2.45	2.36	2.29	2.24
29	4.18	3.33	2.93	2.70	2.55	2.43	2.35	2.28	2.22
30	4.17	3.32	2.92	2.69	2.53	2.42	2.33	2.27	2.21
40	4.08	3.23	2.84	2.61	2.45	2.34	2.25	2.18	2.12
60	4.00	3.15	2.76	2.53	2.37	2.25	2.17	2.10	2.04
120	3.92	3.07	2.68	2.45	2.29	2.17	2.09	2.02	2.96
∞	3.84	3.00	2.60	2.37	2.21	2.10	2.01	1.94	1.88

$\alpha=0.05$

n_2	n_1									
	10	12	15	20	24	30	40	60	120	∞
1	241.9	243.9	245.9	248.0	249.1	250.1	251.1	252.2	253.3	254.3
2	19.40	19.41	19.43	19.45	19.45	19.46	19.47	19.48	19.49	19.50
3	8.79	8.74	8.70	8.66	8.64	8.62	8.59	8.57	8.55	8.53
4	5.96	5.91	5.86	5.80	5.77	5.75	5.72	5.69	5.66	5.63
5	4.74	4.68	4.62	4.56	4.53	4.50	4.46	4.43	4.40	4.36
6	4.06	4.00	3.94	3.87	3.84	3.81	3.77	3.74	3.70	3.67
7	3.64	3.57	3.51	3.44	3.41	3.38	3.34	3.30	3.27	3.23
8	3.35	3.28	3.22	3.15	3.12	3.08	3.04	3.01	2.97	2.93
9	3.14	3.07	3.01	2.94	2.90	2.86	2.83	2.79	2.95	2.71
10	2.98	2.91	2.85	2.77	2.74	2.70	2.66	2.62	2.58	2.54
11	2.85	2.79	2.72	2.65	2.61	2.57	2.53	2.49	2.45	2.40
12	2.75	2.69	2.62	2.54	2.51	2.47	2.43	2.38	2.34	2.30
13	2.67	2.60	2.53	2.46	2.42	2.38	2.34	2.30	2.25	2.21
14	2.60	2.53	2.46	2.39	2.35	2.31	2.27	2.22	2.18	2.13
15	2.54	2.48	2.40	2.33	2.29	2.25	2.20	2.16	2.11	2.07
16	2.49	2.42	2.35	2.28	2.24	2.19	2.15	2.11	2.06	2.01
17	2.45	2.38	2.31	2.23	2.19	2.15	2.10	2.06	2.01	1.96
18	2.41	2.34	2.27	2.19	2.15	2.11	2.06	2.02	1.97	1.92
19	2.38	2.31	2.23	2.16	2.11	2.07	2.03	1.98	1.93	1.88
20	2.35	2.28	2.20	2.12	2.08	2.04	1.99	1.95	1.90	1.84
21	2.32	2.25	2.18	2.10	2.05	2.01	1.96	1.92	1.87	1.81
22	2.30	2.23	2.15	2.07	2.03	1.98	1.94	1.89	1.84	1.78
23	2.27	2.20	2.13	2.05	2.01	1.96	1.91	1.86	1.81	1.76
24	2.25	2.18	2.11	2.03	1.98	1.94	1.89	1.84	1.79	1.73
25	2.24	2.16	2.09	2.01	1.96	1.92	1.87	1.82	1.77	1.71
26	2.22	2.15	1.07	1.99	1.95	1.90	1.85	1.80	1.75	1.69
27	2.20	2.13	1.06	1.97	1.93	1.88	1.84	1.79	1.73	1.67
28	2.19	2.12	1.04	1.96	1.91	1.87	1.82	1.77	1.71	1.65
29	2.18	2.10	1.03	1.94	1.90	1.85	1.81	1.75	1.70	1.64
30	2.16	2.09	2.01	1.93	1.89	1.84	1.79	1.74	1.68	1.62
40	2.08	2.00	1.92	1.84	1.79	1.74	1.69	1.64	1.58	1.51
60	1.99	1.92	1.84	1.75	1.70	1.65	1.59	1.53	1.47	1.39
120	1.91	1.83	1.75	1.66	1.61	1.55	1.50	1.43	1.35	1.25
∞	1.83	1.75	1.67	1.57	1.52	1.46	1.39	1.32	1.22	1.00

$\alpha = 0.01$

n_2	n_1 = 1	2	3	4	5	6	7	8	9
1	4052	4999.5	5403	5626	5764	5859	5928	5982	6062
2	98.50	99.00	99.17	99.25	99.30	99.33	99.36	99.37	99.39
3	34.12	30.82	29.46	28.71	28.24	27.91	27.67	27.49	27.35
4	21.20	18.00	16.69	15.98	15.52	15.21	14.98	14.80	14.66
5	16.26	13.27	12.06	11.39	10.97	10.67	10.46	10.29	10.16
6	13.75	10.92	9.78	9.15	8.75	8.47	8.46	8.10	7.98
7	12.25	9.55	8.45	7.85	7.46	7.19	6.99	6.84	6.72
8	11.26	8.65	7.59	7.01	6.63	6.37	6.18	6.03	5.91
9	10.56	8.02	6.99	6.42	6.06	5.80	5.61	5.47	5.35
10	10.04	7.56	6.55	5.99	5.64	5.39	5.20	5.06	4.94
11	9.65	7.21	6.22	5.67	5.32	5.07	4.49	4.74	4.63
12	9.33	6.93	5.95	5.41	5.06	4.82	4.64	4.50	4.39
13	9.07	6.70	5.74	5.21	4.86	4.62	4.44	4.30	4.19
14	8.86	6.51	5.56	5.04	4.69	4.46	4.28	4.14	4.03
15	8.68	6.36	5.42	4.89	4.56	4.32	4.14	4.00	3.89
16	8.53	6.23	5.29	4.77	4.44	4.20	4.03	3.39	3.78
17	8.40	6.11	5.18	4.67	4.34	4.10	3.93	3.79	3.68
18	8.29	6.01	5.09	4.58	4.25	4.01	3.84	3.71	3.60
19	8.18	5.93	5.01	4.50	4.17	3.94	3.77	3.63	3.52
20	8.10	5.85	4.94	4.43	4.10	3.87	3.70	3.56	3.46
21	8.02	5.78	4.87	4.37	4.04	3.81	3.64	3.51	3.40
22	7.95	5.72	4.82	4.31	3.99	3.76	3.59	3.45	3.35
23	7.88	5.66	4.76	4.26	3.94	3.71	3.54	3.41	3.30
24	7.82	5.61	4.72	4.22	3.90	3.67	3.50	3.36	3.26
25	7.77	5.57	4.68	4.18	3.85	3.63	3.46	3.32	3.22
26	7.72	5.53	4.64	4.14	3.82	3.59	3.42	3.29	3.18
27	7.68	5.49	4.60	4.11	3.78	3.56	3.39	3.26	3.15
28	7.64	5.45	4.57	4.07	3.75	3.53	3.36	3.23	3.12
29	7.60	5.42	4.54	4.04	3.73	3.50	3.33	3.20	3.09
30	7.56	5.39	4.51	4.02	3.70	3.47	3.31	3.17	3.07
40	7.31	5.18	4.31	3.83	3.51	3.29	3.12	2.99	2.89
60	7.08	4.98	4.13	3.65	3.34	3.12	3.95	2.82	2.72
120	6.85	4.79	3.95	3.48	3.17	2.96	2.79	2.96	2.56
∞	6.63	4.61	3.78	3.32	3.02	2.80	2.64	2.51	2.41

$\alpha=0.01$

n_2	n_1									
	10	12	15	20	24	30	40	60	120	∞
1	6056	6106	6157	6209	6235	6261	6287	6313	6339	6366
2	99.40	99.42	99.43	99.45	99.46	99.47	99.47	99.48	99.49	99.50
3	27.33	27.05	26.87	26.69	26.60	26.50	26.41	26.32	26.22	26.13
4	14.55	14.37	14.20	14.02	13.93	13.84	13.75	13.65	13.56	13.46
5	10.05	9.29	9.72	9.55	9.47	9.38	9.29	9.20	9.11	9.02
6	7.87	7.72	7.56	7.40	7.31	7.23	7.14.01	7.06	6.97	6.88
7	6.62	6.47	6.31	6.16	6.07	5.99	5.91	5.82	5.74	5.65
8	5.81	5.67	5.52	5.36	5.28	5.20	5.12	5.03	4.95	4.86
9	5.26	5.11	4.96	4.81	4.73	4.65	4.57	4.48	4.40	4.31
10	4.85	4.71	4.56	4.41	4.33	4.25	4.17	4.08	4.00	3.91
11	4.54	4.40	4.25	4.10	4.02	3.95	3.86	3.78	3.69	3.60
12	4.30	4.16	4.01	3.86	3.78	3.70	3.62	3.54	3.45	3.36
13	4.10	3.96	3.82	3.66	3.59	3.51	3.43	3.34	3.25	3.17
14	3.94	3.80	3.66	3.51	3.43	3.35	4.27	3.18	3.09	3.00
15	3.80	3.67	3.52	3.37	3.29	3.21	3.13	3.05	2.96	2.87
16	3.69	3.55	3.41	3.26	3.18	3.10	3.02	2.93	2.84	2.74
17	3.59	3.46	3.31	3.16	308	3.00	2.92	2.83	2.75	2.65
18	3.51	3.37	3.23	3.08	3.00	2.92	2.84	2.75	2.66	2.57
19	3.34	3.30	3.15	3.00	2.92	2.84	2.76	2.67	2.58	2.49
20	3.37	3.23	3.09	2.94	2.86	2.78	2.69	2.61	2.52	2.42
21	3.31	3.17	3.03	2.88	2.80	2.72	2.64	2.55	2.46	2.36
22	3.26	3.12	2.98	2.83	2.75	2.67	2.58	2.50	2.40	2.31
23	3.21	3.07	2.93	2.78	2.70	2.62	2.54	2.45	2.35	2.26
24	3.17	3.03	2.89	2.74	2.66	2.58	2.49	2.40	2.31	2.21
25	3.13	2.99	2.85	2.70	2.62	2.54	2.45	2.36	2.27	2.17
26	3.09	2.96	2.81	2.66	2.58	2.50	2.42	2.33	2.23	2.13
27	3.06	2.93	2.78	2.63	2.55	2.47	2.38	2.29	2.20	2.10
28	3.03	2.90	2.75	2.60	2.52	2.44	2.35	2.26	2.17	2.06
29	3.00	2.87	2.73	2.57	2.49	2.41	2.33	2.23	2.14	2.03
30	2.98	2.84	2.70	2.55	2.47	2.39	2.30	2.21	2.11	2.01
40	2.80	2.66	2.52	2.37	2.29	2.20	2.11	2.02	1.92	1.80
60	2.63	2.50	2.35	2.20	2.12	2.03	1.94	1.84	1.78	1.60
120	2.47	2.34	2.19	2.03	1.95	1.86	1.76	1.66	1.53	1.38
∞	2.32	2.18	2.04	1.88	1.79	1.70	1.59	1.47	1.32	1.00

References

[1] LARSON R, FARBER B. Elementary statistics: picturing the world [M]. 6th ed. New York: Pearson Education, Inc., 2016.

[2] DEGROOT M H, SCHERVISH M J. Probability and statistics [M]. 4th ed. New York: Pearson Education, Inc., 2012.

[3] CASELLA G, BERGER R L. Statistical inference [M]. 2nd ed. Massachusetts: Duxbury Press, 2002.

[4] LOCK R H, LOOK P F, MORGAN K L, etc. Statistics: unlocking the power of data[M]. New Jersey: John Wiley & Sons, Inc., 2013.